The Odyssey

HOMER

Translated by George Herbert Palmer

DOVER PUBLICATIONS, INC.
Mineola, New York

DOVER THRIFT EDITIONS

GENERAL EDITOR: PAUL NEGRI
EDITOR OF THIS VOLUME: SUSAN L. RATTINER

Copyright

Copyright © 1999 by Dover Publications, Inc.
All rights reserved.

Bibliographical Note

This Dover edition, first published in 1999, is an unabridged republication of the George Herbert Palmer translation of *The Odyssey*, as published by Houghton Mifflin Company, Boston and New York, in 1912.

Library of Congress Cataloging-in-Publication Data

Homer.
   [Odyssey. English]
   The odyssey / Homer ; translated by George Herbert Palmer.
      p.   cm. — (Dover thrift editions)
   ISBN-13: 978-0-486-40654-1
   ISBN-10: 0-486-40654-7
   1. Epic poetry, Greek—Translations into English. 2. Odysseus (Greek mythology)—Poetry. I. Palmer, George Herbert, 1842–1933. II. Title. III. Series.
PA4025.A5P35   1999
883'.01—dc21
                                        98–50940
                                           CIP

Manufactured in the United States by Courier Corporation
40654710
www.doverpublications.com

Contents

Preface

IN THIS translation of the Odyssey I have had the following aims:—

To give to the thought of Homer a more direct and simple expression than has hitherto been judged admissible; to be at once minutely faithful to the Greek original and to keep out of sight the fact that either an original or a translator exists; to present especially the objective, unreflective, realistic, and non-literary features of the primitive story; to report in all their delicacy the events which Homer reports, to exhibit his attitude of mind toward them, and to produce again the impression produced by him that things did happen just so; in the wording, to discard originality and to make free use of the fortunate phrases of preceding translators; but to employ persistently the veracious language, the language of prose, rather than the dream language, the language of poetry; and still to confess that the story, unlike a bare record of fact, is throughout, like poetry, illuminated with an underglow of joy; to mark gently this permeating joy by a simple rhythm, a rhythm so unobtrusive and so free from systematic arrangement that no one need turn from the matter to mark the movement; above all, to discharge a debt of gratitude to the great friend who for twenty-five years has been showing me the beauty of himself and of the world; and finally, to make it plain that I cannot attain these aims, and to commend them to others as alluring and impossible.

CAMBRIDGE, *February* 21, 1891.

iii

Introduction

WHEN THE poems of Homer were written, no man knows. We shall not
be far wrong if we say they came into being a thousand years before the
Christian era, or about as early as we find the Greek race. At the dawn
of authentic history portions of them were chanted about the cities of
the Grecian mainland, southern Italy, Sicily, the islands of the Ægean,
and the coast of Asia Minor. Throughout the continuance of Greek civilization they were the chief ingredient in the education of the young
and the chief literary delight of the men of mature years. So universally
did they enter into the making of the Greek mind that it is no exagger-
ation to say that every one of that race of whom we have certain historical knowledge was "by this vision splendid upon his way attended."
Yet unfortunately we have little knowledge of their author, a circumstance due in part to his greatness. Founders are seldom known. Buddha,
Theseus, King Alfred, Shakespeare, John Harvard, are shadowy figures
standing at the dim beginning of important eras largely created by
themselves. By the time the importance of such men is comprehended
and we turn to inspect their personality, they are gone, hidden behind
the majesty of their works.

Moreover, the question When and by whom was the Odyssey written? is not so simple as it sounds. A great work has many sources. Its
creator, however creative, finds much of his material already prepared.
Shakespeare invented few of his plots. He took characters, scenes, and
conversations from novels and histories where their power had already
been proved. Sometimes he altered old plays. In deference to later taste
his own have frequently been altered. A poem, therefore, even in the
clear light of modern times and among a people possessing strong

v

notions of literary birthright, may not be constructed throughout by a
single author nor contain within itself security against change. How
much more, then, in an age accustomed to tradition and careless of
individual performance, may we expect the substance of a poem to
bear the marks of many minds. Into the Odyssey has gone a mass of histories, legends, mythologies, genealogies, ideals of character, manners,
modes of life, which must have required centuries to mature. The book
is an epitome of a civilization, with all that civilization's variegated
dreams, records, and inventions.

To what extent this accumulated material was already shaped before
its appearance here we cannot say. Possibly enough fragments of early
song contribute something to the large harmony, and later times may
also have admitted interpolations. Peculiarities of style and diction
which mark portions of the poem might in this way be most easily
explained. Here and there, too, critics have suspected such incon-
gruities in the narrative, or have found a single action or character
thrown into such questionable prominence, that they have imagined it
possible to tell where the piecing has occurred. But while an abundance of this sharp-sighted criticism has been spent upon the poem, no
critic has had any large success in convincing others of his conclusions.
All are at least agreed that in the Odyssey more than in the Iliad there
is a prevailing evenness of style, firmness of plot, and harmony in the pre-
sentation of characters and situations. Whatever diverse poetic materials
were originally employed, the resulting unity is conspicuous and aston-
ishing. The Odyssey is no chance conglomerate. It is a masterpiece of
poetic art, beautiful in its parts, and no less beautiful in its structure,
bearing throughout the impress of a single mind—his whom we rightly
call Homerus, the Joiner, the Composer.

The poem presupposes the events of the Trojan war, a war which
fifty years ago was believed to be mythical, but which the excavations
of Dr. Schliemann at the site of the city have shown to have historic
basis. The incidents referred to are these: Paris, the son of Priam, King
of Troy, carried off to Troy Helen, the wife of Menelaus, King of
Lacedæmon. At the summons of his brother, Agamemnon, King of
Argos and Mycenæ, the princes of Greece and the neighboring islands
united in an expedition for her recovery. Troy, too, summoned its allies
and for ten years endured a close siege. The Greek camp lay along the
seashore where a landing was first effected. Between this and the city
stretched a plain on which fighting was almost constant. Dissensions
and pestilence at last broke out in the Greek army and were followed
by the series of battles described in the Iliad. Despairing of capturing
the city by force, the Greeks resorted to stratagem. They sailed away,
leaving upon the shore a huge wooden horse in which were hidden

Menelaus and a band of resolute men. The Trojans foolishly dragged
the trophy within their walls. The following night the men within it crept
from their ambush, threw open the gates of Troy to the returning Greeks,
and carried fire and slaughter through the rich city. The objects of the
joint expedition were now accomplished; and each surviving chief, taking his share of plunder, assembled his ships, sailed away, and was soon
established once more in his former home.

Or rather, all but one came safely home. Among the men in the wooden
horse was Odysseus, — Ulysses, as the Romans afterwards called him, —
the ruler of the little island of Ithaca. Ten years before, he had left in
Ithaca his young wife, Penelope, and his infant son, Telemachus. For
ten years more he was to be parted from them, wandering among seas
and islands, whose god, Poseidon, he had offended. When half that
time was gone, and Odysseus did not — like the other leaders — return,
reports of his death were spread, and Penelope was urged to take another husband. In the remote state of Ithaca when the rightful sovereign was absent, the prince but a boy, and the ruler a beautiful and
wealthy woman, disorganization easily set in. The princes of the country and of the neighboring islands gathered at the palace, and, under
excuse of wooing Penelope, lived at free quarters there, wasting the substance of Odysseus and corrupting nearly all his retainers. Penelope,
powerless to restrain their lawlessness, but believing Odysseus still alive,
could defend herself from the dreaded marriage only by matching
woman's wit against dull force and numbers.

This, then, is the twofold story of the Odyssey: the story of a loyal
wife, sagaciously watching through years of turmoil for the coming of
the husband in whose power she trusts; and the story of that resource-
ful husband himself, who, when men, gods, and nature are arrayed
against him, triumphs over all and by cool intelligence, patient
courage, and a tenacious heart that ever rejoiced in danger, forces a
way single-handed — one man against the world, but obedient to the
voice of wisdom — until he wins once more his wife, child, and kingdom.
The theme of the Odyssey is the dominance of mind over circumstance,
a theme deeply fixed in the genius of the Greek race, and continually
emphasized by Homer in the standing epithets attached to his three
leading characters: Odysseus is "the wise" ($\pi o\lambda\acute{\upsilon}\mu\eta\tau\iota\varsigma$), Penelope "the
heedful" ($\pi\varepsilon\rho\acute{\iota}\phi\rho\omega\nu$), and Telemachus "the discreet" ($\pi\varepsilon\pi\nu\upsilon\mu\acute{\varepsilon}\nu o\varsigma$). The form
given to the poem by this ethical motive is naturally that of a story of
adventure, a story matchless in its combination of plainness, profundity,
and range of human interest, and one that has probably affected western
civilization more deeply than any piece of writing outside the Bible.

The poem naturally divides itself into two Parts, widely contrasted in
subject, method, and movement. The twelve Books of the First Part

relate the experiences of Odysseus on his homeward journey—at sea, among lands and peoples who are not Greek, in regions where marvels happen easily, where gods, beings half human, and phantoms of the dead, show themselves without exciting much surprise. In this First Part the pages are crowded with events, and here are found most of the single incidents which make the Odyssey famous. Each Book has its independent interest, and fragmentary readers who seek detachable incidents are chiefly attracted to this Part.

In the twelve Books of the Second Part, reporting the recovery by Odysseus of his island kingdom, the events pass on land, at home, among familiar Greek customs from which the marvelous is for the most part banished. Here the struggle is with wicked men, not with divine or physical powers. The interest of this Part is dramatic rather than incidental, each incident finding its principal significance through its bearing on the final catastrophe—the slaughter of the suitors and the reinstatement of Odysseus. To catch the sweep of inevitable dramatic vengeance here it is necessary to read several Books together. But when connectedly read, this Part reveals a sustained psychologic power which is not found in the earlier portion.

Within these two large divisions the Books group themselves in sets of four, each little group having its distinctive theme, and making its needful contribution to the common plot. That plot is orderly, firm in texture, and well calculated to hold the attention of the hearer. It begins with depicting the situation at once in Heaven and in Ithaca. It is now the twentieth year since Odysseus left his home, the tenth since he sailed from Troy. During three years of the homeward voyage the avenging god Poseidon delayed him on the sea. For the past seven years the nymph Calypso has held him as her unwilling guest in the island of Ogygia. At last (B. I) the protectress of his family, the goddess Athene, protests to Zeus against permitting further wrong to one so wise and pious, and urges Zeus to send the messenger Hermes to Calypso with orders of release. Athene herself goes disguised to Ithaca and encourages Telemachus, now just coming of age, to assert himself against the suitors. Telemachus (B. II) in an assembly bids the suitors depart from Ithaca, and begs of them a ship with which he may search for tidings of his father. Scornfully they refuse. By Athene's aid, however, he obtains ship and crew, sails to Pylos, and learns (B. III) from King Nestor the little he knows about the wanderings of Odysseus. Peisistratus, the son of Nestor, joining him, the two young men go overland to Lacedæmon, to the palace of Menelaus and Helen. Menelaus (B. IV) has been at home but two years. He recounts his own wanderings, and relates how he heard from the old man of the sea that Odysseus is a captive in Ogygia. The suitors at Ithaca lie in wait to catch Telemachus on his return.

When we have thus become familiar with the state of affairs in Ithaca, the scene changes (B. V) to Ogygia. A second council of the gods is held, or we are reminded of the previous one. Hermes takes flight with his message, delivers it, and Calypso unwillingly consents to the departure of Odysseus. He builds a raft and sets sail, but on the eighteenth day of his voyage is discovered by his enemy Poseidon, who wrecks him on the island of Phæacia. Naked and fainting, he struggles ashore at a river's mouth, and falls asleep in a thicket. The country (B. VI) is ruled by King Alcinoüs. His daughter, Nausicaä, in obedience to a dream, persuades her father to allow her and her maidens to make a washing expedition to the neighboring river. Their sportive cries awake Odysseus who, without disclosing his name, wins from Nausicaä a promise of aid. She conducts him to the city and bids him make appeal to her mother Arete. After admiring (B. VII) the house and gardens of Alcinoüs, he presents himself to the Queen, who listens kindly to the account of his shipwreck. At an assembly (B. VIII) it is decided to send Odysseus onward. He shows his strength at the games; but when at the following banquet the bard sings a song of Troy, he cannot restrain his tears, he discloses his name, and is entreated to tell the tale of his wanderings.

By this device Homer enlivens his poem, and breaks the long account of the homeward voyage into two easy sections. It is the journey's second section, that from Ogygia through Phæacia, of which we first learn. This is performed before our very eyes. But of the earlier section, that from Troy to Ogygia, we know only by hearsay. Odysseus narrates it, telling a traveler's tale which fills four breathless Books with marvels. His story begins (B. IX) with the departure from Troy. He plundered the Ciconians, he visited the Lotus-eaters; he was in the cave of Polyphemus; his men (B. X) turned the winds of helpful Æolus to harm. From the subsequent attack of the Læstrygonians only one ship escaped and reached the isle of Circe. Here followed still stranger events, and Odysseus learned from Circe that the Prophet Teiresias in the land of the dead must direct his farther course. To the dim region (B. XI) beyond the Ocean-stream he accordingly steered, talked there with his dead sailor, with his mother, with a group of great men's wives and daughters, with his former comrades of the Trojan war, with the mythical heroes of his race, and with Teiresias, who warned him against deeds of impiety. Returning to Circe (B. XII) and receiving from her supplies and instructions, he set sail once more, passed the Sirens in safety, lost six of his men under the crag of Scylla, and landed at last on the island where the herds of the Sun were pastured. In spite of the warnings of Teiresias, these sacred cattle were killed and eaten by his men. To avenge their death Zeus sent upon the ship a tempest which wrecked it, leaving Odysseus alone alive. He clung to the keel, even when sucked down by the whirlpool of Charybdis, and after ten days of drifting reached Calypso's island, where we found him at the beginning of B. V.

Part Second now begins, yet not abruptly. Wonders of the sea still mark the early pages of B. XIII. The Phæacians are delighted with Odysseus's story. They give him abundant gifts, and set him on one of their marvelous ships, which lands him after a single night's sail on the Ithacan coast, Poseidon taking a final and impotent vengeance by sinking the ship as it returns to Scheria. Athene appears, instructs Odysseus how to store his goods, warns him of the coming struggle with the suitors, and bids him, while concerting plans, to take shelter with the swineherd Eumæus, the one among his retainers who has kept him in most loyal remembrance. To prevent likelihood of recognition, she transforms his garb and person into those of an aged beggar. By Eumæus (B. XIV) he is hospitably received. At table he tells of fictitious wanderings, in the course of which he had heard of Odysseus, who, as he thinks, will soon return. As they lie down for the night Odysseus commends himself further to Eumæus by a story of the Trojan war. Telemachus meanwhile (B. XV), under guidance of Athene, leaves Menelaus, joins his ship at Pylos, safely passes the suitors' ambuscade, but instead of going to the palace seeks the lodge of Eumæus. Welcomed there (B. XVI), he sends Eumæus to Penelope, to inform her of his return; then alone with the pretended beggar he describes the hardships endured at the palace by himself and his mother. Odysseus, through the transforming power of Athene becoming once more a king, reveals himself to his son, and together they plan the overthrow of the suitors. Eumæus, after delivering his message at the palace and finding the suitors there foiled in their ambuscade, returns to the lodge.

It is the purpose of the next group of Books to delay the action, to make us see Odysseus calmly enduring outrage under his own roof, and by thus bringing before us the immensity of the suitors' insolence to prepare our minds to accept with exultation the tremendous vengeance at the close. Telemachus (B. XVII), departing at dawn to the town, reports to Penelope what Menelaus had told him of Odysseus. Theoclymenus, too, an Argive prophet who had come to Ithaca on the ship of Telemachus, declares that Odysseus is already in the land. But Penelope doubts. And now Odysseus, a beggar once more, is conducted by Eumæus to the palace, being insulted on the way by a goatherd Melanthius. In the courtyard lies his old neglected dog, Argos, who dies in recognizing his master. Entering the hall, Odysseus asks alms of the suitors and for a time obtains it, until Antinoüs, one of their leaders, breaking into abuse hurls a stool at him. Penelope in her own room, hearing that a man is hurt, is indignant and sends Eumæus to fetch him. But the beggar, though professing to have tidings of Odysseus, postpones the meeting till evening. While Odysseus sits by the threshold (B. XVIII), the privileged beggar Irus appears. Angry at being supplanted, and cheered on by the suitors, he provokes Odysseus to a combat. Odysseus fells him with a single blow, drags him into the courtyard, and warns Amphinomus, a leader of the suitors who had shown signs of kindness, to avoid impending doom. Penelope stands at the door, allures the suitors by her beauty, and, declaring that she must soon make her choice among them, obtains rich gifts. Odysseus meets with further insult from the handmaid Melantho and from Eurymachus. When the suitors have departed for the night, leaving Telemachus and Odysseus behind, the two (B. XIX) remove to another room all weapons found in the hall. Telemachus then goes to rest, while Penelope comes with her women to the appointed meeting with Odysseus. In answer to her questions, he gives a feigned account of seeing Odysseus in Crete and moves her to tears by the minuteness of his description. Odysseus will be in Ithaca, he asserts, before the new year. She offers him a bed and bath, and he is compelled to allow the old nurse Eurycleia to wash his feet. There was a scar upon his knee, the result of a wound given by a boar when he was but a youth. On touching this, Eurycleia recognizes him, but is checked in her cry by Odysseus. Athene diverts for the moment the attention of Penelope, who soon relates a dream which may portend the overthrow of the suitors. She also tells of the trial of the bow that to-morrow must decide which of the suitors shall become her unwelcome husband. Night (B. XX) brings little sleep to Odysseus and Penelope. In her restless dreams she beholds her husband once more beside her; while he, full of rage at the shameless suitors, and perceiving the need of instant action, is dismayed at the odds against him. Athene promises aid and Zeus sends him an omen. For the festival of the archer god Apollo the house is in the morning set in order. Wood, water, swine, and goats are brought. Odysseus learns that Philœtius, a goatherd, loyally desires his master's return. The suitors soon gather, with murder in their hearts against Telemachus, but are restrained by signs from Zeus. At the morning meal brawling breaks out. When Odysseus receives from Telemachus a portion like the rest, Ctesippus flings an ox-hoof at him, and a demand is uttered that Penelope at once make her decision. Telemachus assents, but hideous premonitions fill the hall.

Penelope now (B. XXI) brings from the storeroom the great bow of Odysseus, the sight of which moves Eumæus and Philœtius to tears. Telemachus sets up the row of axes through which the archers are to shoot, and, announcing that he too will compete, attempts to string the bow. He almost succeeds, but is stopped by a sign from Odysseus. Others also failing, they heat and grease the bow. To no effect; they have not strength to string it. Meanwhile Odysseus, following Eumæus and Philœtius to the court, reveals himself to them and gives his final orders. They all return, and find that neither Antinoüs nor Eurymachus can bend the bow. Odysseus asks it. The suitors insultingly refuse, and Penelope intervenes. Telemachus, sending her to her chamber, allows Odysseus to try the bow, who shoots an arrow through the axes. Taking his stand before the door (B. XXII), he shoots down Antinoüs, and declares himself Odysseus. The frightened suitors, who have only their swords, try to propitiate him, to flee, to rush upon him. One after one they fall. From the armory Telemachus brings weapons to be used when the quiver of arrows shall be spent. Melanthius also succeeds in obtaining twelve spears for the suitors. These they let fly at Odysseus and his men. But Athene frustrates their missiles, guides those hurled against them, and spreads a panic which brings slaughter on them all. None are spared except the bard Phemius and the herald Medon. And now Eurycleia, at the bidding of Odysseus, summons twelve guilty handmaids, who are forced to carry out the bodies and to aid in cleansing the great hall and then are hanged in the courtyard. With fumes of sulphur Odysseus purifies the house, while loyal handmaids rejoice over his return. During the struggle Athene has kept Penelope in a deep sleep. Eurycleia (B. XXIII) now goes to waken her, bearing to her tidings of the return of Odysseus and the slaughter of the suitors. It is more than Penelope can believe. If the men are dead, they have been slain by some god through anger at their crimes. Yet she descends and meets Odysseus, but is speechless with joy and indecision. Telemachus upbraids her. Odysseus, perceiving that time is needed for the recognition, turns to other things. Dance and song must continue the festival, or from the stillness the townspeople will discover what has happened. While the bard plays, Odysseus bathes, and in his own dress once more presents himself before Penelope. She tries if it is he by bidding Eurycleia move out a great bed for him from the bridal chamber he had formerly built. A growing tree wrought into its frame made it immovable. Of this none knew except her maid, herself, and Odysseus. The angry question of Odysseus whether in his absence the olive trunk had been cut assures her that it is in truth her husband, and she throws herself into his arms. As they lie in bed that magical night each tells the other what has passed in the long separation. At dawn Odysseus rises, calls Telemachus and the two herdsmen, and sets off for the farm of his father Laërtes. An interlude, possibly an interpolation (B. XXIV), shows Hermes conducting the souls of the suitors to Hades, where, surrounded by a group of dead Greek chieftains, Agamemnon contrasts the stately burial of Achilles with his own pitiful end. From one of the suitors he learns how the long fidelity of Penelope has been rewarded with triumph.

At the farm Odysseus gradually reveals himself to his aged and impov-
erished father. But a rumor of the slaughter of the suitors runs through
the town, and their kinsmen quickly gather. Led by the father of
Antinoüs they attack the house of Laërtes. Laërtes strikes down their
leader, and all are put to rout. Athene intervenes in guise of Nestor and
makes between the foes a lasting peace.

The action of the Odyssey occupies about six weeks. At a few points
the days are doubtful, but the most probable scheme is that of Faesi,
who divides as follows:—

1st day. Council of the gods. Athene visits Ithaca. B. I.
2nd day. Calling of the Ithacan assembly and the departure of Telemachus. B. II.
3rd day. Visit to Pylos. B. III.
4th day. Sacrifice at Pylos. Departure to Lacedæmon. Arrival at Pheræ. B. III.
5th day. Arrival at Lacedæmon and welcome by Menelaus. B. III–IV.
6th day. Stay in Lacedæmon. Plot of the suitors in Ithaca against Telemachus.
   B. IV.
7th day. Second council of the gods. Hermes sent to Calypso. B. V.
8th–11th day. Building of the raft. B. V.
12th–28th day. Odysseus departing from Ogygia continues his voyage safely for
   seventeen days. B. V.
29th–31st day. The Phæacian mountains come in sight. Storm, shipwreck, and
   two days of drifting on the sea. Odysseus lands on the coast of Scheria and
   falls asleep in a thicket. B. V.
32nd day. Meeting of Nausicaä and Odysseus. His coming to the palace of
   Alcinoüs. B. VI–VII.
33rd day. Second day at Scheria. Banquet. Games. Story of Odysseus.
   B. VIII–XIII.
34th day. Third day at Scheria. Gifts are brought to the ship of Odysseus,
   which sails at night. B. XIII.
35th day. Odysseus wakes in Ithaca and goes to Eumæus. From Lacedæmon
   Athene summons Telemachus, who sleeps at Pheræ. B. XIII–XV.
36th day. By night Telemachus passes Pheæ and Elis. Stay of Odysseus with
   Eumæus. B. XV.
37th day. Telemachus lands in Ithaca and meets Odysseus at the lodge of
   Eumæus. B. XV–XVI.
38th day. Telemachus goes to the town, followed by Odysseus. The fight with
   Irus. The recognition by Eurycleia and talk with Penelope. B. XVII–XX.
39th day. The trial of the bow. The slaughter of the suitors and the recognition
   by Penelope. B. XX–XXIII.
40th day. The recognition by Laërtes and the conclusion of peace. B. XXIII–end.

The scenes of the Odyssey are not, like those of the Iliad, drawn from
war and camps. They have for the most part a domestic and social character. When the heroes of the Iliad have nothing else to do, they fight;
under similar circumstances those of the Odyssey eat. These are the

distinctive occupations of the two poems. That of the Odyssey is the nobler, for it is connected with home, friendship, reflection, women's influence. A wider range of motive is consequently opened in the Odyssey.

Odysseus is the central character, a man wise not through the posses- sion of large knowledge (Nestor is that) but through sagacity, resource- fulness, and self-command. Other men—Telemachus, Eumæus, Antinoüs, and Eurymachus—bear important parts. But the dominant forces of the poem are women. The prime mover is a goddess. Those most influential over the journey home are the nymphs Calypso and Circe, perhaps we should add Ino and Leucothea. In Phæacia Queen Arete is of larger consequence than King Alcinoüs. Among the mighty dead whom Odysseus meets in Hades there are as many women as men. Eurycleia, Eurynome, and the forward handmaid Melantho are conspicuous figures of the Ithacan household; while, exalted above them all appear the three eternal types of womanhood: Nausicaä, the unconquered girl; Helen, the accomplished lady; Penelope, the faithful wife. In the Odyssey, in short, woman is the comrade of man, respected as his equal in intellectual power, administrative capacity, and artistic skill. It is usually assumed that Homer's women lived in isolation, hav- ing an apartment to themselves, the gynæcæum or harem of Eastern nations; and certainly this was usual in the historic ages of Greece. But in the Odyssey I find no clear trace of such an arrangement, while the psychologic evidence against it is strong. Though Penelope and her maids generally withdraw from the riotous suitors to rooms of their own, they enter the hall with freedom, even when men are there; and it is there at night that Penelope talks with Odysseus. Helen sits in the hall of Menelaus and receives guests there. So does Arete in the hall of Alcinoüs. Arete attends a public banquet. Penelope would have been present at the trial of the bow had she not for prudential reasons been dismissed by Telemachus. Nausicaä and her maids drive unattended into the country; and when she comes home from washing, it is her brother who carries her clothing to her chamber. These are not harem manners. To find anything like them in their combination of freedom and dignity we must cross the intervening ages and talk with the women of our own time.

The style of Homer is radiant with the freshness of the early world. He seems always to be thinking of everything for the first time. Grave and weighty though he is, he has a simplicity and swiftness that are the despair of translators. His common cast of phrase is inexplicably felicitous. "There's magic in the web of it," but there is no constraint. He does not, like Milton, "build the lofty line." His little words fall into their places as if they belonged there—unremarkable, unalterable, efficient, and lingering long in the mind when the sight of them is gone. His sentence is seldom an organic whole like the modern period, the parts mutually dependent; it can generally be cut in several places and still give a tolerable sense. When describing an event, he ordinarily mentions what happened as a series of separate facts, strung together with "and, and." Qualifying clauses he usually places subsequently, like afterthoughts; not where rhetoricians say they should be placed, before the introduction of the thing qualified. Like the Elizabethan dramatists he frequently employs constructions intelligible only to the interested listener, not to the grammarian; nouns are omitted; pronouns serve in places where our critics call them ambiguous; doors for misconception are again and again left open for those who care to misconceive. Everywhere is seen a syntax full of beauty when thought of as that of living speech; full of defect, if judged by the canons of the schools. In the very forms of the language there is extraordinary flexibility; a syllable is prolonged here, clipped there; a consonant is doubled or left single; the commoner vowels have alternative forms. All is plastic. Literary conventions have not yet sprung up. This freedom from conventional trammels is an immense artistic advantage to Homer, and he uses it to the full. What portion of the thought should fall on the mind first he knows as nobody else has ever known, and this is the portion that he places first. He fixes his eye on the object, and as its different parts present themselves he tells us of them. In reading him, we must think of the prowling lion and the starting ship rather than of the printed words. Repetition is with him, as with the child, a genuine poetic resource. He has all the child's delight in "saying it again," and he always prefers the old story to the new. The individual aspects of object or person he is fond of fixing once for all in an epithet, whose recurrence may convey a pleasure somewhat similar to that which we moderns receive in rhyme,—a pleasure enlarged by the repetition of phrases, or even of whole passages. The appropriateness of these to their new situation is secured by changes in the turn of a word or two. Similes are common, metaphors rare; the thing and that with which it is compared remain two and unblended, exactly as in life.

In the whole body of Homeric poetry there are about thirty thousand lines: sixteen thousand in the Iliad, twelve thousand in the Odyssey, and two or three thousand in the Hymns—a collection of separate hexameter poems, addressed to various gods, and now believed to be the product of a later age. The most convenient school edition of the Odyssey is that of W. W. Merry, in two volumes, published by the Clarendon Press. In it the Greek text is broken at intervals by an English line descriptive of the matter, and there are careful notes and introductions. The large edition of H. Hayman, three volumes,

London, D. Nutt & Co., is especially valuable for its summaries of the narrative, its full notes, its marginal references, and its analyses of the characters. The handiest Homeric dictionary is that of Autenrieth, translated by R. P. Keep, and published by Harper. Dunbar's "Concordance of the Odyssey," Clarendon Press, cites passages, though with many inaccuracies. Gladstone's "Primer of Homer," his "Juventus Mundi," both published by Macmillan, and A. M. Clerke's "Familiar Studies in Homer," published by Longman, are entertaining, but not, like R. C. Jebb's "Introduction to Homer," published by Ginn & Co., altogether trustworthy. A. J. Church, in his "Stories from Homer," published by Harper, has preserved much of the Homeric spirit.

There are twenty-three English translations of the Odyssey. Between the earliest of them—the brilliant version of George Chapman, 1615, in five iambics, couplet rhyme—and the year 1861, when Matthew Arnold published his stimulating essays "On Translating Homer," a new rendering of the Odyssey appeared about every thirty years. Since that time the rate of issue has been ten times more rapid. Among these translations the most important are those of Alexander Pope, 1725, five iambics, couplet rhyme; William Cowper, 1791, five iambics, blank verse; Henry Cary, 1823, prose; P. S. Worsley, 1861, Spenserian stanza; W. C. Bryant, 1872, five iambics, blank verse; S. H. Butcher and A. Lang, A world's book like the Odyssey cannot be exhausted, nor can any one person completely report it. It has as many aspects as it has translators. Hobbes commended it to his readers as a series of lessons in morals; to Worsley it was the world's great fairy tale; to Butcher and Lang it is an archaic "historical document." Others have found in it a philological interest, a mythological, a grammatical. However broad-minded a student may be, his sympathies are sure to reach a limit somewhere short of the compass of Homer. I have approached the Odyssey from the philosophic and poetic side, delighting in Homer's unique mental attitude. Notwithstanding his extraordinary powers of observation and utterance, he seems to me to confront the world like a child. Turning to him, I escape from our complicated and introspective world, and am refreshed.

THE ODYSSEY

I.

THE COUNCIL OF THE GODS AND THE SUMMONS
TO TELEMACHUS

SPEAK TO me, Muse, of the adventurous man who wandered long after he sacked the sacred citadel of Troy. Many the men whose towns he saw, whose ways he proved; and many a pang he bore in his own breast at sea while struggling for his life and his men's safe return. Yet even so, by all his zeal, he did not save his men; for through their own perversity they perished—fools! who devoured the kine of the exalted Sun. Wherefore he took away the day of their return. Of this, O goddess, daughter of Zeus, beginning where thou wilt, speak to us also.

Now all the others who were saved from utter ruin were at home, safe both from war and sea. Him only, longing for his home and wife, the potent nymph Calypso, a heavenly goddess, held in her hollow grotto desiring him to be her husband. Nay, when the time had come in the revolving years at which the gods ordained his going home to Ithaca, even then, among his kin, he was not freed from trouble. Yet the gods felt compassion, all save Poseidon, who steadily strove with godlike Odysseus till he reached his land.

But Poseidon now was with the far-off Ethiopians, the remotest of mankind, who form two tribes, one at the setting of the Exalted one, one at his rising; awaiting there a sacrifice of bulls and rams. So sitting at the feast he took his pleasure. The other gods, meanwhile, were gathered in the halls of Zeus upon Olympus, and thus began the father of men and gods; for in his mind he mused of gentle Aegisthus, whom Agamemnon's far-famed son, Orestes, slew. Mindful of him, he thus addressed the immortals:

"Lo, how men blame the gods! From us, they say, spring troubles. But through their own perversity, and more than is their due, they meet with sorrow; even as now Aegisthus, pressing beyond his due, married the lawful wife of the son of Atreus and slew her husband on his coming home. Yet he well knew his own impending ruin; for we ourselves forewarned him, dispatching Hermes, our clear-sighted Speedy-comer, and told him not to slay the man nor woo the wife. 'For because of the son of Atreus shall come vengeance from Orestes when he is grown and longs for his own land.' This Hermes said, but did not turn the purpose of Aegisthus by his kindness. And now Aegisthus makes atonement for it all."

Then answered him the goddess, clear-eyed Athene: 'Our father, son of Kronos, most high above all rulers, that man assuredly lies in befitting ruin. So perish all who do such deeds! Yet is my heart distressed for wise Odysseus, hapless man, who, long cut off from friends, is meeting hardship upon a sea-girt island, the navel of the sea. Woody the island is, and there a goddess dwells, daughter of wizard Atlas who knows the depths of every sea and through his power holds the tall pillars which keep earth and sky asunder. It is his daughter who detains this hapless, sorrowing man, ever with tender and insistent words enticing to forgetfulness of Ithaca. And still Odysseus, through longing but to see the smoke spring from his land, desires to die. Nevertheless, your heart turns not, Olympian one. Did not Odysseus seek your favor beside the Argive ships and offer sacrifice upon the plain of Troy? Why then are you so wroth against him, Zeus?"

Then answered her cloud-gathering Zeus, and said: "My child, what word has passed the barrier of your teeth? How could I possibly forget princely Odysseus, who is beyond all mortal men in wisdom, beyond them too in giving honor to the immortal gods, who hold the open sky? Nay, but Poseidon, the girder of the land, is ceaselessly enraged because Odysseus blinded of his eye the Cyclops, god-like Polyphemus, who of all Cyclops has the greatest power. A nymph, Thoösa, bore him, daughter of Phorcys, lord of the barren sea, for she within the hollow caves united with Poseidon. And since that day the earth-shaking Poseidon does not indeed destroy Odysseus, but ever drives him wandering from his land. Come then, let us all here plan for his turning home. So shall Poseidon lay by his anger, unable, in defiance of us all, to strive with the immortal gods alone."

Then answered him the goddess, clear-eyed Athene: "Our father, son of Kronos, most high above all rulers, if it now please the blessed gods that wise Odysseus shall return to his own home, let us send Hermes forth—the Guide, the Speedy-comer—into the island of Ogygia, straightway to tell the fair-haired nymph our steadfast purpose, that hardy Odysseus shall set forth upon his homeward way. I in the mean while go to Ithaca, to rouse his son yet more and to put vigor in his breast; that, summoning to an assembly the long-haired Achaeans, he may denounce the troop of suitors, men who continually butcher his thronging flocks and swing-paced, crook-horned oxen. And I will send him to Sparta and to sandy Pylos, to try to learn of his dear father's coming, and so to win a good report among mankind."

Saying this, under her feet she bound her beautiful sandals, immortal, made of gold, which carry her over the flood and over the boundless land swift as a breath of wind. She took her ponderous spear, tipped with sharp bronze, thick, long, and strong, with which she vanquishes the ranks of men,—of heroes, even,—when this daughter of a mighty sire is roused against them. Then she went dashing down the ridges of Olympus and in the land of Ithaca stood at Odysseus' gate, on the threshold of his court. Holding in hand a brazen spear, she seemed the stranger Mentes, the Taphian leader. Here then she found the haughty suitors. They were amusing themselves with games of draughts before the palace door, seated on hides of oxen which they themselves had slain. Their pages and busy squires were near; some mixing wine and water in the bowls, others with porous sponges washing and laying tables, while others still carved them abundant meat.

By far the first to see Athene was princely Telemachus. For he was sitting with the suitors, sad at heart, picturing in mind his noble father,—how he might come from somewhere, make a scattering of the suitors, take to himself his honors, and be master of his own. Thus thinking while he sat among the suitors, Athene met his eye. Straight to the door he went, being at heart ashamed to have a stranger stand so long before his gate. So drawing near and grasping her right hand, he took her brazen spear, and speaking in winged words he said: "Hail, stranger, here with us you shall be welcome; and by and by when you have tasted food, you shall make known your needs."

Saying this, he led the way, and Pallas Athene followed. When they were come within the lofty hall, he carried the spear to a tall pillar and set it in a well-worn rack, where also stood many a spear of hardy Odysseus. Athene herself he led to a chair and seated, spreading a linen cloth below. Good was the chair and richly wrought; upon its lower part there was a rest for feet. Beside it, for himself, he set a sumptuous seat apart from all the suitors, for fear the stranger, meeting rude men and worried by their din, might lose his taste for food; and then that he might ask him, too, about his absent father. Now water for the hands a servant brought in a beautiful pitcher made of gold, and poured it out over a silver basin for their washing, and spread a polished table by their side. And the grave housekeeper brought bread and placed before them, setting out food of many a kind, freely giving of her store. The carver, too, took platters of meat, and placed before them, meat of all kinds, and set their golden goblets ready; while a page, pouring wine, passed to and fro between them.

And now the haughty suitors entered. These soon took seats in order, on couches and on chairs. Pages poured water on their hands, maids heaped them bread in baskets, and young men brimmed the bowls with drink; and on the food spread out before them they laid hands. So after they had stayed desire for drink and food, then in their thoughts they turned to other things, the song and dance; for these attend a feast. A page put a beautiful harp into the hands of Phemius, who sang perforce among the suitors; and touching the harp, he raised his voice and sang a beautiful song. Then said Telemachus to clear-eyed Athene, his head bent close, that others might not hear:

"Good stranger, will you feel offense at what I say? These things are all their care,—the harp and song,—an easy care when, making no amends, they eat the substance of a man whose white bones now are rotting in the rain, if lying on the land, or in the sea the waters roll them round. Yet were they once to see him coming home to Ithaca, they all would pray rather for speed of foot than stores of gold and clothing. But he, instead, by some hard fate is gone, and naught remains to us of comfort—no, not if any man on earth shall say he still will come. Passed is his day of coming. But now declare me this and plainly tell, who are you? Of what people? Where is your town and kindred? On what ship did you come? And how did sailors bring you to Ithaca? Whom did they call themselves? For I am sure you did not come on foot. And tell me truly this, that I may know full well if for the first time now you visit here, or are you my father's friend? For many foreigners once sought our home; because Odysseus also was a rover among men."

Then said to him the goddess, clear-eyed Athene: "Well, I will very plainly tell you all: Mentes I call myself, the son of wise Anchialus, and I am lord of the oar-loving Taphians. Even now I put in here, with ship and crew, when sailing over the wine-dark sea to men of a strange speech, to Temesê, for bronze. I carry glittering iron. Here my ship lies, just off the fields outside the town, within the bay of Reithron under woody Neïon. Hereditary friends we count ourselves from early days, as you may learn if you will go and ask old lord Laërtes, who, people say, comes to the town no more, but far out in the country suffers hardship, an aged woman his attendant, who supplies him food and drink whenever weariness weighs down his knees, as he creeps about his slope of garden ground. Even now I came, for I was told your father was at home. But, as I see, the gods delay his journey; for surely nowhere yet on earth has royal Odysseus died; living, he lingers somewhere still on

the wide sea, upon some sea-girt island, and cruel men constrain him—
some savage folk, who hold him there against his will. Nay, I will prophesy such things as the immortals bring to mind, things which I think
will happen; although I am no prophet and have no skill in birds. Not
long shall he be absent from his own dear land, though iron fetters bind
him. Some means he will devise to come away; for many a shift has he.
But now, declare me this and plainly tell, if you indeed—so tall—are
the true son of Odysseus. In head and beautiful eyes you surely are
much like him. So often we were together before he embarked for
Troy, where others too, the bravest of the Argives, went in their hollow
ships. But since that day I have not seen Odysseus, nor he me."

Then answered her discreet Telemachus: "Yes, stranger, I will plainly
tell you all. My mother says I am his child; I myself do not know; for
no one ever yet knew his own parentage. Yet would I were the son of
some blest man on whom old age had come amongst his own possessions. But now, the man born most ill-fated of all human kind—of him
they say I come, since this you ask me."

Then said to him the goddess, clear-eyed Athene: "Surely the gods
meant that your house should not lack future fame, when to such son
as you Penelope gave birth. Nevertheless declare me this and truly tell,
what is the feast? What company is this? And what is your part here?
Some drinking bout or wedding? It surely is no festival at common cost.
So rude they seem, and wanton, feasting about the hall. A man of sense
must be indignant who comes and sees such outrage."

Then answered her discreet Telemachus: "Stranger,—since now you
ask of this and question me,—in former days this house bade fair to be
wealthy and esteemed, so long as he was here; but the hard-purposed
gods then changed their minds and shut him from our knowledge more
than all men beside. For were he dead, I should not feel such grief, if
he had fallen among comrades in the Trojan land, or in the arms of
friends when the skein of war was wound. Then would the whole
Achaean host have made his grave, and for his son in after days a great
name had been gained. Now, silently the robber winds have swept him
off. Gone is he, past all sight and hearing, and sighs and sorrows he has
left to me. Yet now I do not grieve and mourn for him alone; because
the gods have brought me other sore distress. For all the nobles who
bear sway among the islands,—Doulichion, Same, and woody
Zacynthos,—and they who have the power in rocky Ithaca, all woo my
mother and despoil my home. She neither declines the hated suit nor
has she power to end it; while they with feasting impoverish my home
and soon will bring me also to destruction."

Stirred into anger, Pallas Athene spoke: "Alas! in very truth you
greatly need absent Odysseus, to lay hands on the shameless suitors.

What if he came even now and here before his house stood at the outer gate, with helmet, shield, and his two spears,—even such as when I saw him first at my own home, drinking and making merry, on his return from Ephyra, from Ilus, son of Mermerus. For thither on his swift ship went Odysseus, seeking a deadly drug in which to dip his brazen arrows. And Ilus did not give it, for he feared the immortal gods; my father, however, gave it, for he held him strangely dear. If as he was that day Odysseus now might meet the suitors, they all would find quick turns of fate and bitter rites of marriage. Still, in the gods' lap it lies to say if he shall come and wreak revenge within his halls; but yours it is to plan to thrust the suitors from your door. Give me your ear and heed my words. To-morrow, summoning to an assembly the Achaean lords, announce your will to all and call the gods to witness! Bid the suitors all disperse, each to his own. And for your mother, if her heart inclines to marriage, let her return to her strong father's hall. They there shall make the wedding and provide the many gifts which should accompany a well-loved child. Then for yourself I offer sound advice, if you will hearken. Man the best ship you have with twenty oarsmen, and go and gather tidings of your long-absent father. Perhaps some man may tell you, or you may catch a rumor sent from Zeus, which oftenest carries tidings. First go to Pylos, and question royal Nestor. Then on to Sparta, to light-haired Menelaus; for he came last of all the mailed Achaeans. And if you hear your father is alive and coming home, then, worn as you are, you might endure for one year more. But if you hear that he is dead,—no longer with the living—you shall at once return to your own native land, and pile his mound and pay the funeral rites, full many, as are due, and you shall give your mother to a husband. Moreover, after you have ended this and finished all, within your mind and heart consider next how you may slay the suitors in your halls, whether by stratagem or open force. You must not hold to childish ways, because you are no longer now the child you were. Have you not heard what fame royal Orestes gained with all mankind, because he slew the slayer, wily Aegisthus, who had slain his famous father? You too, my friend,—for certainly I find you fair and tall,—be strong, that men hereafter born may speak your praise. Now I will go to my swift ship and to my comrades, who greatly chafe at waiting. Rely upon yourself. Heed what I say."

Then answered her discreet Telemachus: "Stranger, in this you speak with kindness, even as a father to a son. Never shall I forget it. But tarry now, though eager for your journey. Bathe, and refresh your soul; then glad at heart turn to your ship, bearing a gift of value, very beautiful, to be to you a keepsake from myself, even such a thing as dear friends give to friends."

Then answered him the goddess, clear-eyed Athene: "Do not detain me longer now, when I am anxious for my journey. And any gift your heart may bid you give, give when I come again, for me to carry home. Choose one exceeding beautiful; it shall be matched in the exchange."

Saying this, clear-eyed Athene passed away, even as a bird—a sea-hawk—takes its flight. Into his heart she had brought strength and courage, turning his thoughts upon his father more even than before. As he marked this in his mind, an awe came on his heart; he knew a god was with him. Straightway he sought the suitors, godlike himself.

To them the famous bard was singing, while they in silence sat and listened. He sang of the return of the Achaeans, the sad return, which Pallas Athene had appointed them on leaving Troy.

Now from her upper chamber, there heard this wondrous song the daughter of Icarius, heedful Penelope, and she descended the long stairway from her room, yet not alone; two damsels followed her. And when the royal lady reached the suitors, she stood beside a column of the strong-built roof, holding before her face her delicate wimple, the while a faithful damsel stood upon either hand. Then bursting into tears, she said to the noble bard:

"Phemius, many another tale you know to charm mankind, exploits of men and gods, which bards make famous. Sit and sing one of these. The rest drink wine in silence. But cease this song, this song of woe, which harrows evermore the soul within my breast; because on me has fallen grief that cannot be forgotten. So dear a face I miss, ever remembering one whose fame is wide through Hellas and mid-Argos."

Then answered her discreet Telemachus: "My mother, why forbid the honored bard to cheer us in whatever way his mind is moved? The bards are not to blame, but rather Zeus, who gives to toiling men even as he wills to each. And for the bard, there is no ground for censure if he sings the Danaäns' cruel doom. The song which men most heartily applaud is that which comes the newest to their ears. Then let your heart and soul submit to listen; for not Odysseus only lost the day of his return at Troy, but many another perished also. Nay, seek your chamber and attend to matters of your own,—the loom, the distaff,—and bid the women ply their tasks. Words are for men, for all, especially for me; for power within this house rests here."

Amazed, she turned to her own room again, for the wise saying of her son she laid to heart. And coming to the upper chamber with her maids, she there bewailed Odysseus, her dear husband, till on her lids clear-eyed Athene caused a sweet sleep to fall.

But the suitors broke into uproar up and down the dusky hall. Each prayed to lie beside her. But thus discreet Telemachus began to speak: "You suitors of my mother, overweening in your pride, let us enjoy our feast and have no brawling now. For a pleasant thing it is to hear a bard like this, one who is like the gods in voice. But in the morning let us all take seats in the assembly, where I may unreservedly announce my will that you shall quit my halls. Seek other tables and eat what is your own, changing from house to house! Or if it seems to you more profitable and better to ruin the living of one man without amends, go wasting on! But I will call upon the gods that live forever and pray that Zeus may grant deeds of requital. Then beyond all amends, here in this house you shall yourselves be ruined."

He spoke, and all with teeth set in their lips marveled because Telemachus had spoken boldly. Then said Antinoüs, Eupeithes' son: "Telemachus, surely the gods themselves are training you to be a man of lofty tongue and a bold speaker. But may the son of Kronos never make you king in sea-girt Ithaca, although it is by birth your heritage!"

Then answered him discreet Telemachus: "Antinoüs, will you feel offense at what I say? This I would gladly take, if Zeus would grant it. Do you suppose the kingship is the worst fate in the world? Why, it is no bad thing to be a king! Soon the house of a king grows rich and he himself is honored more. Still, as to kings of the Achaeans, here in sea-girt Ithaca are many others young and old, some one of whom may take the place, since royal Odysseus now is dead. But I myself will be the lord of our own house and of the slaves which royal Odysseus won for me."

Then answered him Eurymachus, the son of Polybus: "Telemachus, in the gods' lap it lies to say which one of the Achaeans shall be king in sea-girt Ithaca. Your substance may you keep and of your house be lord; may the man never come who, heedless of your will, shall strip you of that substance while men shall dwell in Ithaca. But, good sir, I would ask about this stranger—whence the man comes, and of what land he calls himself. Where are his kinsmen and his native fields? Does he bring tidings of your father's coming, or is he come with hope of his own gains? How hastily he went! Not waiting to be known! And yet he seemed no low-born fellow by the face."

Then answered him discreet Telemachus: "Eurymachus, as for my father's coming, that is at an end. Tidings I trust no longer, let them come whence they may. Nor do I care for divinations, such as my mother seeks, summoning a diviner to the hall. This stranger is my father's friend, a man of Taphos; Mentes he calls himself, the son of wise Anchialus, and he is lord of the oar-loving Taphians."

So spoke Telemachus, but in his mind he knew the immortal goddess. Meanwhile the suitors to dancing and the gladsome song turned merrily, and waited for the evening to come on. And on their merriment dark evening came. So then, desiring rest, they each departed homeward.

But Telemachus himself, where on the beautiful court his chamber was built high upon commanding ground, went to his bed with many doubts in mind. And walking by his side, with blazing torch, went faithful Eurycleia, daughter of Ops, Peisenor's son, whom once Laërtes purchased with his substance when she was but a girl, and paid the price of twenty oxen. Her equally with his faithful wife he honored at the palace, but he never sought her bed, avoiding a wife's anger. Now she it was who bore the blazing torch beside Telemachus; for she of all the handmaids loved him most and was his nurse when little. He opened the doors of the strong chamber, sat down upon the bed, pulled his soft tunic off, and laid it in the wise old woman's hands. Folding and smoothing out the tunic, she hung it on a peg beside the well-bored bedstead, then left the chamber, and by its silver ring pulled to the door, drawing the bolt home by its strap. So there Telemachus, all the night long, wrapped in a fleece of wool, pondered in mind the course Athene counseled.

II.

THE ASSEMBLY AT ITHACA AND THE DEPARTURE
OF TELEMACHUS

SOON AS the early, rosy-fingered dawn appeared, the dear son of Odysseus rose from bed, put on his clothes, slung his sharp sword about his shoulder, under his shining feet bound his fair sandals, and came forth from his chamber in bearing like a god. Straightway he bade the clear-voiced heralds summon to an assembly the long-haired Achaeans. Those summoned, and these gathered very quickly. So when they were assembled and all had come together, he went himself to the assembly, holding in hand a brazen spear,—yet not alone, two swift dogs followed after,—and marvelous was the grace Athene cast about him, that all the people gazed as he drew near. He sat down in his father's seat; the elders made him way.

The first to speak was lord Aegyptius, a man bowed down with age, who knew a thousand things. His dear son Antiphus, a spearman, had gone with god-like Odysseus in the hollow ships to Ilios, famed for horses. The savage Cyclops killed him in the deep cave and on him made a supper last of all. Three other sons there were; one joined the suitors,—Eurynomus—and two still kept their father's farm. Yet not because of these did he forget to mourn and miss that other. With tears for him, he thus addressed the assembly, saying:

"Hearken now, men of Ithaca, to what I say. Never has our assembly once been held, no single session, since royal Odysseus went away in hollow ships. Who is it calls us now, in such a fashion? Who has such urgent need? Young or old is he? Has he heard tidings of the army's coming, which he would plainly tell to us so soon as he has learned? Or has he other public matter to announce and argue? At any rate, good seems the man to me—a blessed man. May Zeus accomplish all the good his mind intends!"

10

As thus he spoke, the dear son of Odysseus rejoiced at what was said and kept his seat no longer. He burned to speak. He rose up in the midst of the assembly, and in his hand a herald placed the sceptre,—a herald named Peisenor, discreet of understanding. Then turning first to the old man, he thus addressed him:

"Sire, not far off is he, as you full soon shall know, who called the people hither; for it is I especially whom grief befalls. No tidings of the army's coming have I heard, which I would plainly tell to you so soon as I have learned; nor have I other public matter to announce and argue. Rather it is my private need, ill falling on my house in twofold wise. For first I lost my noble father, who was formerly your king,—kind father as e'er was—and now there comes a thing more grievous still, which soon will utterly destroy my home and quite cut off my substance. Suitors beset my mother sorely against her will, sons of the very men who are the leaders here. They shrink from going to the house of Icarius, her father, to let him count the bride-gifts of his daughter and give her then to whom he will, whoever meets his favor; but haunting this house of ours day after day, killing our oxen, sheep, and fatted goats, they hold high revel, drinking sparkling wine with little heed. Much goes to waste, for there is no man here fit like Odysseus to keep damage from our doors. We are not fit ourselves to guard the house; attempting it, we should be pitiful, unskilled in conflict. Guard it I would, if only strength were mine. For deeds are done not to be longer borne, and with no decency my house is plundered. Shame you should feel yourselves, and some respect as well for neighbors living near you, and awe before the anger of the gods, lest haply they may turn upon you, vexed with your evil courses. Nay, I entreat you by Olympian Zeus, and by that Justice which dissolves and gathers men's assemblies, forbear, my friends! Leave me to pine in bitter grief alone, unless indeed my father, good Odysseus, ever in malice wronged the mailed Achaeans, and in return for that you now with malice do me wrong, urging these people on. Better for me it were you should yourselves devour my stores and herds. If you devoured them, perhaps some day there might be payment made; for we would constantly pursue you through the town, demanding back our substance till all should be restored. Now, woes incurable you lay upon my heart."

In wrath he spoke, and dashed the sceptre to the ground, letting his tears burst forth, and pity fell on all the people. So all the rest were silent; no man dared to make Telemachus a bitter answer. Antinoüs alone made answer, saying:

"Telemachus, of the lofty tongue and the unbridled temper, what do you mean by putting us to shame? On us you would be glad to fasten guilt. I tell you the Achaean suitors are not at all to blame; your mother is to blame, whose craft exceeds all women's. The third year is gone by, and fast the fourth is going since she began to mock the hearts in our Achaean breasts. To all she offers hopes, has promises for each, and sends us messages, but her mind has a different purpose. Here is the last pretext she cunningly devised. Within the hall she set up a great loom and went to weaving; fine was the web and very large; and then to us said she: 'Young men who are my suitors, though royal Odysseus now is dead, forbear to urge my marriage till I complete this robe,—its threads must not be wasted,—a shroud for lord Laërtes, against the time when the fell doom of death that lays men low shall overtake him. Achaean wives about the land, I fear, might give me blame if he should lie without a shroud, he who had great possessions.' Such were her words, and our high hearts assented. Then in the daytime would she weave at the great web, but in the night unravel, after her torch was set. Thus for three years she hid her craft and cheated the Achaeans. But when the fourth year came, as time rolled on, then at the last one of her maids, who knew full well, confessed, and we discovered her unraveling the splendid web; so then she finished it, against her will, perforce. Therefore to you the suitors make this answer, that you yourself may understand in your own heart, and that the Achaeans all may understand. Send forth your mother! Bid her to marry whomever her father wills and him who pleases her! Or will she weary longer yet the sons of the Achaeans, mindful at heart of what Athene largely gave her, skill in fair works, a noble mind, and such a craft as we have never known in those of old, those who were long ago fair-haired Achaean women,—Tyro, Alcmene, and crowned Mycene,—no one of whom had judgment like Penelope; and yet, in truth, in this she judged not wisely. For just so long shall men devour your life and substance as she retains the mind the gods put in her breast at present. Great fame she brings herself, but brings on you the loss of large possessions; for we will never go to our estates, nor elsewhere either, till she shall marry an Achaean—whom she will."

Then answered him discreet Telemachus: "Antinoüs, against her will I cannot drive from home the one who bore me and who brought me up. My father is away,—alive or dead,—and hard it were to pay the heavy charges to Icarius which I needs must, if of my will alone I sent my mother forth. For from her father's hand I shall meet ills, and Heaven will send me more, when my mother calls upon the dread Avengers as she forsakes the house; blame too will fall upon me from mankind. Therefore that word I never will pronounce; and if your hearts chafe at your footing here, then quit my halls! Seek other tables and eat what is your own, changing from house to house! Or if it seems to you more profitable and better to ruin the living of one man without amends, go wasting on! But I will call upon the gods that live forever and pray that Zeus may grant deeds of requital. Then beyond all amends, here in this house you shall yourselves be ruined!"

So spoke Telemachus, and answering him far-seeing Zeus sent forth a pair of eagles, flying from a mountain peak on high. These for a time moved on along the wind, close by each other and with outstretched wings; but as they reached the middle of the many-voiced assembly, wheeling about they briskly flapped their wings, glared at the heads of all, and death was in their eyes. Then with their claws tearing each other's cheek and neck, they darted to the right, across the town and houses. Men marveled at the birds, as they beheld, and pondered in their hearts what they might mean. And to the rest spoke old lord Halitherses, the son of Mastor; for he surpassed all people of his time in understanding birds and telling words of fate. He with good will addressed them thus, and said:

"Hearken now, men of Ithaca, to what I say; and to the suitors especially I speak, for over them rolls a great wave of woe. Odysseus will not long be parted from his friends, but even now is near, sowing the seeds of death and doom for all men here. Ay, and on many others too shall sorrow fall, on many of us who live in far-seen Ithaca! But long ere that, let us consider how to check these men, or rather, let them check themselves; that shall be soon their gain. And not as inexpert I prophesy, but with sure knowledge. For this I say: all has come true which I declared that day the Argive host took ship for Ilios, and with them also wise Odysseus went. I said that after suffering much, and losing all his men, unknown to all, in the twentieth year he should come home; and now it all comes true."

Then answered him Eurymachus, the son of Polybus: "Well, well, old man, go home and play the prophet to your children, or else they may have trouble in the days to come! About these matters I can prophesy much better than yourself. Plenty of birds flit in the sunshine, but not all are fateful. As for Odysseus, he died far away; and would that you had perished with him! You would not then be prating so of reading signs, nor would you, when Telemachus is wroth, thus press him on, looking for him to send your house some gift. But this I tell you, and it shall be done; if you, who know all that an old man knows, delude this youth with talk and urge him on to anger, it shall be in the first place all the worse for him, and he shall accomplish nothing by aid of people here, while on yourself, old man, we will inflict a fine which it will grieve you to the soul to pay. Bitter indeed shall be your sorrow. And to Telemachus, here before all, I give this warning. Let him instruct his mother to go to her father's house. They there shall make the wedding and arrange the many gifts which should accompany a well-loved child; for not, I think, till then will the sons of the Achaeans quit their rough courtship. No fear have we of any man, not even of Telemachus, so full of talk. Nothing we care for auguries which you, old man, idly declare, making yourself the more detested. So now again, his substance shall be miserably devoured, and no return be made, so long as she delays the Achaeans with her marriage. Moreover, waiting here day after day, as rivals for her charms, we will not seek out other women whom it might well become a man to marry."

Then answered him discreet Telemachus: "Eurymachus and all you other lordly suitors, this will I urge no longer; I have no more to say; for now the gods and all the Achaeans understand. But give me a swift ship with twenty comrades, to help me make a journey up and down the sea; for I will go to Sparta and to sandy Pylos, to learn about the coming home of my long-absent father. Perhaps some man may tell me, or I may catch a rumor sent from Zeus, which oftenest carries tidings. If I shall hear my father is alive and coming home, worn as I am, I might endure for one year more. But if I hear that he is dead,—no longer with the living,—I will at once return to my own native land, and pile his mound and pay the funeral rites, full many, as are due, and I will give my mother to a husband."

So saying, he sat down; and up rose Mentor, who was the friend of gallant Odysseus. On going with the ships, Odysseus gave him charge of all his house, that they should heed their elder and he keep all things secure. He with good will addressed them thus, and said:

"Hearken now, men of Ithaca, to what I say. Never again let sceptred king in all sincerity be kind and gentle, nor let him in his mind heed righteousness. Let him instead ever be stern, and work unrighteous deeds; since none remembers princely Odysseus among the people whom he ruled, kind father though he was. Yet I make no complaint against the haughty suitors for doing deeds of violence in insolence of heart; for they at hazard of their heads thus violently devour the household of Odysseus, saying he comes no more. But with the rest of the people I am wroth, because you all sit still, and, uttering not a word, you do not stop the suitors,—they so few and you so many."

Then answered him Evenor's son, Leiocritus: "Infernal Mentor, crazywitted, what do you mean by urging these to stop us? Hard would it be, for many more than we, to fight with us on question of our food! Indeed, should Ithacan Odysseus come himself upon us lordly suitors feasting in his house, and be resolved at heart to drive us from the hall, his wife would have no joy, however great her longing, over his coming; but here he should meet shameful death, fighting with more than he. You spoke unwisely! Come, people, then, turn to your own affairs! For this youth here, Mentor shall speed his voyage, and Halitherses too, for they are from of old his father's friends; but I suspect he still will sit about, gather his news in Ithaca, and never make the voyage."

He spoke, and hastily dissolved the assembly. So they dispersed, each to his house; but the suitors sought the house of princely Odysseus.

Telemachus, however, walked alone along the shore, and, washing his hands in the foaming water, prayed to Athene: "Hear me, thou god who camest yesterday here to our home, and badst me go on shipboard over the misty sea to ask about the coming home of my long-absent father. All thy commands the Achaeans hinder, the suitors most of all in wicked insolence."

So spoke he in his prayer, and near him came Athene, likened to Mentor in her form and voice, and speaking in winged words she said:

"Telemachus, henceforth you shall not be a base man nor a foolish, if in you stirs the brave soul of your father, and you like him can give effect to deed and word. Then shall this voyage not be vain and ineffective. But if you are no son of him and of Penelope, then am I hopeless of your gaining what you seek. Few sons are like their fathers; most are worse, few better than the father. Yet because you henceforth will not be base nor foolish, nor has the wisdom of Odysseus wholly failed you, therefore there is a hope you will one day accomplish all. Disregard, then, the thoughts and plans of the mad suitors, for they are in no way wise or upright men. Nothing they know of death and the dark doom which now is near, so that they all shall perish in a day. But for yourself, the journey you desire shall not be long delayed. So truly am I your father's friend, I will provide you a swift ship and be myself your comrade. But go you to the palace, mix with the suitors, and prepare the stores, securing all in vessels,—wine in jars, and barley-meal, men's marrow, in tight skins,—while I about the town will soon collect a willing crew. The ships are many in sea-girt Ithaca, ships new and old. Of these I will select the best, and quickly making ready we will sail the open sea."

So spoke Athene, daughter of Zeus. No longer then lingered Telemachus when he heard the goddess speak. He hastened to the house, though with a heavy heart, and at the palace found the haughty suitors flaying goats and singeing swine within the court. Antinoüs laughingly came forward to Telemachus, and holding him by the hand he spoke, and thus addressed him:

"Telemachus, of the lofty tongue and the unbridled temper, do not again grow sore in heart at what we do or say! No, eat and drink just as you used to do. All you have asked of course the Achaeans will provide,— the ship and the picked crew,—to help you quickly find your way to hallowed Pylos, seeking for tidings of your noble father."

Then answered him discreet Telemachus: "Antinoüs, it is not possible to sit at table quietly with you rude men and calmly take my ease. Was it not quite enough that in the days gone by you suitors wasted much good property of mine, while I was still a helpless child? But now that I am grown and hear and understand what people say, the spirit swells within me, and I will try to bring upon your heads an evil doom whether I go to Pylos or remain here in this land. But go I will—not vain shall be the voyage of which I speak—a passenger with others, since I can have command of neither ship nor crew. And this was what a while ago you judged was best."

He spoke, and from the hand of Antinoüs quietly drew his own. Meanwhile, the suitors in the house were busy at their meal. They mocked him, jeering at him in their talk, and a rude youth would say:

"Really, Telemachus is plotting for our ruin! He will bring champions from sandy Pylos; or even from Sparta, so deeply is he stirred; or else he means to go to Ephyra, that fruitful land, and fetch thence deadly drugs to drop into our wine-bowl and so destroy us all."

Then would another rude youth answer thus: "If he goes off upon a hollow ship and wanders far from friends, who knows but he too may be lost just as Odysseus was! And that would make us more ado; for all his goods we then must share, and to his mother give the house, for her to keep—her and the man who marries her."

So ran their talk. Meanwhile Telemachus passed down the house into his father's large and high-roofed chamber, where in a pile lay gold and bronze, clothing in chests, and stores of fragrant oil. Great jars of old delicious wine were standing there, holding within pure liquor fit for gods, in order ranged along the wall, in case Odysseus, after all his woes, ever came home again. Shut were the folding-doors, close-fitting, double; and here both night and day a housewife stayed, who in her watchful wisdom guarded all—Eurycleia, daughter of Ops, Peisenor's son. To her now spoke Telemachus, calling her to the room:

"Good nurse, come draw me wine in jars, sweet wine that is the choicest next to the wine you keep, thinking that ill-starred man will one day come—high-born Odysseus—safe from death and doom. Fill twelve and fit them all with covers. Then pour me barley into well-sewn sacks. Let there be twenty measures of ground barley-meal. None but yourself must know. Get all together, and I to-night will fetch them, so soon as my mother goes to her chamber seeking rest; for I am going to Sparta and to sandy Pylos, to try to learn of my dear father's coming."

As he said this, his dear nurse Eurycleia cried aloud and sorrowfully said in winged words: "Ah, my dear child, how came such notions in your mind? Where will you go through the wide world, our only one, our darling! High-born Odysseus is already dead, far from his home in some strange land. And now these men, the instant you are gone, will plot against you harm, that you by stealth may be cut off, and they thus share with one another all things here. No, stay you here at ease among your own! You have no need to suffer hardship, roaming over barren seas."

Then answered her discreet Telemachus: "Courage, good nurse! for not without God's warrant is my purpose. But swear to speak no word of this to my dear mother until the eleventh or twelfth day comes, or until she shall miss me and hear that I am gone, that so she may not stain her beautiful face with tears."

Thus did he speak, and the old woman swore by the gods a solemn oath. Then after she had sworn and ended all that oath, she straightway drew him wine in jars, and poured him barley into well-sewn sacks. Telemachus, meanwhile, passed to the house and joined the suitors.

Now a new plan the goddess formed, clear-eyed Athene. In likeness of Telemachus, she went throughout the town, and, approaching one and another man, gave them the word, bidding them meet by the swift ship at eventide. Noëmon next, the gallant son of Phronius, she begged for a swift ship; and this he freely promised.

Now the sun sank and all the ways grew dark. And now she drew the swift ship to the sea and put in all the gear that well-benched vessels carry; she moored her by the harbor's mouth; the good crew gathered round about, and the goddess gave them zeal.

Then a new plan the goddess formed, clear-eyed Athene. She hastened to the house of princely Odysseus, there on the suitors poured sweet sleep, confused them as they drank, and made the cups fall from their hands. They hurried off to rest throughout the town, and did not longer tarry, for sleep fell on their eyelids. Then to Telemachus spoke clear-eyed Athene, calling him forth before the stately hall, likened to Mentor in her form and voice:

"Telemachus, already your mailed comrades sit at the oar and wait your starting. Come, let us go, and not lose time upon the way."

Saying this, Pallas Athene led the way in haste, and he walked after in the footsteps of the goddess. But when they came to the ship and to the sea, they found upon the shore their long-haired comrades, to whom thus spoke revered Telemachus:

"Come, friends, and let us fetch the stores; all are collected at the hall. My mother knows of nothing, nor do the handmaids either. One alone had my orders."

So saying, he led the way, the others followed after; and bringing all the stores into their well-benched ship they stowed them there, even as the dear son of Odysseus ordered. Then came Telemachus aboard; but Athene led the way, and at the vessel's stern she sat her down, while close at hand Telemachus was seated. The others loosed the cables, and coming aboard themselves took places at the pins. A favorable wind clear-eyed Athene sent, a brisk west wind that sang along the wine-dark sea. And now Telemachus, inspiriting his men, bade them lay hold upon the tackling, and they hearkened to his call. Raising the pinewood mast, they set it in the hollow socket, binding it firm with forestays, and tightened the white sail with twisted oxhide thongs. The wind swelled out the belly of the sail, and round the stem loudly the rippling water roared as the ship started. Onward she sped, forcing a passage through the waves. Making the tackling fast throughout the swift black ship, the men brought bowls brimming with wine, and to the gods, that never die and never have been born, they poured it forth—chiefest of all to her, the clear-eyed child of Zeus. So through the night and early dawn did the ship cleave her way.

III.

AT PYLOS

AND NOW the sun, leaving the beauteous bay, rose to the brazen sky, to shine for the immortals and for mortal men upon the fruitful fields; and the two drew near to Pylos, the stately citadel of Neleus. The townsfolk here were offering a sacrifice upon the shore, slaying black bulls to the dark-haired Earth-shaker. Nine groups there were, five hundred men in each, and nine bulls were presented for each group. When the inward parts were tasted and the thighs were burning to the god, the two ran swiftly in, hauled up and furled their trim ship's sail, brought her to anchor, and came forth themselves. So from the ship came forth Telemachus, but Athene led the way, and thus began the goddess, clear-eyed Athene:

"Telemachus, no shyness now! For to accomplish this you crossed the sea, to make inquiry for your father and to learn where he lies buried and what fate he met. Go then straight forward to the horseman Nestor, and let us know what is the wisdom hidden in his breast. Beg him yourself to tell the very truth. Falsehood he will not speak; truly upright is he."

Then answered her discreet Telemachus: "Mentor, how can I go? How importune him? In subtleties of speech I am not practised. Shyness is fitting in a youth when questioning his elders."

Then said to him the goddess, clear-eyed Athene: "Telemachus, some promptings you will find in your own breast, and Heaven will send still more; for, certainly, not unbefriended of the gods have you been born and bred."

Saying this, Pallas Athene led the way in haste, and he walked after in the footsteps of the goddess. So they approached the gathering of the men of Pylos and the group where Nestor sat among his sons. Round him his people, making the banquet ready, were roasting meats and

19

putting pieces on the spits. But as they saw the strangers, all the men crowded near, gave hands in welcome, and asked them to sit down; and Nestor's son Peisistratus, approaching first, took each one by the hand and placed them at the feast on some soft fleeces laid upon the sands, beside his brother Thrasymedes and his father. He gave them portions of the inward parts, poured out some wine into a golden cup, and, offering welcome, said to Pallas Athene, daughter of ægis-bearing Zeus:

"Here, stranger, make a prayer to lord Poseidon. It is his feast you find at this your coming. Then, after you have poured and prayed as is befitting, give this man too the cup of honeyed wine for him to pour; for I suppose he also prays to the immortals. All men have need of gods. But he is the younger, young as I myself; so I will give you first the golden chalice."

Saying this, he placed the cup of sweet wine in her hand. And Athene was pleased to find the man so wise and courteous, pleased that he gave her first the golden chalice. Forthwith she prayed a fervent prayer to lord Poseidon:

"Hearken, Poseidon, thou girder of the land, and count it not too much to give thy suppliants these blessings. First upon Nestor and his sons bestow all honor; then to the rest grant gracious recompense, to all the men of Pylos, for their splendid sacrifice; and grant still farther that Telemachus and I may sail away having accomplished that for which we came upon our swift black ship."

Thus did she pray, and was herself fulfilling all. To Telemachus she passed the goodly double cup, and in like manner also prayed the dear son of Odysseus. But when the rest had roasted the outer flesh and drawn it off, dividing the portions, they held a glorious feast. And after they had stayed desire for drink and food, then thus began the Gerenian horseman Nestor:

"Now, then, it is more suitable to prove our guests and ask them who they are, since they are refreshed with food. Strangers, who are you? Where do you come from, sailing the watery ways? Are you upon some business? Or do you rove at random, as the pirates roam the seas, risking their lives and bringing ill to strangers?"

Then answered him discreet Telemachus, plucking up courage; for Athene herself put courage in his heart to ask about his absent father and to win a good report among mankind:

"O Nestor, son of Neleus, great glory of the Achaeans, you ask me whence we are, and I will tell you. We are of Ithaca, under Mount Neïon. Our business is our own, no public thing, as I will show. I come afar to seek some tidings of my father, royal hardy Odysseus, who once, they say, fought side by side with you and sacked the Trojan town. For as to all the others who were in the war at Troy we have already learned

where each man met his mournful death; but this man's death the son
of Kronos left unknown. No one can surely say where he has died;
whether he was borne down on land by foes, or on the sea among the
waves of Amphitrite. Therefore I now come hither to your knees to ask
if you will tell me of my father's mournful death, in case you saw it for
yourself with your own eyes, or from some other heard the story of his
wanderings; for to exceeding grief his mother bore him. Use no mild
word nor yield to pity from regard for me, but tell me fully all you
chanced to see. I do entreat you, if ever my father, good Odysseus, in
word or deed kept covenant with you there in the Trojan land where
you Achaeans suffered, be mindful of it now; tell me the very truth."

Then answered him the Gerenian horseman Nestor: "Ah, friend,
you make me call to mind the pains we bore when in that land, un-
tamed in spirit as we sons of the Achaeans were—all we endured on
shipboard on the misty sea, coasting for plunder where Achilles led;
and all our fightings round the stronghold of King Priam, where so
many of our bravest perished. There warlike Ajax lies, and there
Achilles. There too Patroclus, the peer of gods in wisdom. There my
own son, so strong and gallant, Antilochus, exceeding swift of foot, a
famous fighter. And many other woes we had, added to these. What
mortal man could count them? Nay, should you tarry five or six years
here to ask what woes the great Achaeans suffered, you would return to
your own land, wearied ere I could tell.

"For nine years long we plotted their destruction, busy with craft of
every kind; yet still the son of Kronos hardly brought us through. With
one man then none sought to vie in wisdom; for far beyond us all in
craft of every kind was royal Odysseus, your father,—if you are indeed
his child. I am amazed to see. And yet, how fitting are your words! One
would not say a youth could speak so fitly. There, all that while, royal
Odysseus and I never once disagreed in the assembly or the council;
but with one heart, with will and steadfast purpose, we planned how all
might best be ordered for the Argives.

"Yet after we overthrew the lofty town of Priam, when we went away
in ships and God dispersed the Achaeans, ah, then Zeus purposed in
his mind a sad voyage for the Argives! For nowise prudent and upright
were all. So, many a one came to an evil end, through the fell wrath of
the dread father's clear-eyed child, who caused a strife betwixt the sons
of Atreus. For these two summoned to an assembly all the Achaeans, in
haste, not in due order, at the setting sun; and heavy with wine the
young Achaeans came. Then each declared the reason why he called
the host together. Now Menelaus exhorted all the Achaeans to turn
their thoughts toward going home on the broad ocean-ridges; but this
pleased Agamemnon not at all. He wished to stay the host and offer

sacred hecatombs, that so he might appease the dread wrath of Athene,—ah, fool! who did not know she might not be persuaded; for a purpose is not lightly changed in gods who live forever. Thus stood the brothers exchanging bitter words, while up sprang other mailed Achaeans in wild din and both the plans found favor. That night we rested, nursing in our breasts hard thoughts of one another. Zeus was preparing us the ill that comes from wrong. At dawn we dragged our ships into the sacred sea, and put therein our goods and the low-girdled women. Half of the host held back, remaining with the son of Atreus, Agamemnon, the shepherd of the people; while we, the other half, embarked and sailed. Swiftly our ships ran on; God smoothed the billowy deep. Arrived at Tenedos, we offered sacrifices to the gods, as homeward bound; but Zeus had not yet willed our coming home,—cruel! to waken bitter strife a second time. Part turned their curved ships back and sailed away after Odysseus, keen and crafty, again to proffer aid to Agamemnon, son of Atreus. I, with the company of ships which followed me, pressed onward, for I knew some power intended ill. On pressed the warlike son of Tydeus, too, inspiriting his men. Later upon our track came light-haired Menelaus, who overtook us while at Lesbos we debated on the long sea voyage, doubtful if we should sail above steep Chios, by way of the island Psyria, with Chios on our left, or under Chios and past windy Mimas. We therefore begged of God to show some sign; and he made plain our way, bidding us cut the centre of the sea straight of Euboea, if we would soonest flee from danger. The whistling wind began to blow, and swiftly along the swarming water sped our ships, and touched at night Geraestus, where on Poseidon's altar we laid many thighs of bulls, thankful that we had compassed the wide sea. It was the fourth day when the crews of Diomed the horseman, son of Tydeus, moored their trim ships at Argos. I still held on toward Pylos, nor did the breeze once fall after the god first sent it forth to blow.

"And thus it was I came, dear child, bringing no tidings; nothing I know about the rest of the Achaeans, which were saved and which were lost. But all that I have learned while sitting here at home, this, as is proper, you shall know; I will hide nothing from you. Safely, they say, returned the spearmen of the Myrmidons, whom the proud son of fierce Achilles led; safely, too, Philoctetes, the gallant son of Poias; and back to Crete Idomeneus brought all his men,—all who escaped the war, the sea took not a man. About the son of Atreus you yourselves have heard, though you live far away; how he returned, and how Aegisthus plotted his mournful death. And yet a fearful reckoning Aegisthus paid! When a man dies, how good it is to leave a son! That son took vengeance on the slayer, wily Aegisthus, who had slain his famous father. You too, my friend,—for certainly I find you fair and tall,—be strong, that men hereafter born may speak your praise."

Then answered him discreet Telemachus: "O Nestor, son of Neleus, great glory of the Achaeans, stoutly that son took vengeance, and the Achaeans shall spread his fame afar, that future times may know. Oh, that to me as well the gods would give the power to pay the suitors for their grievous wrongs, for they with insult work me abominations! But no such boon the gods bestowed on me and on my father. Now, therefore, all must simply be endured."

Then answered him the Gerenian horseman Nestor: "Friend,— since you turn my thoughts that way by your own words,—they say that many suitors of your mother, heedless of you, work evil in your halls. Pray tell me, do you willingly submit, or are the people of your land adverse to you, led by some voice of God? Who knows but yet Odysseus may return and recompense their crimes, either alone, or all the Achaeans with him? Ah, might clear-eyed Athene be pleased to be your friend as formerly she aided great Odysseus, there in the Trojan land where we Achaeans suffered! For I never knew the gods to show such open friendship as Pallas Athene showed in standing by Odysseus. If now to you she would be such a friend and heartily give aid, it might be some of these men here would cease to think of marriage."

Then answered him discreet Telemachus: "Nay, sire, not soon, I think, will words like these come true. Too great is what you say; I am astonished. Hope what I might, such things could never be, not if the gods should will them."

Then said to him the goddess, clear-eyed Athene: "Telemachus, what word has passed the barrier of your teeth? Easily may a god, who will, bring a man safe from far. But I myself would gladly meet a multitude of woes, if thus I might go home and see my day of coming, and not return and fall beside my hearth as Agamemnon fell, under the plottings of his own wife and Aegisthus. Yet death, the common lot, gods have no power to turn even from one they love, when the fell doom of death that lays men low once overtakes him."

Then answered her discreet Telemachus: "Mentor, let us talk of this no more, sad as we are. For him no real return can ever be; long time ago the immortals fixed his death and his dark doom. At present I would trace a different story and question Nestor, since beyond all men else he knows the right and wise. Three generations of mankind they say that he has ruled, and as I now behold him he seems like an immortal. O Nestor, son of Neleus, relate to me the truth! How did the son of Atreus die, wide-ruling Agamemnon? And where was Menelaus? What was the deadly plot wily Aegisthus laid to kill a man much braver than himself? Was Menelaus absent from Achaean Argos, traveling to men afar, that so Aegisthus, taking courage, did the murder?"

Then answered him the Gerenian horseman Nestor: "Well, I will tell you all the truth, my child. Indeed, you yourself guess how it had fallen out if the son of Atreus, light-haired Menelaus, had found Aegisthus living in the palace when he returned from Troy. Then over dead Aegisthus, men had heaped no mound of earth, but dogs and birds had feasted on him where he lay upon the plain outside the town, and no Achaean woman had made lament for him; for monstrous was the deed he wrought. At Troy we tarried, bringing to fulfillment many toils, while he, at ease, hidden in grazing Argos, strove hard to win the wife of Agamemnon by his words. At first, indeed, she scorned ill-doing, this royal Clytaemnestra, being of upright mind. Moreover, a bard was with her whom the son of Atreus strictly charged, on setting forth for Troy, to guard his wife. But when at last the doom of gods constrained her to her ruin, then did Aegisthus take the bard to a lone island and leave him there the prey and prize of birds, while her, as willing as himself, he led to his own home. And many a thigh-piece did he burn upon the sacred altars of the gods, and many an offering render, woven stuffs and gold, at having achieved such monstrous deed as in his heart he had not hoped.

"Now as we came from Troy, the son of Atreus and myself set sail together full of loving thoughts; but when we were approaching sacred Sunion, a cape of Athens, Phoebus Apollo smote the helmsman of Menelaus and slew him with his gentle arrows while he held the rudder of the running ship within his hands. Phrontis it was, Onetor's son, one who surpassed all humankind in piloting a ship when winds were wild. So Menelaus tarried, though eager for his journey, to bury his companion and to pay the funeral rites. But when he also, sailing in his hollow ships over the wine-dark sea, reached in his course the steep height of Maleia, from that point on far-seeing Zeus gave him a grievous way. He poured forth blasts of whistling winds and swollen waves as huge as mountains. Dividing the ships, he brought a part to Crete, where the Cydonians dwelt around the streams of Iardanus. Here is a cliff, smooth and steep toward the water, at the border land of Gortyn, on the misty sea, where the south wind drives in the heavy waves on the western point toward Phaestus, and this small rock holds back the heavy waves. Some came in here, and the men themselves hardly escaped destruction; their ships the waves crushed on the ledges. But the five other dark-bowed ships wind and wave bore to Egypt. So Menelaus gathered there much substance and much gold, coasting about on ship-board to men of alien speech; and all this time at home Aegisthus foully plotted. Seven years he reigned in rich Mycene when he had slain the son of Atreus. The people were held down. But in the eighth ill came; for royal Orestes came from Athens and slew the slayer, wily Aegisthus, who had slain his famous father. The slaughter done, he held a funeral banquet for the Argives, over his hateful mother and spiritless Aegisthus, and on that self-same day came Menelaus, good at the war-cry, bringing a store of treasure, all the freight his ships could bear.

"You too, dear friend, wander not long and far from home, leaving your wealth behind and persons in your house so insolent as these; for they may swallow all your wealth, sharing with one another, while you are gone a fruitless journey. And yet, I say, go visit Menelaus. Indeed, I bid you go; for he is lately come from foreign lands and from those nations whence one could not really hope to come, when once the storms had swept him off into so vast a sea,—a sea from which birds travel not within a year, so vast it is and fearful. Go then at once with your own ship and crew, or if you like by land; chariot and horses are ready for you, and ready too my sons to be your guides to sacred Lacedaemon, where lives light-haired Menelaus. Beg him yourself to tell the very truth. Falsehood he will not speak; truly upright is he."

As he thus spoke the sun went down and darkness came, and the goddess, clear-eyed Athene, said to them:

"Sire, certainly these words of yours are fitly spoken. But come, cut up the tongues and mix the wine, that after we have poured libations to Poseidon and the rest of the immortals we seek our rest, since it is time for that. For now the day has turned to dusk, and surely it is not well to tarry long at the gods' feast; rather to rise and go."

So spoke the daughter of Zeus; and they hearkened to her saying. Pages poured water on their hands; young men brimmed bowls with drink and served to all, with a first pious portion for the cup; they themselves threw the tongues into the flame and, rising, poured libations. So after they had poured and drunk as their hearts would, then would Athene and princely Telemachus set off together for their hollow ship. But Nestor checked them and rebuked them, saying:

"Zeus and the other immortal gods forbid that you should leave my house and turn to a swift ship! As if I were a man quite without clothes and poor, a man who had not robes and rugs enough at home for himself and friends to sleep in comfort! But in my house are goodly robes and rugs. And never, surely, shall the son of that Odysseus lie on ship's deck while I am living, or while within my halls children remain to entertain such guests as visit house of mine."

Then said to him the goddess, clear-eyed Athene: "Well have you said in this, kind sir, and good it were Telemachus should heed, for it is far more seemly so. Nay, he shall now attend you and sleep within your halls. But as for me, I go to the black ship to cheer my men and tell their duties, for I am the only man of years among them all; the others, younger men, follow me out of friendship, and all are of the age of bold Telemachus. There would I lay me down by the black hollow ship to-night; but in the morning I will go to the bold Cauconians where there are debts now due me, not recent ones nor small. As for Telemachus who stays with you, send him upon his way by chariot with your son, and give him horses that have swiftest speed and best endurance."

Saying this, clear-eyed Athene passed away, in likeness of an osprey. Awe fell on all who saw. The old man marveled as he gazed, grasped by the hand Telemachus, and said as he addressed him:

"Dear friend, you will not prove, I trust, a base man, lacking spirit, if when so young the gods become your guides. This is none else of those who have their dwelling on Olympus than the daughter of Zeus, the Plunderer, Tritogeneia, who honored your good father too amongst the Argives. Ah, queen, be gracious and vouchsafe me fair renown,—me and my children and my honored wife,—and I will give to thee a glossy heifer, broad of brow, unbroken, one no man ever brought beneath the yoke. Her I will give, tipping her horns with gold."

So spoke he in his prayer, and Pallas Athene heard. Then the Gerenian horseman Nestor led sons and sons-in-law to his fair palace. And they on reaching the far-famed palace of the king, took seats in order on couches and on chairs; and the old man mixed at their coming a vessel of sweet wine, which, now eleven years old, the housewife opened, loosening the lid. A bowl of this the old man mixed, and fervently he prayed, pouring libation to Athene, daughter of ægis-bearing Zeus.

Then after they had poured and drunk as their hearts would, desiring rest, they each departed homeward; but in the house itself the Gerenian horseman Nestor prepared the bed of Telemachus, the son of princely Odysseus, upon a well-bored bedstead beneath the echoing portico. By him he placed Peisistratus, that sturdy spearman, one ever foremost, he who was still the bachelor among the sons at home. But Nestor slept in the recess of the high hall; his wife, the Queen, making her bed beside him.

Soon as the early rosy-fingered dawn appeared, the Gerenian horseman Nestor rose from bed, and coming forth sat down on the smooth stones which stood before his lofty gate, white, glistening as with oil. On them in former days Neleus had sat, the peer of gods in wisdom; but long ago he met his doom and went to the house of Hades, and now Gerenian Nestor sat thereon, as warder of the Achaeans, holding the sceptre. Round him his sons collected in a group, on coming from their chambers,—Echephron and Stratius, Perseus, Aretus, and gallant Thrasymedes, and sixth and last came lord Peisistratus. Then they led

forward godlike Telemachus, and set him by their side, and thus began
the Gerenian horseman Nestor:

"Hasten, dear children, and fulfill my vow; that first of all the gods I
satisfy Athene, who came to me in open presence at the gods' high
feast. Go one among you to the field and have a heifer quickly brought,
and let the neat-herd drive her up. One go to the black ship of bold
Telemachus, and bring here all his crew. Leave only two behind. Let
one again summon the smith Laërces hither, to tip with gold the
heifer's horns. The rest of you stay here together. But tell the maids
within our famous palace to spread a feast, to fetch some seats, some
logs of wood, and some fresh water."

He spoke; away went all in breathless haste. And now there came the
heifer from the field; there came from the swift balanced ship the crew
of brave Telemachus; there came the smith, with his smith's tools in
hand, his implements of art, anvil and hammer and the shapely tongs,
with which he works the gold; there came Athene, too, to meet the sacrifice. Then the old horseman Nestor furnished gold, and so that other
welded it round the heifer's horns, smoothing it till the goddess might
be pleased to view the offering. Now by the horns Stratius and noble
Echephron led up the heifer; Aretus brought lustral water in a flowered
basin from the store-room, and in his other hand held barley in a basket; and dauntless Thrasymedes, a sharp axe in his hand, stood by to fell
the heifer, while Perseus held the blood-bowl. Then the old horseman
Nestor began the opening rites, of washing hands and sprinkling meal.
And fervently he prayed Athene at beginning, casting the forelocks in
the fire.

So after they had prayed and strewn the barley-meal, forthwith the
son of Nestor, ardent Thrasymedes, drew near and dealt the blow. The
axe cut through the sinews of the neck and broke the heifer's power. A
cry went up from the daughters of Nestor, the sons' wives, and his own
honored wife, Eurydice, the eldest of the daughters of Clymenus. The
sons then raised the beast up from the trodden earth and held her so,
the while Peisistratus, ever the foremost, cut the throat. And after the
black blood had flowed and life had left the carcase, they straightway
laid it open, quickly cut out the thighs, all in due order, wrapped them
in fat in double layers and placed raw flesh thereon. On billets of wood
the old man burned them, and poured upon them sparkling wine,
while young men by his side held five-pronged forks. So after the thighs
were burned and the inward parts were tasted, they sliced the rest, and
stuck it on the forks and roasted all, holding the pointed forks in hand.

Meanwhile to Telemachus fair Polycaste gave a bath, she who was
youngest daughter of Nestor, son of Neleus. And after she had bathed
him and anointed him with oil and put upon him a goodly robe and

tunic, forth from the bath he came, in bearing like the immortals; and he went and sat by Nestor, the shepherd of the people.

The others, too, when they had roasted the outer flesh and drawn it off, sat down and fell to feasting. Men of degree attended them, pouring the wine into their golden cups. So after they had stayed desire for drink and food, then thus began the Gerenian horseman Nestor: "My sons, go fetch the full-maned horses for Telemachus and yoke them to the car, that he may make his journey."

So he spoke, and willingly they heeded and obeyed. Quickly they harnessed the swift horses to the car. The housewife put in bread and wine and dainties, such things as heaven-descended princes eat. And now Telemachus mounted the goodly chariot, and Nestor's son Peisistratus, ever the foremost, mounted the chariot too, and took the reins in hand. He cracked the whip to start, and not unwillingly the pair flew off into the plain, left the steep citadel of Pylos, and all day long they shook the yoke they bore between them.

Now the sun sank and all the ways grew dark, and the men arrived at Pherae, before the house of Diocles, the son of Orsilochus, whose father was Alpheius. There for the night they rested; he gave them entertainment.

Then as the early rosy-fingered dawn appeared, they harnessed the horses, mounted the gay chariot, and off they drove from porch and echoing portico. Peisistratus cracked the whip to start, and not unwillingly the pair flew off. So into the plain they came where grew the grain; and through this, by and by, they reached their journey's ending. So fast their horses sped them. Then the sun sank and all the ways grew dark.

IV.

AT LACEDAEMON

INTO THE low land now they came of caverned Lacedaemon and drove to the palace of famous Menelaus. They found him holding a wedding feast for all his kin in honor of the son and gentle daughter of his house. To the son of Achilles, that breaker of men's ranks, he gave his daughter; for long ago, at Troy, he pledged himself to give her, and now the gods brought round their wedding. Accordingly to-day with horses and with chariots he sent her forth to the famed city of the Myrmidons, whose king her bridegroom was. Then for his son he took to wife Alector's daughter out of Sparta, his son being now full grown, strong Megapenthes, the child of a slave mother. The gods gave Helen no more issue after she in the early time had borne her lovely child, Hermione, who had the grace of golden Aphrodite.

Thus at the feast in the great high-roofed house, neighbors and kinsmen of famous Menelaus sat and made merry. Among them sang the sacred bard and touched his lyre; a pair of dancers went whirling down the middle as he began the song.

Now at the palace gate two youths and their horses stopped, princely Telemachus and the proud son of Nestor. Great Eteoneus came forth and saw them, — he was a busy squire of famous Menelaus, — and hastened through the hall to tell the shepherd of the people, and standing close beside him he said in winged words:

"Here are two strangers, heaven-descended Menelaus, and they are like the seed of mighty Zeus. Say, shall we unharness their swift horses, or shall we send them forth for some one else to entertain?"

Then, deeply moved, said light-haired Menelaus: "You were no fool, Boëthoüs' son, Eteoneus, before this time, but now you chatter folly like a child! Only because as guests we often had our food of strangers, are we here; and we must look to Zeus henceforth to keep us safe from harm. No! take the harness from the strangers' horses and bring the men themselves within to share our feast."

He spoke, and Eteoneus hastened along the hall and called on other busy squires to follow. They took the sweating horses from the yoke, tied them securely at the mangers, threw them some corn and mixed therewith white barley, then tipped the chariot up against the bright face-wall, and brought the men into the lordly house. And they, beholding, marveled at the dwelling of the heaven-descended king; for a sheen as of the sun or moon played through the high-roofed house of famous Menelaus. Now after they had satisfied their eyes with gazing, they went to the polished baths and bathed. And when the maids had bathed them and anointed them with oil, and put upon them fleecy coats and tunics, they took their seats by Menelaus, son of Atreus. And water for the hands a servant brought in a beautiful pitcher made of gold, and poured it out over a silver basin for their washing, and spread a polished table by their side. Then the grave housekeeper brought bread and placed before them, setting out food of many a kind, freely giving of her store. The carver, too, took platters of meat and placed before them, meat of all kinds, and set their golden goblets ready. And greeting the pair said light-haired Menelaus:

"Break bread, and have good cheer! and by and by when you have eaten, we will ask what men you are. Surely the parent line suffers no loss in you; but you are of some line of heaven-descended sceptred kings. For common men have no such children."

So saying, he set before them fat slices of a chine of beef, taking up in his hands the roasted flesh which had been placed before him as the piece of honor; and on the food spread out before them they laid hands. But after they had stayed desire for drink and food, Telemachus said to Nestor's son,—his head bent close, that others might not hear:

"O son of Nestor, my heart's delight, notice the blaze of bronze throughout the echoing halls, the gold, the amber, silver, and ivory! The court of Olympian Zeus within must be like this. What untold wealth is here! I am amazed to see."

What he was saying light-haired Menelaus overheard, and speaking in winged words he said: "Dear children, no! No mortal man could vie with Zeus; eternal are his halls and his possessions; but one of humankind to vie with me in wealth there may or may not be. Through many woes and wanderings I brought it in my ships, and I was eight years on the way. Cyprus, Phœnicia, Egypt, I wandered over; I came to the Ethiopians, Sidonians, and Erembians, and into Libya, where the lambs are full-horned at their birth. Three times a year the flocks bear young. No prince or peasant there lacks cheese, meat, or sweet milk, but the ewes always give their milk the whole year round. While I was gathering thereabouts much wealth and wandering on, a stranger slew my brother while off his guard, by stealth, and through the craft of his accursed wife. Here too I have no joy as lord of my possessions. But from your fathers you will have heard that tale, whoever they may be; for great was my affliction, and desolate my house which once stood fair and stored with many blessings. Would I were here at home with but the third part of my wealth, and they were safe to-day who fell on the plain of Troy, far off from grazing Argos! But no! and for them all I often grieve and mourn when sitting in my halls. Now with a sigh I ease my heart, then check myself; soon comes a surfeit of benumbing sorrow. Yet in my grief it is not all I so much mourn as one alone, who makes me loathe my sleep and food when I remember him; for no Achaean met the contests that Odysseus met and won. And still on him it was appointed woe should fall, and upon me a ceaseless pain because of him; so long he tarries, whether alive or dead we do not know. For him now mourn the old Laërtes, steadfast Penelope, and Telemachus, whom he left at home a new-born child."

So he spoke, and stirred in Telemachus yearnings to mourn his father. Tears from his eyelids dropped upon the ground when he heard his father's name, and he held with both his hands his purple cloak before his eyes. This Menelaus noticed, and hesitated in his mind and heart whether to leave him to make mention of his father or first to question him and prove him through and through.

While he thus doubted in his mind and heart, forth from her fragrant high-roofed chamber Helen came, like golden-shafted Artemis. For her, Adraste placed a carven chair; Alcippe brought a covering of soft wool, and Phylo a silver basket which Alcandra gave, the wife of Polybus, who lived at Thebes in Egypt, where abundant wealth is in the houses. He gave to Menelaus two silver bath-tubs, a pair of kettles, and ten talents of gold. And then, besides, his wife gave Helen beautiful gifts; she gave a golden distaff and a basket upon rollers, fashioned of silver, and its rim finished with gold. This her attendant Phylo now brought and set beside her, filled with a fine-spun yarn; across it lay the distaff, charged with dark wool. Seated upon her chair,—upon whose lower part there was a rest for feet,—she straightway questioned thus her husband closely:

"Do we know, heaven-descended Menelaus, who these men here assert themselves to be? Shall I disguise my thought or speak it plainly? My heart bids speak. None have I ever seen, I think, so like another— no man, no woman; amazed am I to see!—as this man here is like the son of brave Odysseus, even like Telemachus, whom his father left at home a new-born child, when you Achaeans, for the sake of worthless me, came under the walls of Troy, eager for valorous fighting."

Then, answering her, said light-haired Menelaus: "Now I too note it, wife, even as you suggest; such were Odysseus' feet and hands, his turn of eye, his head, and hair above. And even now, as I began to call to mind Odysseus and to tell what grievous toils he bore in my behalf, this youth let fall a bitter tear from under his brows and held his purple cloak before his eyes."

Then Nestor's son, Peisistratus, made answer: "O son of Atreus, heaven-descended Menelaus, leader of hosts, this is in truth his son, as you have said; but he is modest and too bashful in his heart to make display of talk on his first coming here, before you too, whose voice we both enjoy as if it were a god's. The Gerenian horseman, Nestor, sent me forth to be his guide; for he desired to see you, hoping that you might give him aid by word or deed. Ah, many a grief the son of an absent father meets at home, when other helpers are not by. So with Telemachus; the one is gone, and others there are none throughout the land to ward off ill."

Then, answering him, said light-haired Menelaus: "What! Is there then within my house the son of one so dear, one who for me bore many a conflict! I used to say I should rejoice over his coming home far more than over that of all the other Argives, if through the seas Olympian far-seeing Zeus let our swift ships find passage. In Argos I would have granted him a city, and would here have built his house, and I would have brought him out of Ithaca,—him and his goods, his child, and all his people,—clearing its dwellers from some single city that lies within my neighborhood and owns me as its lord. So living here we had been much together; and nothing further could have parted then our joyous friendship till death's dark cloud closed round. But God himself must have been envious of a life like this, and made that hapless man alone to fail of coming."

So he spoke, and stirred in all a yearning after tears. Then Argive Helen wept, the child of Zeus; Telemachus too wept, and Menelaus, son of Atreus; nor yet did Nestor's son keep his eyes tearless. For in his mind he mused on good Antilochus, whom the illustrious son of the bright dawn had slain. Remembering whom, he spoke in winged words:

"O son of Atreus, that you were wise beyond the wont of men old Nestor used to say, when we would mention you at home, talking with one another. And now if it is well, give heed to me; for after a feast I do not like to sit and grieve. There is to-morrow. Not that I think it ill to weep for one who dies, when he has met his doom. It is the only honor sorrowing men can pay, to cut the hair and let the tear fall down the cheek. A brother of mine once died, one not the meanest of the Argives. You must have known him. I never myself looked on his face and never knew him; but Antilochus, they say, was very swift of foot, a famous fighter."

Then answering him said light-haired Menelaus: "Friend, you have said just what a man of understanding might say and even do, were he indeed your elder; for sprung from such a father you too talk with understanding. Easily is his offspring known to whom the son of Kronos allots a boon in birth and marriage. And thus has he blessed Nestor continually, all his days, granting him hale old age at home and children who are youths of wisdom, mighty with the spear. Let us then check the lamentation which arose a while ago and turn once more to feasting. Let them pour water on our hands. Again, to-morrow, for Telemachus and me there will be tales to tell."

He spoke, and Asphalion poured water on their hands,—he was a busy squire of famous Menelaus,—then on the food spread out before them they laid hands.

Now elsewhere Helen turned her thoughts, the child of Zeus. Straightway she cast into the wine of which they drank a drug which quenches pain and strife and brings forgetfulness of every ill. He who should taste it, mingled in the bowl, would not that day let tears fall down his cheeks although his mother and his father died, although before his door a brother or dear son fell by the sword and his own eyes beheld. Such cunning drugs had the daughter of Zeus, drugs of a healing virtue, which Polydamna gave, the wife of Thon, in Egypt, where the fruitful soil yields drugs of every kind, some that when mixed are healing, others deadly. There every one is a physician, skillful beyond all humankind; for they are of the race of Paeon. So after she had cast the drug into the bowl and bidden pour, then once more taking up the word, she said:

"Heaven-descended son of Atreus, Menelaus, and you too, you sons of worthy men, though Zeus to one in one way, to another in another, distributes good and ill and is almighty, yet for the present sit and feast within the hall and cheer yourselves with tales. One fitting well the time I will relate. Fully I cannot tell, nor even name the many feats of hardy Odysseus. But this is the sort of deed that brave man did and dared there in the Trojan land where you Achaeans suffered. Marring himself with cruel blows, casting a wretched garment round his shoulders, and looking like a slave, he entered the wide-wayed city of his foes; and other than his own true self he made himself appear in this disguise, even like a beggar, far as he was from such an one at the Achaean ships. In such a guise, he entered the Trojans' town; they took no notice, one and all; I alone knew him for the man he was and questioned him. He shrewdly tried to foil me. But after I had bathed him and anointed him with oil and given him clothing, when I had sworn a solemn oath not to make known Odysseus to the Trojans till he should reach the swift ships and the huts of the Achaeans, then he described the whole

Achaean plot. So, slaying many Trojans with his trenchant sword, he went off to the Argives and carried back much knowledge. Thereat the other Trojan women raised a loud lament. My soul was glad; for my heart already turned toward going home again, and I would mourn the blindness Aphrodite brought when she lured me thither from my native land and bade me leave my daughter, my chamber, and my husband,—a man who lacked for nothing, either in mind or person."

Then, answering her, said light-haired Menelaus: "Yes, all your tale, my wife, is told right well. I have in days gone by tested the wisdom and the will of many heroes, and I have traveled over many lands; but never have I beheld a soul so true as hardy Odysseus. This also is the sort of deed that brave man did and dared within the wooden horse where all we Argive chiefs were lying, bearing to the Trojans death and doom. Erelong you passed that way,—some god must have impelled you who sought to bring the Trojans honor; godlike Deïphobus was following after. Thrice walking round our hollow ambush, touching it here and there, you called by name the Danaän chiefs, feigning the voice of every Argive's wife. Now I and the son of Tydeus and royal Odysseus, crouched in the middle, heard your call, and we two, starting up, were minded to go forth, or else to answer straightway from within; but Odysseus held us back and stayed our madness. Then all the other sons of the Achaeans held their peace. Anticlus only was determined to make answer to your words; but Odysseus firmly closed his mouth with his strong hands, and so saved all the Achaeans. All through that time he held him thus, till Pallas Athene led you off."

Then answered him discreet Telemachus: "O son of Atreus, heaven-descended Menelaus, leader of hosts, so much the harder is it; all was of no avail against a mournful death, though an iron heart was his. Nay, bring us to our beds, that so at last, lulled in sweet sleep, we be at ease."

He spoke, and Argive Helen bade the maids to set a bed beneath the portico, to lay upon it beautiful purple rugs, spread blankets over these, and then place woolen mantles on the outside for a covering. So the maids left the hall, with torches in their hands, and spread the bed; and a page led forth the strangers. Thus in the porch slept prince Telemachus and the illustrious son of Nestor. But the son of Atreus slept in the recess of the high wall, and by him long-robed Helen lay, a queen of women.

Soon as the early rosy-fingered dawn appeared, Menelaus, good at the war-cry, rose from bed, put on his clothes, slung his sharp sword about his shoulder, under his shining feet bound his fair sandals, and came forth from his chamber in bearing like a god. Then seating himself beside Telemachus, he thus addressed him, saying:

"What is it that has brought you here, my lord Telemachus, to sacred

what the suitors are
doing in his house
The Odyssey 35

Lacedaemon on the broad ocean-ridges? A public need or private? Tell
me the very truth."

Then answered him discreet Telemachus: "O son of Atreus, heaven-
descended Menelaus, leader of hosts, I came to see if you could tell me
tidings of my father. My home is swallowed up, my rich estate is
wasted; with men of evil hearts my house is filled, men who continually butcher my thronging flocks and swing-paced, crook-horned oxen,—
the suitors of my mother, overweening in their pride. Therefore I now
come hither to your knees to ask if you will tell me of my father's
mournful death, in case you saw it for yourself with your own eyes or
from some other heard the story of his wanderings; for to exceeding
grief his mother bore him. Use no mild word nor yield to pity from
regard for me, but tell me fully all you chanced to see. I do entreat you,
if ever my father, good Odysseus, in word or deed kept covenant with
you there in the Trojan land where you Achaeans suffered, be mindful
of it now; tell me the very truth."

Then, deeply moved, said light-haired Menelaus: "Heavens! In a
very brave man's bed they sought to lie, the weaklings! As when in the
den of a strong lion a hind has laid asleep her new-born sucking fawns,
then roams the slopes and grassy hollows seeking food, and by and by
into his lair the lion comes and on both hind and fawns brings ghastly
doom; so shall Odysseus bring a ghastly doom on these. Ah, father
Zeus, Athene, and Apollo! if with the power he showed one day in
stately Lesbos, when he rose and wrestled in a match with Philomeleides,
and down he threw him heavily, while the Achaeans all rejoiced,—if as
he was that day Odysseus now might meet the suitors, they all would
find quick turns of fate and bitter rites of marriage. But as to what you
ask thus urgently, I will not turn to talk of other things, and so deceive
you; but what the unerring old man of the sea told me, in not a word
will I disguise or hide from you.

"At the river of Egypt, eager as I was to hasten hither, the gods still
held me back, because I did not make the offerings due; and the gods
wish us ever to be mindful of their precepts. Now in the surging sea an
island lies,—Pharos they call it,—distant as far from the Egyptian
stream as a hollow ship runs in a day when a whistling wind blows after.
By it there lies a bay with a good anchorage, from which they send the
trim ships off to sea after supplying them with drinking water. Here the
gods kept me twenty days; not once came winds that blow along the sea
and serve for aid to ships on the broad ocean-ridges. So all my stores
would have been spent and my men's courage, had not a certain goddess pitied and preserved me. This was Eidothea, the daughter of
mighty Proteus, the old man of the sea; for I deeply moved her heart as
she met me on my solitary way apart from my companions; for they

were ever roaming round the island, fishing with crooked hooks, and hunger pinched their bellies. She, drawing near me, spoke and thus she said: 'Are you so very helpless, stranger, and unnerved, or do you willingly give way, taking a pleasure in your pains? So long you have been pent within the island, unable to discover an escape, while fainter grows the courage of your comrades.'

"So she spoke, and answering her said I: 'Then let me tell you, whatsoever goddess you may be, that I remain here through no will of mine, but I must have given offense to the immortals, who hold the open sky. Rather tell me,—for gods know all,—which of the immortals chains me here and bars my progress; and tell me of my homeward way, how I may pass along the swarming sea.'

"So I spoke, and straight the heavenly goddess answered: 'Well, stranger, I will plainly tell you all. There haunts this place a certain old man of the sea, unerring and immortal, Proteus of Egypt, who knows the depths of every sea, and is Poseidon's minister. He is, men say, my father, who begot me. If you could only lie in wait and seize on him, he would tell you of your course, the stages of your journey, and of your homeward way, how you may pass along the swarming sea. And he would tell you, heaven-descended man, if you desire, all that has happened at your home, of good or ill, while you have wandered on your long and toilsome way.'

"So she spoke, and answering her said I: 'Do you instruct me how to lie in wait for the old god, lest he foreseeing or foreknowing may escape. Hard is a god for mortal man to master.'

"So I spoke, and straight the heavenly goddess answered: 'Well, stranger, I will truly tell you all. When now the sun has reached midheaven, forth from the water comes the unerring old man of the sea at a puff of the west wind and veiled in the dark ripple. When he is come, he lays him down under the caverned cliffs; while round him seals, the brood of a fair sea nymph, huddle and sleep, on rising from the foaming water, and pungent is the scent they breathe of the unfathomed sea. There will I bring you at the dawn of day and lay you in the line. Meantime do you choose carefully for comrades the three best men you have among the well-benched ships. And I will tell you all the old man's magic arts. First he will count the seals and go their round; and when he has told them off by fives and found them all, he will lie down among them like a shepherd with his flock. As soon as you see him sleeping, summon all your might and main and hold him fast, although he strive and struggle to escape. He will make trial of you, turning into whatsoever moves on earth, to water even, and heaven-kindled fire; yet hold unflinchingly and clasp the more. But when at length he questions you in his own shape,—in the same shape as when you saw him sleeping,—

then, hero, cease from violence and set the old man free, but ask what god afflicts you, and ask about your homeward way, how you may pass along the swarming sea.'

"Saying this, she plunged into the surging sea. I to the ships which lay along the sands turned me away, and as I went my heart grew very dark. But when I came to the ship and to the sea and we had made our supper and the immortal night drew near, we laid us down to sleep upon the beach. Then as the early rosy-fingered dawn appeared, along the shore of the wide-stretching sea I went with many supplications to the gods. I took three comrades with me, men whom I trusted most in every undertaking.

"She, in the mean time, having plunged into the sea's broad bosom, brought from the deep four skins of seals; all were fresh-flayed; and she prepared the plot against her father. She had scooped hollows in the sands, and sat awaiting us. Near her we drew. She made us all lie down in order and threw a skin on each. Then might our ambuscade have proved a hard one; for the pestilent stench of the sea-born seals oppressed us sorely. And who would make his bed beside a monster of the sea? But she preserved us and contrived for us great ease. Under the nose of each she set ambrosia, very sweet of smell, and this destroyed the creature's stench. So all the morning did we wait with patient hearts. At last the seals came trooping from the sea and soon lay down in order on the beach. At noon out of the sea came the old man, found his fat seals, went over all, and told their number, telling us first among the creatures, and never in his heart suspected there was fraud. At length he too lay down. Then with a shout we sprang and threw our arms about him, and the old man did not forget his crafty wiles: for first he turned into a bearded lion, then to a dragon, leopard, and huge boar; he turned into liquid water, into a branching tree; still we held firm, with patient hearts. But when at last the old man wearied, skillful though he was in magic arts, in open speech he questioned me and said:

"'Which of the gods, O son of Atreus, aided your plot to seize me here against my will, by ambuscade? What would you have?'

"So he spoke, and answering him said I: 'You know, old man,—why put me off with such a question?—how long a time I am confined upon this island, unable to discover an escape, while fainter grows my heart within. Rather tell me,—for gods know all,—which of the immortals chains me here and bars my progress; and tell me of my homeward way, how I may pass along the swarming sea.'

"So I spoke, and straightway answering me said he: 'Nay, but to Zeus and to the other gods you should have made good offerings on setting forth, if you would quickly reach your land, sailing the wine-dark sea; for now it is appointed you to see your friends no more nor reach your stately house and native land till you have gone again to Egypt's waters, to its heaven-descended stream, and offered sacred hecatombs to the immortal gods who hold the open sky. Then shall the gods grant you the course which you desire.'

"As thus he spoke, my very soul was crushed within me because he bade me cross again the misty sea and go to Egypt's river, a long and weary way. Yet still I answered thus and said: 'Old man, all that you bid me I will do. Only declare me this and plainly tell, did all the Achaeans with their ships return unharmed, whom Nestor and I left on our setting forth from Troy? Did any die by grievous death at sea or in the arms of friends when the skein of war was wound?'

"So I spoke, and straightway answering me said he: 'Son of Atreus, why question me of this? Better it were you should not see nor comprehend my knowledge; for certainly you will not long be free from tears after you learn the truth. Yes, many were cut off and many spared. Of leaders, only two among the mailed Achaeans died on the journey home,—as for the battle, you yourself were there,—and one, still living, lingers yet on the wide sea. Ajax was lost, he and his long-oared ships. At first Poseidon wrecked him on the great rocks of Gyrae, but saved him from the sea. And so he might have escaped his doom, though hated by Athene, had he not uttered overweening words, puffed up with pride; for he said he had escaped the great gulf of the sea in spite of gods. Poseidon heard his haughty boasting, and straightway, grasping the trident in his sturdy hands, he smote the rock of Gyrae, splitting it open. One part still held its place; the broken piece fell in the sea. It was on this Ajax at first had sat, puffed up with pride. It bore him down into the boundless surging deep. So there he died, drinking the briny water.

"'Your brother escaped his doom and came in safety, he and his hollow ships; for powerful Hero saved him. But when he was about to reach the steep height of Maleia, a sweeping storm bore him once more along the swarming sea, loudly lamenting, to the confines of that country where Thyestes dwelt in former days, but where now dwelt Thyestes' son, Aegisthus. And when at last from this point on his course was clear of danger, and the gods changed the wind about and home they came, then with rejoicing did he tread his country's soil, and he kissed and clasped that soil; and from him many hot tears fell, for he saw the land with gladness. But from a tower a watchman spied him, whom wily Aegisthus posted there and promised him for pay two talents of gold. He had been keeping guard throughout the year, lest unobserved the king might come and try the force of arms. He hastened to the house to tell the shepherd of the people, and soon Aegisthus planned his treacherous craft. Selecting twenty of the bravest in the land, he laid an ambush; and just across the hall bade that a feast be spread. Then he went to welcome Agamemnon, the shepherd of the people, with horses and with chariots, while meditating crimes. He led him up unheeding to his death and slew him at the feast, even as one kills the ox before the manger. Not a follower of the son of Atreus lived, nor a follower of Aegisthus; all died within the hall.'

"As thus he spoke, my very soul was crushed within me, and sitting on the sands I fell to weeping; my heart no longer cared to live and see the sunshine. But when of weeping and of writhing I had had my fill, then said the unerring old man of the sea: 'Do not, O son of Atreus, long and unceasingly thus weep, because we know there is no remedy. Seek rather with all speed to reach your native land; for either you will find Aegisthus still alive, or Orestes will have slain him, so forestalling you, and you may join the funeral feast.'

"So he spoke, and the heart and sturdy spirit in my breast through all my grief again grew warm; and speaking in winged words I said: 'Of these men then I know, but name the third who still alive lingers on the wide sea; or be he dead, spite of my grief I fain would hear.'

"So I spoke, and straightway answering me said he: 'It is Laërtes' son, whose home is Ithaca. I saw him on an island, letting the big tears fall, in the hall of the nymph Calypso, who holds him there by force. No power has he to reach his native land, for he has no ships fitted with oars, nor crews to bear him over the broad ocean-ridges. As for yourself, heaven-favored Menelaus, it is not destined you shall die and meet your doom in grazing Argos; but to the Elysian plain and the earth's limits the immortal gods shall bring you, where fair-haired Rhadamanthus dwells. Here utterly at ease passes the life of men. No snow is here, no winter long, no rain, but the loud-blowing breezes of the west the Ocean-stream sends up to bring men coolness; for you have Helen and are counted son-in-law of Zeus.'

"Saying this, he plunged into the surging sea. I with my gallant comrades turned to our ships, and as I went my heart grew very dark. But when we came to the ship and to the sea, and we had made our supper, and the immortal night drew near, we laid us down to sleep upon the beach. Then as the early rosy-fingered dawn appeared, we in the first place launched our ships into the sacred sea, put masts and sails in the trim ships, the men embarked themselves, took places at the pins, and sitting in order smote the foaming water with their oars. So back again to Egypt's waters, to its heaven-descended stream, I brought my ships and made the offerings due. And after appeasing the anger of the gods that live forever, I raised a mound to Agamemnon, that his fame might never die. This done, I sailed away; the gods gave wind and brought me swiftly to my native land. But come, remain awhile here at

my hall until eleven or twelve days pass. Then I will send you forth with
honor, giving you splendid gifts, three horses and a polished car.
Moreover, I will give a goodly chalice, that as you pour libations to the
immortal gods you may be mindful all your days of me."

Then answered him discreet Telemachus: "O son of Atreus, keep me
no long time here, though I could be content to stay a year, and no
desire for kindred or for home would ever come; for I find a wonderful
pleasure in hearing your tales and talk. But already friends at hallowed
Pylos are uneasy, and you still hold me here. As for the gift that you
would give, pray let it be some keepsake. Horses I will not take to
Ithaca, but leave them as an honor here for you; for you rule open
plains, where lotus is abundant, marsh-grass and wheat and corn, and
the white broad-eared barley. In Ithaca there are no open runs, no
meadows; a land for goats, and pleasanter than grazing country. Not
one of the islands is a place to drive a horse, none has good meadows,
of all that rest upon the sea; Ithaca least of all."

He spoke, and Menelaus, good at the war-cry, smiled, patted him
with his hand, and said:

"Of noble blood you are, dear child, as your words show. Yes, I will
make the change, for well I can. And out of all the gifts stored in my
house as treasures I will give you that which is most beautiful and precious: I will give a well-wrought bowl. It is of solid silver, its rim finished
with gold, the work of Hephaestus. Lord Phaedimus, the king of the
Sidonians, gave it to me, when his house sheltered me upon my homeward way. And now to you I gladly give it."

So they conversed together. But banqueters were coming to the
palace of the noble king. Men drove up sheep, and brought the cheering wine, and their veiled wives sent bread. Thus they were busied with
their dinner in the hall.

Meanwhile before the palace of Odysseus the suitors were making
merry, throwing the discus and the hunting spear upon the level pavement, holding riot as of old. Here sat Antinoüs and god-like
Eurymachus, the leaders of the suitors; for they in manly excellence
were quite the best of all. To them Noëmon, son of Phronius, now drew
near; and questioning Antinoüs thus he spoke:

"Antinoüs, do we know, or do we not, when Telemachus will come
from sandy Pylos? He took a ship of mine and went away, and now I
need her for crossing to broad Elis where I keep my twelve brood
mares. The hardy mules, their foals, are still unbroken; one I would
fetch away and break him in."

So he spoke. The others were amazed. They did not think Telemachus
was gone to Pylos, to the land of Neleus; they thought he was still somewhere at the farm, among the flocks, or with the swineherd.

Then said Antinoüs, Eupeithes son: "Tell me precisely when he went and what young men were with him. Picked men of Ithaca, or did he take his hirelings and slaves? That indeed he might do! And tell me truly this, that I may know it well; did he with violence, against your will, take the black ship? Or did you give it willingly, because he begged?"

Then answered him Noëmon, son of Phronius: "I gave it willingly. What could one do when a man like him, with troubles on his heart, entreated? Hard would it be to keep from giving. The youths who next to us are noblest in the land are his companions. I marked their captain as he went on board, and it was Mentor or a god exactly like him. Yet this is strange. Here I saw noble Mentor yesterday in the morning; and there he was embarking on the ship for Pylos."

So saying, he departed to his father's house. But the proud spirits of the two were stirred. They made the suitors seat themselves and stop their sports. And then Antinoüs, Eupeithes' son, addressed them in displeasure. With great passion was his dark soul filled. His eyes were like bright fire.

"Well! Well! Here is a monstrous action impudently brought to pass, this journey of Telemachus. We said it should not be; and here in spite of all of us this young boy simply goes, launching a ship and picking out the best men of the land. Before we think, he will begin to be our bane. But may Zeus blast his power before he reaches man's estate! Come then, and give me a swift ship with twenty comrades, and I will lie in wait upon his way, and guard the strait twixt Ithaca and rugged Samos. So to his grief he cruises off to find his father." He spoke, and all approved and urged him on. And presently they rose and entered the hall of Odysseus.

But now Penelope, no long time after, learned of the plans on which the suitors' hearts were brooding. For the page Medon told her, who overheard the plot as he stood outside the court, while they within it framed their scheme. He hastened through the palace with the tidings to Penelope; and as he crossed her threshold Penelope thus spoke:

"Page, why have the lordly suitors sent you here? Was it to tell the maids of the princely Odysseus to put by work and lay their table? Oh that they had not wooed or gathered here, or that they here to-day might eat their last and latest meal! You troop about and squander all our living, even all the estate of wise Telemachus. To your fathers of old you gave no heed when you were children, nor heard what sort of man Odysseus was among your elders, how he did no wrong by deed or word to any in the land. And that is the common way with high-born kings; one man they hate and love another. But he wrought no iniquity to any man. Yet what your disposition is, and what your shameful deeds, is plain to see. There is no gratitude for good deeds done."

Then Medon spoke, a man of understanding: "Ah, Queen, I would that were our greatest ill; but weightier matters yet, a sorer evil, the suitors now propose—which may the son of Kronos hinder! They have resolved to slay Telemachus with the keen sword, as he sails home. He went away for tidings of his father, to hallowed Pylos and to sacred Lacedaemon."

As he thus spoke, her knees grew feeble and her very soul. Long time a speechless stupor held her; her two eyes filled with tears, her full voice stayed. But at the last she answered thus and said: "Page, why is my child gone? What need had he to mount the coursing ships, which serve men for sea-horses and cross the mighty flood? Was it to leave no name among men here?"

Then answered Medon, that man of understanding: "I do not know whether a god impelled him, or if his own heart stirred within to go to Pylos, to gather tidings of his father's coming or there to learn what fate he met."

So saying, he departed along the hall of Odysseus. But upon her heart-eating anguish fell. No longer had she power to sit upon a chair, though many were in the room, but down she sank upon the floor of her rich chamber, pitifully moaning. Round about, her maids were sobbing—all her household, young and old. And with repeated cries, Penelope thus spoke:

"Listen, dear maids! Surely the Olympian gave me exceeding sorrow, beyond all women born and bred my mates. For I in former days lost my good husband, a man of lion heart, for every excellence honored among the Danaäns—good man! his fame is wide through Hellas and mid-Argos. Moreover now my darling son the winds have snatched away, silently, from my halls; I heard not of his going. Hard-hearted maids! No one of you took thought to rouse me from my bed, though well your own hearts knew when he embarked on the black hollow ship. Ah, had I learned that he was purposing this journey, surely he would have stayed, however eager for the journey, or else he should have left me dead within the hall. But now let some one haste and call old Dolius, the slave my father gave when I came here, who tends my orchard trees; that he may quickly go, seat himself by Laërtes and, telling all, learn if Laërtes can devise a way to come before the people and cry out against the men who seek to crush his race and that of great Odysseus."

Then answered her the good nurse Eurycleia: "Dear lady, slay me with the ruthless sword or leave me in the hall; I will not hide my story. I knew of all. I gave him what he wanted, bread and sweet wine. But he exacted from me a solemn oath to speak no word to you until twelve days were past, or until you should miss him and hear that he was gone,

that so you might not stain your beautiful face with tears. Now therefore bathe, and putting on fresh garments, go to your upper chamber
with your maids, and offer prayer to Athene, daughter of ægis-bearing
Zeus; for thus she may preserve him safe from death. Vex not an old
man, vexed already. Surely I cannot think the Arceisian line is wholly
hateful to the blessed gods. Nay, one shall still survive to hold the high-
roofed house and the fat fields around."

She spoke, and lulled the other's cries and stayed her eyes from tears.
Penelope bathed, and putting on fresh garments went to her upper chamber with her maids, took barley in a basket, and thus she prayed Athene:

"Hear me, thou child of ægis-bearing Zeus, unwearied one! If ever
wise Odysseus when at home burned the fat thighs of ox or sheep to
thee, thereof be mindful now; preserve me my dear son. Guard him
against the cruel suitors' wrongs."

Thus having said, she raised the cry, and the goddess heard her
prayer. But the suitors broke into uproar up and down the dusky hall,
and a rude youth would say: "Ha, ha! at last the long-wooed queen
makes ready for our marriage. Little she thinks that for her son death is
in waiting." So they would say, but knew not how things were.

And now Antinoüs addressed them, saying: "Good sirs, beware of
haughty talk of every kind, or some one may report it indoors too.
Come, rather, let us rise and quietly as we may let us effect the scheme
which pleased the hearts of all."

So saying, he chose the twenty fittest men, who went to the swift ship
and to the shore. They in the first place launched the ship into deep
water, put mast and sail in the black ship, fitted the oars into their leathern slings, all in due order, and up aloft spread the white sail. Stately
squires carried their armor. Out in the stream they moored the boat,
they themselves disembarked, took supper there, and waited for the
evening to come on.

But in her upper chamber heedful Penelope still lay fasting, tasting
neither food nor drink, anxious whether her gentle son would escape
death, or by the audacious suitors be borne down; as doubts a lion in a
crowd of men, in terror as they draw the crafty circle round him. To her
in such anxiety sweet slumber came, and lying back she slept and every
joint relaxed.

Now a new plan the goddess formed, clear-eyed Athene. She shaped
a phantom fashioned in a woman's form, even like Iphthime, daughter
of brave Icarius, her whom Eumelus married, that had his home at
Pherae. And this she sent to the house of princely Odysseus, that it
might make Penelope, mourning and sighing now, cease from her
griefs and tearful cries. It came into the chamber past the bolt-strap,
stood by her head and thus addressed her:

"Are you asleep, Penelope, dear troubled heart? No, never shall the gods that live at ease leave you to weep and pine; for still your son is destined to return, since in the gods' sight he is no transgressor."

Then answered heedful Penelope, very sweetly slumbering at the gates of dreams: "Why, sister, have you come? You never before were with me, because your home is very far away. And you bid me cease from grief and all the pangs that vex my mind and heart, me who in former days lost my good husband, a man of lion heart, for every excellence honored among the Danaäns—good man! his fame is wide through Hellas and mid-Argos. Moreover now my darling son is gone on a hollow ship, a mere boy too, but little skilled in cares and counsels. Therefore for him I mourn even more than for that other. For him I tremble, and I fear that he may meet with ill, either from those within the land where he is gone, or on the sea. For many evil-minded men now plot against him and seek to cut him off before he gains his native land."

And answering her, said the dim phantom: "Take heart, and be not in your mind too sore afraid. So true a guide goes with him as other men have prayed for aid—for powerful is she—Pallas Athene. Seeing you grieve, she pities you, and it was she who sent me here to tell you so."

Then heedful Penelope said to her: "If you are a god and have obeyed some heavenly bidding, come tell me also of that hapless one, if he still lives and sees the sunshine; or is he now already dead and in the house of Hades?"

And answering her, said the dim phantom: "Of him I will not speak at length, be he alive or dead. To speak vain words is ill."

So saying, it glided past the door-post's bolt into the airy breezes. And out of sleep awoke Icarius' daughter, and her very soul was warmed, so clear a dream was sent her in the dead of night.

Meanwhile the suitors, embarking in their ship, sailed on their watery journey, purposing in their minds the speedy murder of Telemachus. Now in mid-sea there is a rocky island, midway from Ithaca to rugged Samos—Star Islet called—of no great size. It has a harbor, safe for ships, on either side; and here it was the Achaeans waited, watching.

V.

THE RAFT OF ODYSSEUS

Read
In
class

DAWN FROM her couch by high Tithonus rose to bring light to immortals and to men; and now the gods sat down to council. With them was Zeus, who thunders from on high, whose power is over all; and to them Athene, ever mindful of Odysseus, told of his many woes; for she was troubled by his stay at the dwelling of the nymph.

"O Father Zeus, and all you blessed gods that live forever, never again let sceptred king in all sincerity be kind and gentle, nor let him in his mind heed righteousness. Let him instead ever be stern and work unrighteous deeds; since none remembers princely Odysseus among the people whom he ruled, kind father though he was. Upon an island now he lies, deeply distressed, at the hall of the nymph Calypso, who holds him there by force. No power has he to reach his native land, for he has no ships fitted with oars, nor crews to bear him over the broad ocean-ridges. Now, too, men seek to slay his darling son, as he sails home. He went away for tidings of his father, to hallowed Pylos and to sacred Lacedaemon."

Then answering, said cloud-gathering Zeus: "My child, what word has passed the barrier of your teeth? For was it not yourself proposed the plan to have Odysseus crush these men by his return? As for Telemachus, aid him upon his way with wisdom,—as you can,—that he may come unharmed to his own native land, and the suitors in their ship may be turned back again."

He spoke, and said to Hermes, his dear son: "Hermes, since you in all things are my messenger, tell to the fair-haired nymph our steadfast purpose, that hardy Odysseus shall go forth upon his homeward way, not with gods' guidance nor with that of mortal man; but by himself, beset with sorrows, on a strong-built raft, he shall in twenty days reach fertile Scheria, the land of the Phaeacians, who are kinsmen of the gods. There shall they greatly honor him, as if he were a god, and bring him on his way by ship to his own native land, giving him stores of bronze and gold and clothing, more than Odysseus would have won from Troy itself, had he returned unharmed with his due share of spoil. Thus, then, it is his lot to see his friends and reach his high-roofed house and native land."

So he spoke, and the guide, the Speedy-comer, did not disobey; forthwith under his feet he bound his beautiful sandals, immortal, made of gold, which carry him over the flood and over the boundless land swift as a breath of wind. He took the wand with which he charms to sleep the eyes of whom he will, while again whom he will he wakens out of slumber. With this in hand, the powerful Speedy-comer began his flight. On coming to Pieria, out of the upper air he dropped down on the deep and skimmed along the water like a bird, a gull, which down the fearful hollows of the barren sea, snatching at fish, dips its thick plumage in the spray. In such wise, through the multitude of waves, moved Hermes. But when he neared the distant island, there turning landward from the dark blue sea, he walked until he came to a great grotto where dwelt the fair-haired nymph. He found she was within. Upon the hearth a great fire blazed, and far along the island the fragrance of cleft cedar and of sandal-wood sent perfume as they burned. Indoors, and singing with sweet voice, she tended her loom and wove with golden shuttle. Around the grotto, trees grew luxuri-antly, alder and poplar and sweet-scented cypress, where long-winged birds had nests,—owls, hawks, and sea-crows ready-tongued, that ply their business in the waters. Here too was trained over the hollow grotto a thrifty vine, luxuriant with clusters; and four springs in a row were running with clear water, making their way from one another here and there. On every side soft meadows of violet and parsley bloomed. Here, therefore, even an immortal who should come might gaze at what he saw, and in his heart be glad. Here stood and gazed the guide, the Speedy-comer. Then after he had gazed to his heart's fill on all, straightway he entered the wide-mouthed grotto, and at a glance Calypso, the heavenly goddess, failed not to know it was he; for not unknown to one another are immortal gods, although they have their dwellings far apart. But brave Odysseus he did not find within; for he sat weeping on the shore, where, as of old, with tears and groans and griefs racking his heart, he watched the barren sea and poured forth tears. And now Calypso, the heavenly goddess, questioned Hermes, seat-ing him on a handsome, shining chair:

"Pray, Hermes of the golden wand, why are you come, honored and welcome though you are? You were not often with me hitherto. Speak what you have in mind; my heart bids me to do it, if I can do it and it is a thing that can be done. But follow me first, and let me give you entertainment."

So saying, the goddess laid a table, loading it with ambrosia and mixing ruddy nectar; and so the guide, the Speedy-comer, drank and ate. But when he had eaten dinner and stayed his heart with food, then thus he answered her and said:

"Goddess, you question me, a god, about my coming hither, and I will truly tell my story as you bid. Zeus ordered me to come, against my will. Who of his own accord would cross such stretches of salt sea? Interminable! And no city of men at hand to make an offering to the gods and bring them chosen hecatombs. Nevertheless the will of ægis-bearing Zeus no god may cross or set at naught. He says a man is with you, the most unfortunate of all who fought for Priam's town nine years and in the tenth destroyed the city and departed home. They on their homeward way offended Athene, who raised ill winds against them and a heavy sea. Thus all the rest of his good comrades perished, but wind and water brought him here. This is the man whom Zeus now bids you send away, and quickly too, for it is not ordained that he shall perish far from friends; it is his lot to see his friends once more and reach his high-roofed house and native land."

As he said this, Calypso, the heavenly goddess, shuddered, and speaking in winged words she said: "Hard are you gods and envious beyond all, to grudge the goddesses their meeting men in open wedlock, when one makes the man she loves her husband. So when rosy-fingered Dawn had chosen Orion, you gods that live at ease grudged him to her, till in Ortygia chaste gold-throned Artemis attacked and slew him with her gentle arrows. When, too, fair-haired Demeter, following her heart, lay with Iasion in the thrice-ploughed field, not long was Zeus unmindful; for he slew him, hurling his gleaming bolt. So now again, you gods grudge me the mortal tarrying here. Yet it was I who saved him, as he rode astride his keel alone, when Zeus with a gleaming bolt smote his swift ship and wrecked it in the middle of the wine-dark sea. There all the rest of his good comrades perished, but wind and water brought him here. I loved and cherished him, and often said that I would make him an immortal, young forever. But since the will of ægis-bearing Zeus no god may cross or set at naught, let him depart, if Zeus commands and bids it, over the barren sea! Only I will not aid him on his way, for I have no ships fitted with oars, nor crews to bear him over the broad ocean-ridges; but I will freely give him counsel and not hide how he may come unharmed to his own native land."

Then said to her the guide, the Speedy-comer: "Even so, then, let him go! Beware the wrath of Zeus! Let not his anger by and by grow hot against you!"

So saying, the powerful Speedy-comer went his way, while the potent nymph hastened to brave Odysseus, obedient to the words of Zeus. She found him sitting on the shore, and from his eyes the tears were never dried; his sweet life ebbed away in longings for his home, because the nymph pleased him no more. And yet by night he always lay, though by constraint, within the hollow grotto, unwilling by her willing side; but in the daytime, sitting on the rocks and sands, with tears and groans and griefs racking his heart, he watched the barren sea and poured forth tears. Now drawing near, the heavenly goddess said:

"Unhappy man, sorrow no longer here, nor let your days be wasted, for I at last will freely let you go. Come, then, hew the long timbers and fashion with your axe a broad-beamed raft; build a high bulwark round, and let it bear you over the misty sea. I will supply you bread, water, and the ruddy wine you like, to keep off hunger; I will provide you clothing and will send a wind to follow, that you may come unharmed to your own native land,—if the gods will, who hold the open sky, for they are mightier than I to purpose or fulfill."

As she said this, long-tried royal Odysseus shuddered, and speaking in winged words he said:

"Some other purpose, goddess, you surely have in this than aid upon my way, when you thus bid me cross on a raft that great gulf of the sea— terrible, toilsome—which trim ships cannot cross, although they speed so fast, glad in the breeze of Zeus. But I will never, notwithstanding what you say, set foot upon a raft till you consent, goddess, to swear a solemn oath that you are not meaning now to plot me further woe."

He spoke; Calypso, the heavenly goddess, smiled, caressed him with her hand and spoke thus, saying:

"You are a cunning rogue, never inclined to folly! How could you think of uttering such words! Hear this, then, Earth, and the broad Heaven above, and thou down-flowing water of Styx,—which is the strongest and most dreaded oath among the blessed gods,—I am not meaning now to plot you further woe. Nay, that I have in mind, and that I here propose, which I would seek for my own good were such need laid on me. Indeed, my thoughts are upright; no iron heart is in my breast, but one of pity."

So saying, the heavenly goddess led the way in haste, and he walked after in the footsteps of the goddess. And now to the hollow grotto came the goddess and the man, and he sat down upon the chair whence Hermes had arisen. The nymph then set before him all food to eat and drink which men are wont to use, and took her seat over against princely Odysseus, while maids set forth for her ambrosia and nectar; then on the food spread out before them they laid hands. So after they were satisfied with food and drink, then thus began Calypso, the heavenly goddess:

"High-born son of Laërtes, ready Odysseus, do you so wish to go at once home to your native land? Farewell, then, even so! But if at heart you knew how many woes you must endure before you reach that native land, you would remain with me, become the guardian of my home, and be immortal, spite of your wish to see your wife, whom you are always longing for day after day. Yet not inferior to her I count myself, either in form or stature. Surely it is not likely that mortal women rival the immortals in form and beauty."

Then wise Odysseus answered her and said: "Powerful goddess, do not be wroth at what I say. Full well I know that heedful Penelope, compared with you, is poor to look upon in height and beauty; for she is human, but you are an immortal, young forever. Yet even so, I wish—yes, every day I long—to travel home and see my day of coming. And if again one of the gods shall wreck me on the wine-dark sea, I will be patient still, bearing within my breast a heart well-tried with trouble; for in times past much have I borne and much have I toiled, in waves and war; to that, let this be added."

As he thus spoke, the sun went down and darkness came;

* * * * * * *
Read in class

Soon as the early rosy-fingered dawn appeared, quickly Odysseus dressed in coat and tunic; and the nymph dressed herself in a long silvery robe, finespun and graceful, she bound a beautiful golden girdle round her waist, and put a veil upon her head. Then she prepared to send forth brave Odysseus. She gave him a great axe, which fitted well his hands; it was an axe of bronze, sharp on both sides, and had a beautiful olive handle, strongly fastened; she gave him too a polished adze. And now she led the way to the farther shore of the island where the trees grew tall, alder and poplar and sky-stretching pine, long-seasoned, very dry, that would float lightly. When she had shown him where the trees grew tall, homeward Calypso went, the heavenly goddess, while he began to cut the logs. The work was quickly done. Twenty in all he felled, and trimmed them with the axe, smoothed them with skill, and leveled them to the line. Meanwhile, Calypso, the heavenly goddess, brought him augers, and so he bored each piece and fitted all, and then with pins and crossbeams fastened the whole together. As when a man skillful in carpentry lays out the floor of a broad freight-ship, of such a size Odysseus built his broad-beamed raft. He raised a bulwark, set with many ribs, and finished with long timbers on the top. He made a mast and sail-yard fitted to it; he made a rudder, too, with which to steer. And then he caulked the raft from end to end with willow withes, to guard against the water, and much material he used. Meanwhile, Calypso, the heavenly goddess, brought him cloth to make the sail, and well did he contrive this too. Braces and halyards and sheet-ropes he set up in her and then with levers heaved her down into the sacred sea.

The fourth day came, and he had finished all. So on the fifth divine Calypso sent him from the island, putting upon him fragrant clothes and giving him a bath. A skin the goddess gave him, filled with dark wine, a second large one full of water, and some provision in a sack. She put upon the raft whatever dainties pleased him and sent along his course a fair and gentle breeze. Joyfully to the breeze royal Odysseus spread his sail, and with his rudder skillfully he steered from where he sat. No sleep fell on his eyelids as he gazed upon the Pleiades, on Boötes which sets late, and on the Bear which men call Wagon too, which turns around one spot, watching Orion, and alone does not dip in the Ocean-stream. For Calypso, the heavenly goddess, bade him to cross the sea with the Bear upon his left; so seventeen days he sailed across the sea. On the eighteenth there came in sight the dim heights of Phaeacia, where nearest him it lay; it seemed a shield laid on the misty sea.

But now the mighty Earth-shaker, coming from Ethiopia, spied him afar from the mountains of the Solymi; for Odysseus came in sight as he sailed along the sea. And Poseidon grew more wroth in spirit, and shaking his head he muttered to his heart:

"Aha! so then the gods have changed their purposes about Odysseus, while I was with the Ethiopians! And here he is close to the land of the Phaeacians, where he is destined to escape from the great coil of evil that surrounds him. Yet still I hope to plunge him into sufficient trouble."

So saying, he gathered clouds and stirred the deep, grasping the trident in his hands; he started tempests of wind from every side, and covered with his clouds both land and sea; night broke from heaven; forth rushed together Eurus and Notus, hard-blowing Zephyrus, and sky-born Boreas, rolling up heavy waves. Then did Odysseus' knees grow feeble, and his very soul, and in dismay he said to his stout heart:

"Ah, woe is me! What will become of me at last? I fear that all the goddess told was true, when she declared that on the sea, before I reached my native land, I should be filled with sorrow. Now all is come to pass. Ah, with what clouds Zeus overcasts the open sky! He stirred the deep, and tempests of wind hurry from every side. Swift death is sure. Thrice, four times happy Danaäns who in the time gone by fell on the plain of Troy to please the sons of Atreus! Would I had died there too, and met my doom the day a multitude of Trojans hurled at me brazen spears over the body of the son of Peleus! Then had I found a burial, and the Achaeans had borne my name afar. Now I must be cut off by an inglorious death."

As thus he spoke, a great wave broke on high and madly plunging whirled his raft around; far from the raft he fell and sent the rudder flying from his hand. The mast snapped in the middle under the fearful tempest of opposing winds that struck, and far in the sea canvas and sail-yard fell. The water held him long submerged; he could not rise at once after the crash of the great wave, for the clothing which divine Calypso gave him weighed him down. At length, however, he came up, spitting from out his mouth the bitter brine which plentifully trickled from his head. Yet even then, spent as he was, he did not forget his raft, but pushing on amongst the waves laid hold of her, and in her middle got a seat and so escaped death's ending. But her the great wave drove along its current, up and down. As when in autumn Boreas drives thistleheads along the plain, and close they cling together, so the winds drove her up and down the deep. One moment Notus tossed her on for Boreas to drive; the next would Eurus give her up for Zephyrus to chase.

But the daughter of Cadmus saw him, fair-ankled Ino, that goddess pale who formerly was mortal and of human speech, but now in the water's depths shares the gods' honors. She pitied Odysseus, cast away and meeting sorrow, and like a petrel on the wing she rose from the sea's trough, and lighting on his strong-built raft spoke to him thus:

"Unhappy man, why is it earth-shaking Poseidon is so furiously enraged that he makes many ills spring up around you? Destroy you shall he not, however wroth he be! Only do this,—you seem to me not to lack understanding. Strip off these clothes, and leave your raft for winds to carry, then strike out with your arms and seek a landing on the Phaeacian coast, where fate allows you safety. Here, spread this wimple underneath your breast. It is immortal; have no fear of suffering or death. But when your hands shall touch the shore, untie and fling the wimple into the wine-dark sea, well off the shore, and so depart."

Saying this, the goddess gave the wimple, and she herself plunged back into the surging sea, in likeness of a petrel. The dark wave closed around. Then hesitated long-tried royal Odysseus, and in dismay he said to his stout heart:

"Ah me! I fear that here again an immortal plots me harm in bidding me leave my raft. I will not yet obey; for in the distance I saw land, where it was said my safety lies. This I will do, for best it seems: so long as the beams hold in the fastenings, here I will stay and bide what I must bear; but when the surge batters my raft to pieces, then I will swim. There is no better plan."

While he thus doubted in his mind and heart, earth-shaking Poseidon raised a great wave, gloomy and grievous, and with bending crest, and launched it on him. And as a gusty wind tosses a heap of grain when it is dry, and some it scatters one way, some another, so were the long beams scattered. But Odysseus mounting a beam, as if he rode a steed, stripped off the clothing which divine Calypso gave, spread quickly the wimple underneath his breast, and plunged down headlong in the sea, with hands outstretched, ready to swim. The great Earth-shaker spied him, and shaking his head he muttered to his heart:

"Thus, after meeting many ills, be tossed about the sea until you join a people who are favorites of Zeus; but even then, I trust, you will not laugh at danger."

Saying this, he lashed his full-maned horses and came to Aegae, where his lordly dwelling stands.

And now Athene, daughter of Zeus, formed a new plan. She barred the pathway of the other winds, bade them to cease and all be laid to rest; but she roused bustling Boreas and before it broke the waves, that safely among the oar-loving Phaeacians might come high-born Odysseus, freed from death and doom.

Then two nights and two days on the resistless waves he drifted; many a time his heart faced death. But when the fair-haired dawn brought the third day, then the wind ceased; there came a breathless calm; and close at hand he spied the coast, as he cast a keen glance forward, upborne on a great wave. As when the precious life is watched by children in a father, who lies in sickness, suffering great pain and slowly wasting,—for a hostile power assails him,—and then the one thus prized the gods set free from danger; so precious in Odysseus' eyes appeared the land and trees. Onward he swam, impatient for his feet to touch the ground. But when he was as far away as one can call, he heard a pounding of the ocean on the ledges; for the great waves roared as on the barren land they madly dashed, and all was whirled in spray. There was no harbor here to hold a ship, no open roadstead; only projecting bluffs, ledges, and reefs. At this Odysseus' knees grew feeble, and his very soul, and in dismay he said to his stout heart:

"Alas! when Zeus now lets me see unlooked for land, and forcing my way along the gulf I finally reach its end, no landing anywhere appears out of the foaming sea. Outside are jagged reefs; around thunder the surging waves, and smooth and steep rises the rocky shore. To the edge the sea is deep, and possible it is not to get a footing with both feet and so escape disaster. If I should try to land, great sweeping waves might dash me on the solid rock; useless would the attempt be! But if I swim still farther, hoping to find a sloping shore and harbors off the sea, I fear a sweeping storm may bear me yet again along the swarming sea, loudly lamenting; or God may send upon me a monster of the deep,— and many such great Amphitrite breeds,—for I know how angry is the great Land-shaker."

While he thus doubted in his mind and heart, a huge wave bore him onward toward the rugged shore. There would his skin have been stripped off and his bones broken, had not the goddess, clear-eyed Athene, given him counsel. Struggling, he grasped the rock with both his hands and clung there, groaning, till the great wave passed. That one he thus escaped, but the back-flowing water struck him again, still struggling, and swept him out to sea. And just as, when a polyp is torn from out its bed, about its suckers clustering pebbles cling, so on the rocks pieces of skin were stripped from his strong hands. The great wave covered him. Then miserably, before his time, Odysseus would have died, if cleared-eyed Athene had not given him ready thought. Rising beyond the waves which thundered on the coast, he swam along outside, eying the land, in hopes to find a sloping shore and harbors off the sea. But when, as he swam, he reached the mouth of a fair-flowing river, there the ground seemed most fit, for it was clear of stones and sheltered from the breeze. He felt the river flowing forth, and in his heart he prayed:

"Hearken, O lord, whoe'er thou art! Thee, long desired, I find, when flying from the sea and from Poseidon's threats. Respected even of immortal gods is he who comes a fugitive, as I here now come to thy current and thy knees through weary toil. Show pity, lord! I call myself thy suppliant."

He spoke, and the god straightway stayed the stream and checked the waves, before him made a calm, and brought him safely into the river's mouth. Both knees hung loose, and both his sturdy arms, for by the sea his spirit had been broken. His body was all swollen, and water gushed in streams out of his mouth and nostrils. So, breathless and speechless, in a swoon he lay and dire fatigue o'ercame him. But when he gained his breath, and in his breast the spirit rallied, then he unbound the wimple of the goddess and dropped it in the river running out to sea; and back a great wave bore it down the stream, and Ino soon received it in her friendly hands. But he, retreating from the river, lay down among the rushes and kissed the bounteous earth, and in dismay he said to his stout heart:

"Ah me! What shall I do? What will become of me even now? If by the stream I watch throughout the weary night, may not the bitter frost and the fresh dew together after this swoon end my exhausted life? The breeze from off a river blows cool toward early morning. But if I climb the hill-side up to the dusky wood and sleep in the thick bushes,—supposing that the chill and weariness depart and pleasant sleep come on,—I am afraid I may become the wild beasts' prey and prize."

Yet on reflecting thus, this seemed the better way: he hastened therefore to the wood. This he found near the water, with open space around. He crept under a pair of shrubs sprung from a single spot; the one was wild, the other common, olive. These no force of wind with its chill breath could pierce, no sunbeams smite, nor rain pass through, they grew so thickly intertwined with one another. Under them crept Odysseus, and quickly with his hands he scraped a bed together, an ample one, for a thick fall of leaves was there, enough to shelter two or three men in winter-time, however severe the weather. This long-tried royal Odysseus saw with joy, and lay down in the midst, heaping the fallen leaves above. As a man hides a brand in a dark bed of ashes, at some outlying farm where neighbors are not near, hoarding a seed of fire to save his seeking elsewhere, even so did Odysseus hide himself in leaves; and on his eyes Athene poured a sleep, quickly to ease him from the fatigue of toil, letting his eyelids close.

VI.

THE LANDING IN PHAEACIA

THUS LONG-TRIED royal Odysseus slumbered here, heavy with sleep and toil; but Athene went to the land and town of the Phaeacians. This people once in ancient times lived in the open Highlands, near that rude folk the Cyclops, who often plundered them, being in strength more powerful than they. Moving them thence, godlike Nausithoüs, their leader, established them at Scheria, far from toiling men. He ran a wall around the town, built houses there, made temples for the gods, and laid out farms; but Nausithoüs had met his doom and gone to the house of Hades, and Alcinoüs now was reigning, trained in wisdom by the gods. To this man's dwelling came the goddess, clear-eyed Athene, planning a safe return for brave Odysseus. She hastened to a chamber, richly wrought, in which a maid was sleeping, of form and beauty like the immortals, Nausicaä, daughter of generous Alcinoüs. Near by two damsels, dowered with beauty by the Graces, slept by the threshold, one on either hand. The shining doors were shut; but Athene, like a breath of air, moved to the maid's couch, stood by her head, and thus addressed her,—taking the likeness of the daughter of Dymas, the famous seaman, a maiden just Nausicaä's age, dear to her heart. Taking her guise, thus spoke clear-eyed Athene:

"Nausicaä, how did your mother bear a child so heedless? Your gay clothes lie uncared for, though the wedding time is near, when you must wear fine clothes yourself and furnish them to those that may attend you. From things like these a good repute arises, and father and honored mother are made glad. Then let us go a-washing at the dawn of day, and I will go to help, that you may soon be ready; for really not much longer will you be a maid. Already you have for suitors the chief ones of the land throughout Phaeacia, where you too were born.

Come, then, beg your good father early in the morning to harness the mules and cart, so as to carry the men's clothes, gowns, and bright-hued rugs. Yes, and for you yourself it is more decent so than setting forth on foot; the pools are far from the town."

Saying this, clear-eyed Athene passed away, off to Olympus, where they say the dwelling of the gods stands fast forever. Never with winds is it disturbed, nor by the rain made wet, nor does the snow come near; but everywhere the upper air spreads cloudless, and a bright radiance plays over all; and there the blessed gods are happy all their days. Thither now came the clear-eyed one, when she had spoken with the maid.

Soon bright-throned morning came, and waked fair-robed Nausicaä. She marveled at the dream, and hastened through the house to tell it to her parents, her dear father and her mother. She found them still in-doors: her mother sat by the hearth among the waiting-women, spinning sea-purple yarn; she met her father at the door, just going forth to join the famous princes at the council, to which the high Phaeacians sum-moned him. So standing close beside him, she said to her dear father:

"Papa dear, could you not have the wagon harnessed for me,—the high one, with good wheels,—to take my nice clothes to the river to be washed, which now are lying dirty? Surely for you yourself it is but proper, when you are with the first men holding councils, that you should wear clean clothing. Five good sons too are here at home,—two married, and three merry young men still,—and they are always want-ing to go to the dance wearing fresh clothes. And this is all a trouble on my mind."

Such were her words, for she was shy of naming the glad marriage to her father; but he understood it all, and answered thus:

"I do not grudge the mules, my child, nor anything beside. Go! Quickly shall the servants harness the wagon for you, the high one, with good wheels, fitted with rack above."

Saying this, he called to the servants, who gave heed. Out in the court they made the easy mule-cart ready; they brought the mules, and yoked them to the wagon. The maid took from her room her pretty clothing, and stowed it in the polished wagon; her mother put in a chest food the maid liked, of every kind, put dainties in, and poured some wine into a goat-skin bottle,—the maid, meanwhile, had got into the wagon,—and gave her in a golden flask some liquid oil, that she might bathe and anoint herself, she and the waiting-women. Nausicaä took the whip and the bright reins, and cracked the whip to start. There was a clatter of the mules, and steadily they pulled, drawing the clothing and the maid,— yet not alone; beside her went the waiting-women too.

When now they came to the fair river's current, where the pools were always full,—for in abundance clear water bubbles from beneath to cleanse the foulest stains,—they turned the mules loose from the wagon, and let them stray along the eddying stream, to crop the hon-eyed pasturage. Then from the wagon they took the clothing in their arms, carried it into the dark water, and stamped it in the pits with rivalry in speed. And after they had washed and cleansed it of all stains, they spread it carefully along the shore, just where the waves washed up the pebbles on the beach. Then bathing and anointing with the oil, they presently took dinner on the river bank and waited for the clothes to dry in the sunshine. And when they were refreshed with food, the maids and she, they then began to play at ball, throwing their wimples off. White-armed Nausicaä led their sport; and as the huntress Artemis goes down a mountain, down long Taÿgetus or Erymanthus, exulting in the boars and the swift deer, while round her sport the woodland nymphs, daughters of ægis-bearing Zeus, and glad is Leto's heart, for all the rest her child o'ertops by head and brow, and easily marked is she, though all are fair; so did this virgin pure excel her women.

But when Nausicaä thought to turn toward home once more, to yoke the mules and fold up the clean clothes, then a new plan the goddess formed, clear-eyed Athene; for she would have Odysseus wake and see the bright-eyed maid, who might to the Phaeacian city show the way. Just then the princess tossed the ball to one of her women, and missing her it fell in the deep eddy. Thereat they screamed aloud. Royal Odysseus woke, and sitting up debated in his mind and heart:

"Alas! To what men's land am I come now? Lawless and savage are they, with no regard for right, or are they kind to strangers and reverent toward the gods? It was as if there came to me the delicate voice of maids—nymphs, it may be, who haunt the craggy peaks of hills, the springs of streams and grassy marshes; or am I now, perhaps, near men of human speech? Suppose I make a trial for myself, and see."

So saying, royal Odysseus crept from the thicket, but with his strong hand broke a spray of leaves from the close wood, to be a covering round his body for his nakedness. He set off like a lion that is bred among the hills and trusts its strength; onward it goes, beaten with rain and wind; its two eyes glare; and now in search of oxen or of sheep it moves, or tracking the wild deer; its belly bids it make trial of the flocks, even by entering the guarded folds; so was Odysseus about to meet those fair-haired maids, all naked though he was, for need constrained him. To them he seemed a loathsome sight, befouled with brine. They hurried off, one here, one there, over the stretching sands. Only the daughter of Alcinoüs stayed, for in her breast Athene had put courage and from her limbs took fear. Steadfast she stood to meet him. And now Odysseus doubted whether to make his suit by clasping the knees of the bright-eyed maid, or where he stood, aloof, in winning words to make that suit, and try if she would show the town and give him clothing. Reflecting thus, it seemed the better way to make his suit in winning words, aloof; for fear if he should clasp her knees, the maid might be offended. Forthwith he spoke, a winning and shrewd speech:

"I am your suppliant, princess. Are you some god or mortal? If one of the gods who hold the open sky, to Artemis, daughter of mighty Zeus, in beauty, height, and bearing I find you likest. But if you are a mortal, living on the earth, most happy are your father and your honored mother, most happy your brothers also. Surely their hearts ever grow warm with pleasure over you, when watching such a blossom moving in the dance. And then exceeding happy he, beyond all others, who shall with gifts prevail and lead you home. For I never before saw such a being with these eyes—no man, no woman. I am amazed to see. At Delos once, by Apollo's altar, something like you I noticed, a young palm-shoot springing up; for thither too I came, and a great troop was with me, upon a journey where I was to meet with bitter trials. And just as when I looked on that I marveled long within, since never before sprang such a stalk from earth; so, lady, I admire and marvel now at you, and greatly fear to touch your knees. Yet grievous woe is on me. Yesterday, after twenty days, I escaped from the wine-dark sea, and all that time the waves and boisterous winds bore me away from the island of Ogygia. Now some god cast me here, that probably here also I may meet with trouble; for I do not think trouble will cease, but much the gods will first accomplish. Then, princess, have compassion, for it is you to whom through many grievous toils I first am come; none else I know of all who own this city and this land. Show me the town, and give me a rag to throw around me, if you had perhaps on coming here some wrapper for your linen. And may the gods grant all that in your thoughts you long for: husband and home and true accord may they bestow; for a better and higher gift than this there cannot be, when with accordant aims man and wife have a home. Great grief it is to foes and joy to friends; but they themselves best know its meaning."

Then answered him white-armed Nausicaä: "Stranger, because you do not seem a common, senseless person,—and Olympian Zeus himself distributes fortune to mankind and gives to high and low even as he wills to each; and this he gave to you, and you must bear it therefore,—now you have reached our city and our land, you shall not lack for clothes nor anything besides which it is fit a hard-pressed suppliant should find. I will point out the town and tell its people's name. The Phaeacians own this city and this land, and I am the daughter of generous Alcinoüs, on whom the might and power of the Phaeacians rests."

She spoke, and called her fair-haired waiting-women: "My women, stay! Why do you run because you saw a man? You surely do not think him evil-minded. The man is not alive, and never will be born, who can come and offer harm to the Phaeacian land: for we are very dear to the immortals; and then we live apart, far on the surging sea, no other tribe of men has dealings with us. But this poor man has come here having lost his way, and we should give him aid; for in the charge of Zeus all strangers and beggars stand, and a small gift is welcome. Then give, my women, to the stranger food and drink, and bathe him in the river where there is shelter from the breeze."

She spoke; the others stopped and called to one another, and down they brought Odysseus to the place of shelter, even as Nausicaä, daughter of generous Alcinoüs, had ordered. They placed a robe and tunic there for clothing, they gave him in the golden flask the liquid oil, and bade him bathe in the stream's currents. Then to the waiting-women said royal Odysseus:

"Women, stand here aside, while by myself I wash the salt from off my back and with the oil anoint me; for it is long since ointment touched my skin. But before you I will not bathe; for I am ashamed to bare myself among you fair-haired maids."

So he spoke; the women went away, and told it to the maid. And now with water from the stream royal Odysseus washed his skin clean of the salt which clung about his back and his broad shoulders, and wiped from his head the foam brought by the barren sea; and when he had thoroughly bathed and oiled himself and had put on the clothing which the chaste maiden gave, Athene, the daughter of Zeus, made him taller than before and stouter to behold, and she made the curling locks to fall around his head as on the hyacinth flower. As when a man lays gold on silver,—some skillful man whom Hephaestus and Pallas Athene have trained in every art, and he fashions graceful work; so did she cast a grace upon his head and shoulders. He walked apart along the shore, and there sat down, beaming with grace and beauty. The maid observed; then to her fair-haired waiting-women said:

"Hearken, my white-armed women, while I speak. Not without purpose on the part of all the gods that hold Olympus is this man's meeting with the godlike Phaeacians. A while ago, he really seemed to me ill-looking, but now he is like the gods who hold the open sky. Ah, might a man like this be called my husband, having his home here, and content to stay! But give, my women, to the stranger food and drink."

She spoke, and very willingly they heeded and obeyed, and set beside Odysseus food and drink. Then long-tried royal Odysseus eagerly drank and ate, for he had long been fasting.

And now to other matters white-armed Nausicaä turned her thoughts. She folded the clothes and laid them in the beautiful wagon, she yoked the stout-hoofed mules, mounted herself, and calling to Odysseus thus she spoke and said:

"Arise now, stranger, and hasten to the town, that I may set you on the road to my wise father's house, where you shall see, I promise you, the best of all Phaeacia. Only do this,—you seem to me not to lack understanding: while we are passing through the fields and farms, here with my women, behind the mules and cart, walk rapidly along, and I will lead the way. But as we near the town,—round which is a lofty rampart, a beautiful harbor on each side and a narrow road between,— there curved ships line the way; for every man has his own mooring-place. Beyond is the assembly near the beautiful grounds of Poseidon, constructed out of blocks of stone deeply imbedded. Further along, they make the black ships' tackling, cables and canvas, and shape out the oars; for the Phaeacians do not care for bow and quiver, only for masts and oars of ships and the trim ships themselves, with which it is their joy to cross the foaming sea. Now the rude talk of such as these I would avoid, that no one afterwards may give me blame. For very for-ward persons are about the place, and some coarse man might say, if he should meet us: 'What tall and handsome stranger is following Nausicaä? Where did she find him? A husband he will be, her very own. Some castaway, perhaps, she rescued from his vessel, some foreigner; for we have no neighbors here. Or at her prayer some long-entreated god has come straight down from heaven, and he will keep her his forever. So much the better, if she has gone herself and found a husband elsewhere! The people of our own land here, Phaeacians, she disdains, though she has many high-born suitors.' So they will talk, and for me it would prove a scandal. I should myself censure a girl who acted so, who, heedless of friends, while father and mother were alive, mingled with men before her public wedding. And, stranger, listen now to what I say, that you may soon obtain assistance and safe conduct from my father. Near our road you will see a stately grove of poplar trees, belonging to Athene; in it a fountain flows, and round it is a meadow. That is my father's park, his fruitful vineyard, as far from the town as one can call. There sit and wait a while, until we come to the town and reach my father's palace. But when you think we have already reached the palace, enter the city of the Phaeacians, and ask for the palace of my father, generous Alcinoüs. Easily is it known; a child, though young, could show the way; for the Phaeacians do not build their houses like the dwelling of Alcinoüs their prince. But when his house and court receive you, pass quickly through the hall until you find my mother. She sits in the firelight by the hearth, spinning sea-purple yarn, a marvel to behold, and resting against a pillar. Her handmaids sit behind her. Here too my father's seat rests on the selfsame pillar, and here he sits and sips his wine like an immortal. Passing him by, stretch out your hands to our mother's knees, if you would see the day of your return in gladness and with speed, although you come from far. If she regards you kindly in her heart, then there is hope that you may see your friends and reach your stately house and native land."

Saying this, with her bright whip she struck the mules, and fast they left the river's streams; and well they trotted, well they plied their feet, and skillfully she reined them that those on foot might follow,—the waiting-women and Odysseus,—and moderately she used the lash. The sun was setting when they reached the famous grove, Athene's sacred ground, where royal Odysseus sat him down. And thereupon he prayed to the daughter of mighty Zeus:

"Hearken, thou child of ægis-bearing Zeus, unwearied one! Oh hear me now, although before thou didst not hear me, when I was wrecked, what time the great Land-shaker wrecked me. Grant that I come among the Phaeacians welcomed and pitied by them."

So spoke he in his prayer, and Pallas Athene heard, but did not yet appear to him in open presence; for she regarded still her father's brother, who stoutly strove with godlike Odysseus until he reached his land.

VII.

THE WELCOME OF ALCINOÜS

HERE, THEN, long-tried royal Odysseus made his prayer; but to the town the strong mules bore the maid. And when she reached her father's famous palace, she stopped before the door-way, and round her stood her brothers, men like immortals, who from the cart unyoked the mules and carried the clothing in. The maid went to her chamber, where a fire was kindled for her by an old Apeirean woman, the chamber-servant Eurymedousa, whom long ago curved ships brought from Apeira; her they had chosen from the rest to be the gift of honor for Alcinoüs, because he was the lord of all Phaeacians, and people listened to his voice as if he were a god. She was the nurse of white-armed Nausicaä at the palace, and she it was who kindled her the fire and in her room prepared her supper.

And now Odysseus rose to go to the city; but Athene kindly drew thick clouds around Odysseus, for fear some bold Phaeacian meeting him might trouble him with talk and ask him who he was. And just as he was entering the pleasant town, the goddess, clear-eyed Athene, came to meet him, disguised as a young girl who bore a water-jar. She paused as she drew near, and royal Odysseus asked:

"My child, could you not guide me to the house of one Alcinoüs, who is ruler of this people? For I am a toil-worn stranger come from far, out of a distant land. Therefore I know not one among the men who own this city and this land."

Then said to him the goddess, clear-eyed Athene: "Yes, good old stranger, I will show the house for which you ask, for it stands near my gentle father's. But follow in silence; I will lead the way. Cast not a glance at any man and ask no questions; for our people do not well endure a stranger, nor courteously receive a man who comes from elsewhere. Yet they themselves trust in swift ships and traverse the great deep, for the Earth-shaker permits them. Swift are their ships as wing or thought."

Saying this, Pallas Athene led the way in haste, and he walked after in the footsteps of the goddess. So the Phaeacians, famed for shipping, did not observe him walking through the town among them, because Athene, the fair-haired powerful goddess, did not allow it, but in the kindness of her heart drew a marvelous mist around him. And now Odysseus admired the harbors, the trim ships, the meeting-places of the lords themselves, and the long walls that were so high, fitted with palisades, a marvel to behold. Then as they neared the famous palace of the king, the goddess, clear-eyed Athene, thus began:

"Here, good old stranger, is the house you bade me show. You will see heaven-descended kings sitting at table here. But enter, and have no misgivings in your heart; for the courageous man in all affairs better attains his end, come he from where he may. First you shall find the Queen within the hall. Arete is her name; sprung from the self-same ancestry as King Alcinoüs. In early days earth-shaking Poseidon begot Nausithoüs by Periboea, the chief of womankind in beauty and youngest daughter of that bold Eurymedon who once was king of the presumptuous giants: but he brought ruin on his impious tribe and on himself. Poseidon lay with Periboea and had by her a son, resolute Nausithoüs, who was king of the Phaeacians. Nausithoüs begot Rhexenor and Alcinoüs; but before Rhexenor had a son, Apollo of the silver bow smote him within his hall, soon after he was wed, and he left behind an only child, Arete. Alcinoüs took Arete for his wife, and he has honored her as no one else on earth is honored among the women who to-day keep houses for their husbands. Thus has she had a heart-felt honor, and she has it still, from her own children, from Alcinoüs himself, and from the people also, who gaze on her as on a god and greet her with welcomes when she walks about the town. For of sound judgment, woman as she is, she has no lack; and those whom she regards, though men, find troubles clear away. If she regards you kindly in her heart, then there is hope that you may see your friends and reach your high-roofed house and native land."

Saying this, clear-eyed Athene passed away, over the barren sea. She turned from pleasant Scheria, and came to Marathon and wide-wayed Athens and entered there the strong house of Erechtheus. Meanwhile Odysseus neared the lordly palace of Alcinoüs, and his heart was deeply stirred so that he paused before he crossed the brazen threshold; for a sheen as of the sun or moon played through the high-roofed house of generous Alcinoüs. On either hand ran walls of bronze from threshold to recess, and round about the ceiling was a cornice of dark metal. Doors made of gold closed in the solid building. The door-posts were of silver and stood on a bronze threshold, silver the lintel overhead, and gold the handle. On the two sides were gold and silver dogs; these had Hephaestus wrought with subtle craft to guard the house of generous Alcinoüs, creatures immortal, young forever. Within were seats planted against the wall on this side and on that, from threshold to recess, in long array; and over these were strewn light fine-spun robes, the work of women. Here the Phaeacian leaders used to sit, drinking and eating, holding constant cheer. And golden youths on massive pedestals stood and held flaming torches in their hands to light by night the palace for the feasters.

In the King's house are fifty serving maids, some grinding at the mill the yellow corn, some plying looms or twisting yarn, who as they sit are like the leaves of a tall poplar; and from the close-spun linen drops the liquid oil. And as Phaeacian men are skilled beyond all others in speeding a swift ship along the sea, so are their women practiced at the loom; for Athene has given them in large measure skill in fair works and noble minds.

Without the court and close beside its gate is a large garden, covering four acres; around it runs a hedge on either side. Here grow tall thrifty trees—pears, pomegranates, apples with shining fruit, sweet figs and thrifty olives. On them fruit never fails; it is not gone in winter or in summer, but lasts throughout the year; for constantly the west wind's breath brings some to bud and mellows others. Pear ripens upon pear, apple on apple, cluster on cluster, fig on fig. Here too the teeming vineyard has been planted, one part of which, the drying place, lying on level ground, is heating in the sun; elsewhere men gather grapes; and elsewhere still they tread them. In front, the grapes are green and shed their flower, but a second row are now just turning dark. And here trim garden-beds, along the outer line, spring up in every kind and all the year are gay. Near by, two fountains rise, one scattering its streams throughout the garden, one bounding by another course beneath the court-yard gate toward the high house; from this the townsfolk draw their water. Such at the palace of Alcinoüs were the gods' splendid gifts.

Here long-tried royal Odysseus stood and gazed. Then after he had gazed to his heart's fill on all, he quickly crossed the threshold and came within the house. He found the Phaeacian captains and councilors pouring libations from their cups to the clear-sighted Speedy-comer, to whom they always offer a last cup when they prepare for bed. Along the hall went long-tried royal Odysseus, still clothed in the thick cloud which Athene drew around him, until he came to Arete and to King Alcinoüs. About Arete's knees Odysseus threw his arms, and then the marvelous cloud retreated from him. Seeing the man, the people of the house were hushed and marveled as they gazed, and thus Odysseus made his supplication:

"Arete, daughter of divine Rhexenor, to your husband I am come, and to your knees, through many toils, and to these feasters too. The gods bestow upon them the blessing of long life, and to his children may each one leave the wealth within his hall and every honor men have given. But quickly grant me aid to reach my native land; for long cut off from friends I have been meeting hardship."

When he had spoken thus, he sat down on the hearth among the ashes by the fire, while all were hushed to silence. At last the old lord Echeneüs spoke, the oldest man of the Phaeacian race, preëminent in speech and full of knowledge of the past. He with good will addressed them thus, and said:

"Alcinoüs, this is not quite honorable to you; it is unseemly that a stranger should be sitting on the hearth among the ashes. Awaiting words of yours, these men hold back. Come then, raise up the stranger, seat him on a silver-studded chair, and bit the pages mix more wine, that we may also pour to Zeus, the Thunderer, who waits on worthy suppliants. And let the housekeeper give supper to the stranger from what she has in store."

Now when revered Alcinoüs heard his word, he took by the hand Odysseus, keen and crafty, raised him from the hearth and placed him on a shining chair, making his son arise, manly Laodamas, who sat beside his father, for his father loved him best. And water for the hands a servant brought in a beautiful pitcher made of gold, and poured it out over a silver basin for their washing, and spread a polished table by their side. And the grave housekeeper brought bread and placed before them, setting out food of many a kind, freely giving of her store. So long-tried royal Odysseus drank and ate. And now to the page revered Alcinoüs said:

"Pontonoüs, mix a bowl and pass the wine to all within the hall, that we may also pour to Zeus, the Thunderer, who waits on worthy suppliants."

He spoke; Pontonoüs stirred the cheering wine and served to all, with a first pious portion for the cup. So after they had poured and drunk as their hearts would, then thus Alcinoüs addressed them, saying:

"Hearken, Phaeacian captains and councilors, and let me tell you what the heart within me bids. After the feast is over, go to your homes and rest; and in the morning we will call more elders hither, and entertain the stranger at the hall, and make fit offering to the gods. Then afterwards we will take thought about his going, so that the stranger, free from toil and trouble, may by our guidance reach his land in gladness and with speed, although he comes from far. So shall he, meanwhile, meet no ill or harm till he set foot in his own land; there, in the days to come, he shall receive whatever fate and the stern spinners wove in his birth-thread when his mother bore him. But if he be some deathless one come down from heaven, then do the gods herein deal with us strangely; for heretofore the gods have always shown themselves without disguise, and when we offer splendid hecatombs they sit beside us at the feast, even like ourselves. And if a man, walking alone, meet them upon his way, they do not hide; for we are of their kin, as are the Cyclops and the wild tribes of Giants."

Then wise Odysseus answered him and said: "Alcinoüs, other thoughts of me be yours! I am not like the deathless ones who hold the open sky, either in form or bearing, but on the contrary I am like men that die; and whomsoever you have known bearing most grief among mankind, his sorrows I could equal. Yes, even more distresses still I might relate which first and last I bore at the gods' bidding. But let me now, though sick at heart, take supper; for nothing is more brutal than an angry belly. Perforce it bids a man attend, sadly though he be worn, though grief be on his mind. Even so, I too have grief upon my mind, and yet this evermore calls me to eat and drink; all I have borne it makes me quite forget, and bids me take my fill. But do you hasten at the dawn of day to land unhappy me in my own country, much as I still must bear; and let life pass when once I have beheld my goods, my slaves, and my great high-roofed house."

He spoke, and all approved and bade send forth the stranger, for rightly had he spoken. Then after they had poured and drunk as their hearts would, desiring rest, they each departed homeward. So in the hall was royal Odysseus left behind; Arete, too, and godlike Alcinoüs sat beside him, while servants cleared away the dishes of the meal. Then thus began white-armed Arete; for when she saw Odysseus she knew his robe and tunic to be the beautiful clothing which she herself had made—she and her waiting-women; and speaking in winged words, she said:

"Stranger, I will myself first ask you this: Who are you? Of what people? Who gave this clothing to you? Did you not say you came to us when lost upon the sea?"

Then wise Odysseus answered her and said: "Hard it were, Queen, fully to tell my woes, because the gods of heaven have given me many; still, what you ask and seek to know I will declare. Ogygia is an island lying far out to sea, where the daughter of Atlas dwells, crafty Calypso, a fair-haired, powerful goddess. Her no one visits, neither god nor mortal man; but hapless me some heavenly power brought to her hearth, and all alone, for Zeus with a gleaming bolt smote my swift ship and wrecked it in the middle of the wine-dark sea. There all the rest of my good comrades perished, but I myself caught in my arms the keel of my curved ship and drifted for nine days. Upon the tenth, in the dark night, gods, brought me to the island of Ogygia, where dwells Calypso, the fair-haired, powerful goddess. Receiving me, she loved and cherished me, and often said that she would make me an immortal, young forever; but she never beguiled the heart within my breast. Here for seven years I lingered, and often with my tears bedewed the immortal robes Calypso gave. But when the eighth revolving year was come, she bade me, even urged me, to depart, whether through message sent from Zeus or that her own mind changed. Upon a strong-built raft she sent me forth, giving abundant food, bread and sweet wine; she clad me in immortal robes and sent along my course a fair and gentle breeze. For seventeen days I sailed across the sea; on the eighteenth there came in sight the dim heights of your coast, and I was glad at heart—ill-fated I, who yet must meet the sore distress which earth-shaking Poseidon brought upon me. For he awoke the winds and barred my progress, stirred marvelously the waters, and the waves did not suffer me, spite of my many groans, to ride my raft. This soon the tempest shattered, but I by swimming forced my way through the flood, till at your coast the wind and water brought me in. Here, as I tried to land, the waves upon the shore might well have overcome me, casting me on great rocks and on forbidding ground; but I turned back and swam until I reached a stream where the ground seemed most fit, so clear of stones and sheltered from the breeze. Gathering my strength, I staggered out, and the immortal night drew near. Off to a distance from the heaven-descended stream I walked, and fell asleep among the bushes, heaping the leaves around; and here God poured upon me a slumber without end. For lying among the leaves and sad at heart, I slept all night till morning, then till noon; the sun was going down as the sweet slumber left me. And now upon the shore I saw your daughter's maids, playing a game, and she among them seemed a goddess. To her I made entreaty, and she did not lack sound judgment, such as you could not hope that a young person meeting you would show; for usually the young are giddy. She gave me bread enough and sparkling wine, she bathed me in the river and gave to me these clothes. Thus, though in trouble, I have told you all the truth."

Then answered him Alcinoüs and said: "Stranger, in this my child behaved not rightly, in that she did not bring you hither with her maids. Yet it was she from whom you first sought aid."

Then wise Odysseus answered him and said: "Sire, do not for this reproach the blameless girl. For she instructed me to follow with the maids; but I would not, for fear and very shame, lest possibly your heart might be offended at the sight. Suspicious creatures are we sons of men on earth."

Then answered him Alcinoüs and said: "Stranger, the heart within my breast is not one lightly troubled. Better, good sense in all things. O

father Zeus, Athene, and Apollo, that such a man as you, so like in
mind to me, might take my child, be called my son-in-law, and here
abide! For I would give you house and goods if you would like to stay.
Against your wish, shall no Phaeacian hold you. That, father Zeus forbid!
Nay, I will fix your setting forth, and you may rest secure; to-morrow
shall it be. And you shall be lying all the time wrapt in a sleep, while
they are speeding you along calm seas until you reach your land and
home or anywhere you please, though that were far beyond Eubœa,
which is called the farthest shore by those among our people who once
saw it when they carried light-haired Rhadamanthus to visit Tityus, the
son of Gaia. So far they went, without fatigue performing all, and on
the self-same day finished the journey home. But you yourself shall
judge how excellent my ships and young men are in tossing up the
water with the oar."

He spoke, and glad was long-tried royal Odysseus, who, making his
prayer, uttered these words and said:

"O father Zeus, all that Alcinoüs has said may he fulfill. Then on the
fruitful earth his name shall never die, and I shall reach my home."

So they conversed together. Meantime white-armed Arete bade her
maids to set a bed beneath the portico, to lay upon it beautiful purple
rugs, spread blankets over these, and then place woolen mantles on the
outside for a covering. So the maids left the hall, with torches in their
hands. And after they had spread the comfortable bed with busy speed,
they summoned Odysseus, drawing near and saying: "Up, stranger,
come to sleep. Your bed is ready." So did they speak, and to him rest
seemed delightful. Thus long-tried royal Odysseus lay down to sleep
upon the well-bored bedstead beneath the echoing portico. But
Alcinoüs slept in the recess of his high hall; his wife, the queen, making her bed beside him.

VIII.

THE STAY IN PHAEACIA

SOON AS the early rosy-fingered dawn appeared, revered Alcinoüs rose from bed, and up rose also high-born Odysseus, spoiler of cities. And now revered Alcinoüs led the way to the assembly-place of the Phaeacians, which lay beside the ships. When they were come, they took their seats on polished stones, set side by side; while Pallas Athene went throughout the town in likeness of the page of wise Alcinoüs, planning a safe return for brave Odysseus; and approaching one and another man, she gave the word:

"Come hither, Phaeacian captains and councilors, come, hasten to the assembly to hear about the stranger who came but lately to the house of wise Alcinoüs, when cast away at sea. In form he is like the immortals."

With words like these she stirred in each a zeal and a desire, and speedily the assembly-place and all its seats were filled with those who came. Then many marveled when they saw the wise son of Laërtes; for Athene cast a wondrous grace about his head and shoulders, and made him taller than before and stouter to behold, that so he might find favor in all Phaeacian eyes as one of power and worth, and that he might win too the many games in which the Phaeacians tried Odysseus. So when they were assembled and all had come together, Alcinoüs thus addressed them, saying:

"Hearken, Phaeacian captains and councilors, and let me tell you what the heart within me bids. This stranger—who he is I do not know— came hither as a wanderer from peoples east or west. He begs us for assistance and prays it be assured. Then let us, even as heretofore, furnish assistance promptly; for never has a stranger reached my halls and tarried long distressed for lack of aid. Come, let us launch into the sacred sea a black ship, freshly fitted, and let the two and fifty youths be chosen from the land who have at former times been found the best. Then after lashing carefully the oars upon the pins, all disembark and take a hasty meal, coming for this to me; I will make good provision for you all. These are my orders to the youths. But for the rest of you, you sceptred kings, come to my goodly palace, that there within my hall we entertain the stranger; let none refuse; and call the sacred bard, Demodocus, for surely God has granted him exceeding skill in song, to cheer us in whatever way his soul is moved to sing."

So saying, he led the way, the sceptred princes followed, and a page went to seek the sacred bard, while two and fifty picked young men departed, as he ordered, to the shore of the barren sea. On coming to the ship and to the sea, they launched the black ship into deep water, put mast and sail in the black ship, fitted the oars into their leathern slings, all in due order, and up aloft spread the white sail. Out in the stream they moored her, then took their way to the great house of wise Alcinoüs. Filled were the porticoes, the courts, and rooms with those already come; many were there, both young and old. In their behalf Alcinoüs sacrificed twelve sheep, eight white-toothed swine, two swing-paced oxen; these the men flayed and served, and made a merry feast.

Meanwhile the page drew near, leading the honored bard. The muse had greatly loved him, and had given him good and ill: she took away his eyesight, but gave delightful song. Pontonoüs placed for him among the feasters a silver-studded chair, backed by a lofty pillar, and hung the tuneful lyre upon its peg above his head, and the page showed him how to reach it with his hands. By him he set a tray and a good table, and placed thereon a cup of wine to drink as need should bid. So on the food spread out before them they laid hands. Now after they had stayed desire for drink and food, the muse impelled the bard to sing men's glorious deeds, a lay whose fame was then as wide as is the sky. He sang the strife of Odysseus with Pelian Achilles,—how they once quarreled at the gods' high feast with furious words, and Agamemnon, king of men, rejoiced in spirit when the bravest of the Achaeans quarreled; for Pheobus Apollo had by oracle declared it so should be, at hallowed Pytho, when Agamemnon crossed its stony threshold to ask for a response. Then was the day the tide of woe began to roll on Trojans and on Danaans, according to the will of mighty Zeus.

So sang the famous bard. Meanwhile Odysseus clutched his great purple cloak in his stout hands and drew it round his head, hiding his beautiful face; for he felt shame before the Phaeacians as from beneath his brow he dropped the tears. But when the sacred bard paused in the song, Odysseus dried his tears, took from his head the cloak, and seizing his double cup poured offerings to the gods. Then as the other would begin again, cheered on to sing by the Phaeacian chiefs,—for they enjoyed the story,—again would Odysseus, covering his head, break into sobs. And thus he hid from all the rest the tears he shed; only Alcinoüs marked him and took heed, for he sat near and heard his deep-drawn sighs; and to the Phaeacians, who delight in oars, he straightway said:

"Hearken, Phaeacian captains and councilors! Now have we satisfied desire for the impartial feast and for the lyre, which is the fellow of the stately feast. Let us then come away and try all kinds of games, so that the stranger, going home, may tell his friends how greatly we surpass all other men in boxing, wrestling, leaping, speed of foot."

So saying, he led the way, the others followed after. The page hung on its peg the tuneful lyre, then took by the hand Demodocus and led him from the hall, guiding his steps along the selfsame road by which the rest of the Phaeacian chiefs went forth to view the games. Thus to the assembly-place they came, a great troop following after, thousands in number; and many a gallant youth stood waiting there. Forth stood Acroneüs, Ocyalus and Elatreus, Nauteus and Prymneus, Anchialus and Eretmeus, Ponteus and Proreus, Thoön, Anabasineüs and Amphialus the son of Polyneüs, son of the carpenter. Forth also stood a youth like murderous Ares, Euryalus, the son of Naubolus, who was the first in beauty and in stature of all Phaeacians after brave Laodamas. Forth stood three sons of good Alcinoüs,—Laodamas, Halius, and matchless Clytoneüs. At first they tried each other in the foot-race. Straight from a mark their track was measured; and all flew swiftly off together, raising the dust along the plain. Best in the race was gallant Clytoneüs; and by such space as at the plough the mule-course runs, so far he shot ahead and reached the crowd; the rest were left behind. Next in the hardy wrestling-match they had a trial, and here Euryalus surpassed all champions. At leaping Amphialus was foremost of them all, while at the discus the leader was Elatreus. In boxing it was Laodamas, the good son of Alcinoüs. So when all hearts were gladdened by the games, up spoke Laodamas, son of Alcinoüs:

"Come, friends, and let us ask the stranger if he knows games and has some skill in any. In build, at all events, he is no common man,— in thighs, and calves, and arms above, strong neck, and massive chest. Fit years he does not lack, only he has been broken down by many hardships; for nothing, I believe, is worse than sea-life for weakening a man, however strong he be."

Then answered him Euryalus, and said: "Laodamas, what you have said is rightly spoken. Go, challenge him yourself, and give the message."

Now when the good son of Alcinoüs heard his words, he went and stood before them all and thus addressed Odysseus:

"Come, good old stranger, do you also try the games, if you have skill in any. Games you should know. There is no greater glory for a man in all his life than what he wins with his own feet and hands. Come then, and try! Drive trouble from your heart! Your journey hence shall not be long delayed. Already the ship is launched, the sailors ready."

Then wise Odysseus answered him and said: "Laodamas, why mock me with this challenge? Sorrow is on my heart far more than games; for in times past much have I borne and much have I toiled, and now I sit in your assembly longing for my home and supplicate your king and all this people."

Then answered back Euryalus, and mocked him to his face: "No indeed, stranger, you do not look like one expert in games, much as these count with men; rather like one busied with ships of many oars, captain of seamen who are traders, one whose mind·is on his cargo, watching freights and greedy gains. You are not like an athlete."

But looking sternly on him wise Odysseus said: "Stranger, your words are rude. You seem a reckless person. So true it is that not to all alike the gods grant grace, in stature, wisdom, and the power of speech. For one man is in look inferior, but God crowns his words with beauty, and men behold him and rejoice; with sure effect he speaks and a sweet modesty; he shines where men are gathered, and as he walks the town men gaze as on some god. And one again in look is like the immortals, but his is not the crowning grace of words. So you, in look, are excellent,—better God could not fashion,—but you are weak in judgment. You stirred the very soul within my breast by talking so unmannerly. No! I am not unskilled in games, as you declare; I was among the best, I think, while I could trust my vigorous age and these my arms. Now I am overwhelmed with pain and trouble; for much have I endured, cleaving my way through wars of men and through the boisterous seas. Still even so, all woe-worn as I am, I will attempt the games, because your words were galling; you provoked me, talking thus."

He spoke, and with his cloak still on he sprang and seized a discus larger than the rest and thick, heavier by not a little than those which the Phaeacians were using for themselves. This with a twist he sent from his stout hand. The stone hummed as it went; down to the ground crouched the Phaeacian oarsmen, notable men at sea, at the stone's cast. Past all the marks it flew, swift speeding from his hand. Athene marked the distances, taking a human form, and thus she spoke and cried aloud:

"A blind man, stranger, could pick you out that mark by feeling merely, because it is not huddled in the crowd, but lies ahead of all. Have a good heart, this bout at least; for no Phaeacian will reach that or overpass it."

She spoke, and glad was long-tried royal Odysseus, pleased that he

saw a true friend in the ring. And now with lighter heart he called to
the Phaeacians:

"Come up to that, young men! Soon I will send another as far, I
think, or farther. And if there is one among you all whose heart and
spirit bids, come, let him try me—for you vexed me very sore—in
boxing, wrestling, or the foot-race even; it matters not to me; let any
Phaeacian try, except Laodamas. He is my host, and who would quarrel
with his entertainer? Witless the man must be, and altogether worthless,
who challenges his host to games when in a foreign land; he hinders
his own welfare. None of the rest I either dread or scorn, but I will
gladly know you all and prove you face to face. Not at all weak am I in
any games men practice. I understand full well handling the polished
bow, and I should be the first to strike my man by sending an arrow in
the throng of foes, however many comrades stood around and shot at
their men too. None except Philoctetes excelled me with the bow at
Troy, when we Achaeans tried the bow. All others I declare I far surpass,
all that are living now and eating bread on earth. The men of former
days I will not seek to rival—Hercules, and Eurytus of Oechalia,—for
these would rival with the bow immortals even. Wherefore great
Eurytus died all too soon; no old age came upon him in his home,
because in wrath Apollo slew him; for Eurytus had challenged him to
try the bow. I send the spear farther than other men an arrow. Only I
fear that in the foot-race some Phaeacian may outstrip me; for rudely
battered have I been on many waters, because I had no ease at sea for
any length of time; therefore my joints are weakened."

So he spoke, and all were hushed to silence; only Alcinoüs answering said: "Stranger, without discourtesy to us is all you say; you merely
seek to show the prowess that is yours, indignant that the man beside
you in the ring insulted you, though surely no man would dispraise
your prowess who knew within his heart what it was fit to say. But listen
now to words of mine, that you may have tales to tell to other heroes
when, feasting in your hall with wife and children, you recollect our
prowess and the feats Zeus has vouchsafed us from our fathers' days till
now. We are not faultless boxers, no, nor wrestlers; but in the foot-race
we run swiftly, and in our ships excel. Dear to us ever is the feast, the
harp, the dance, changes of clothes, warm baths, and bed. Come then,
Phaeacian dancers, the best among you make us sport, that so the
stranger on returning home may tell his friends how we surpass all
other men in sailing, running, in the dance and song. Go, one of you,
forthwith, and fetch Demodocus the tuneful lyre that lies within our hall."

So spoke godlike Alcinoüs, and a page sprang to fetch from the king's
house the hollow lyre. Then rose the appointed umpires, nine in all,
whose public work it was to order all things at the ring; they smoothed

the dancing-ground and cleared a fair wide ring. Meanwhile the page drew near and brought his tuneful lyre to Demodocus, who thereupon stepped to the centre, and round him stood young men in the first bloom of years, skillful at dancing. They struck the splendid dance-ground with their feet; Odysseus watched their twinkling feet, and was astonished.

And now the bard, touching his lyre, began a beautiful song about the loves of Ares and crowned Aphrodite: how at the first they lay together in the palace of Hephaestus, privily; and many a gift he gave, and wronged the bed of lord Hephaestus. Soon to Hephaestus came the tell-tale Sun, who had observed their meeting. And when Hephaestus heard the galling tale, he hastened to his smithy meditating evil in his heart, there set upon its block the mighty anvil and forged him fetters none might break or loose, fetters to hold securely. So after he had wrought his snare, in anger against Ares, hastening to the chamber where his own dear bed was set, around its posts on every side he dropped his toils; and many too hung drooping from the rafter, like delicate spiderwebs which nobody could see, not even the blessed gods, so shrewdly were they fashioned. Then after he had spread the snare all round the bed, he made a show of going off to Lemnos, that stately citadel which in his sight is far the dearest of all spots on earth. Now Ares of the golden rein had kept no careless watch, and so espied craftsman Hephaestus setting forth. He hastened to the house of famed Hephaestus, keen for the love of fair-crowned Cytherea. She, just come home from visiting her sire, the powerful son of Kronos, was sitting down. He came within the door, and holding her by the hand he spoke and thus addressed her:

"Come, dear, to bed, and let us take our pleasure; for Hephaestus is no longer here at home, but gone at last to Lemnos, to the harsh-tongued Sintians."

He spoke, and pleasant it seemed to her to lie beside him. So the pair went and laid them down in bed, and all about them dropped the toils fashioned by shrewd Hephaestus; it was not in their power to move or raise a limb. This they saw only then when there was no escape. But on them came the famous strong-armed god, who had turned back before he reached the land of Lemnos; for in his stead the Sun kept watch and told him all. He hastened to the house, with heavy heart, stood at the porch, wild rage upon him, and raised a fearful cry, calling to all the gods:

"O Father Zeus, and all you other blessed gods that live forever, come see a sight for laughter, deeds not to be endured! For I being lame, this Aphrodite, daughter of Zeus, ever dishonors me and gives her love to deadly Ares, since he is handsome and is sound of limb, while I was born a cripple. Yet nobody is to blame for that but my two parents,—would they had never given me birth! But you shall see where lie the loving pair who stole into my bed. I smart to see them! And yet I think they will not lie much longer thus, however great their love. Shortly they will not wish to sleep together; but still my snare and mesh shall hold them, till her father pays me back the many wedding gifts I gave to get the shameless girl,—seeing his child was fair, though not true-hearted."

He spoke, and the gods gathered at the brazen threshold of his house. Poseidon came, who girds the land, the fortune-bringer Hermes came, and the far-working king Apollo. The goddesses for shame all stayed at home. So at the portal stood the gods, the givers of good things, and uncontrollable laughter broke from the blessed gods as they beheld the arts of shrewd Hephaestus; and glancing at his neighbor one would say:

"Wrong-doing brings no gain. Slow catches swift; as here Hephaestus, who is slow, caught Ares, who is swiftest of the gods that hold Olympus,— catching him by his craft, though lame himself. Now Ares owes the adulterer's fine."

So they conversed together. And now to Hermes spoke the king, the son of Zeus, Apollo: "O Hermes, son of Zeus, guide, giver of good things, would you not like, though loaded down with heavy bonds, to lie in bed by golden Aphrodite?"

Then answered him the guide, the Speedy-comer: "Would it might be, far-shooting king Apollo, though thrice as many bonds, bonds numberless, should hold me fast, and all you gods and goddesses should come and see, would I might lie by golden Aphrodite!"

He spoke, and laughter rose among the immortal gods. But Poseidon did not laugh; he earnestly entreated Hephaestus, the great craftsman, to loosen Ares. And speaking in winged words he said:

"Loose him, and I engage, as you desire, that he shall pay all dues before the immortal gods."

Then said to him the famous strong-armed god:"Poseidon, girder of the land, ask not for this. From triflers, even pledges in the hand are trifles. How could I hold you bound before the immortal gods, if Ares should evade both debt and bond and flee?"

Then said to him the earth-shaker, Poseidon: "Hephaestus, even if Ares does evade the debt and flee, still I myself will pay."

Then answered him the famous strong-armed god: "I cannot and I must not say you nay."

So saying, mighty Hephaestus raised the net, and the pair loosed from out the net, so very strong, sprang up forthwith. He went to Thrace; but she, the laughter-loving Aphrodite, came to Cyprus, into the town of Paphos, where is her grove and fragrant shrine. There did the

Graces bathe her and anoint her with imperishable oil, such as bedews the gods that live forever, and they arrayed her in a dainty robe, a marvel to behold. ← Stoped read here

So sang the famous bard. Odysseus joyed in heart to hear, as did the others also, the Phaeacian oarsmen, notable men at sea.

And now Alcinoüs called on Halius and Laodamas to dance alone, for with them none could vie. So taking in their hands a goodly purple ball, which skillful Polybus had made them, one, bending backward, flung it toward the dusky clouds; the other, leaping upward from the earth, easily caught the ball before his feet touched ground again. Then after they had tried the ball straight in the air, they danced upon the bounteous earth with tossings to and fro. Other young men beat time for them, standing around the ring, and a loud sound of stamping rose. Then to Alcinoüs said royal Odysseus:

"Mighty Alcinoüs, renowned of all, you boasted that your dancers were the best, and now it is proved true. I am amazed to see."

He spoke; revered Alcinoüs was glad, and to the Phaeacians, who delight in oars, he straightway said: "Hearken, Phaeacian captains and councilors! This stranger truly seems a man of understanding. Come then, and let us give such guest-gift as is meet. Twelve honored kings bear sway throughout the land and are its rulers, and a thirteenth am I. Let each present him a spotless robe and tunic and a talent of precious gold. And let us speedily fetch all together, so that the stranger, having these in hand, may come to supper glad at heart. Let too Euryalus give satisfaction to the man, by word and gift, for his speech was unbecoming."

He spoke, and all approved and gave their orders, and for the bringing of the gifts each man sent forth his page. But Euryalus made answer to the king and said: "Mighty Alcinoüs, renowned of all, I will indeed give satisfaction to the stranger, as you bid; for I will give this brazen blade. Its hilt is silver, and a sheath of fresh-cut ivory incloses it. Of great worth he will find it."

So saying, he put into Odysseus' hands the silver-studded sword, and speaking in winged words he said: "Hail, good old stranger! If any word was uttered that was harsh, straight let the sweeping winds bear it away. But the gods grant that you may see your wife and reach your land; for long cut off from friends you have been meeting hardship."

Then wise Odysseus answered him and said: "You too, my friend, all hail! May the gods grant you fortune, and may you never miss the sword you give, making amends besides in what you say."

He spoke, and round his shoulders slung the silver-studded sword. As the sun set, the noble gifts were there; stately pages bore them to the palace of Alcinoüs, where the sons of good Alcinoüs, receiving them, laid the fair gifts before their honored mother. But for the princes revered

Alcinoüs led the way, and entering the house they sat them down on the high seats. Then to Arete spoke revered Alcinoüs:

"Bring hither, wife, a serviceable chest, the best you have, and lay therein a spotless robe and tunic. Then heat upon the fire a caldron for the stranger and warm some water, that, having bathed and seen all gifts put safely by which the gentle Phaeacians brought him, he may enjoy the feast and hear the singer's song. Moreover I will give him my goodly golden chalice, that as he pours libations at his hall to Zeus and to the other gods he may be mindful all his days of me."

He spoke, and Arete told the maids to set a great kettle on the fire as quickly as they could. They set the kettle which supplied the bath upon the blazing fire, they poured in water, put the wood beneath, and lighted. Around the belly of the kettle crept the flame, and so the water warmed. Meanwhile Arete brought the stranger a goodly chest from out the chamber; she put therein the beautiful gifts,—the clothing and the gold which the Phaeacians gave,—and she herself put in a robe and goodly tunic, and speaking in winged words she said:

"Look to the lid yourself and quickly tie the cord, lest some one rob you on the way, when sailing by and by, on the black ship, you rest in pleasant sleep."

When long-tried royal Odysseus heard these words, he straightway fitted on the lid and quickly tied the cunning knot which potent Circe once had taught him. Thereafter the housewife called him to come to the bath and bathe; and he was pleased to see the steaming water, for he was not used to care like this since he had left fair-haired Calypso's home; but there he had as constant care as if he were a god. Now when the maids had bathed him and anointed him with oil and put upon him a goodly coat and tunic, forth from the bath he came and went to join the drinkers, and Nausicaä, with beauty given her of the gods, stood by a column of the strong-built roof and marveled at Odysseus as she looked into his eyes, and speaking in winged words she said:

"Stranger, farewell! When you are once again in your own land, remember me, and how before all others it is to me you owe the saving of your life."

Then wise Odysseus answered her and said: "Nausicaä, daughter of generous Alcinoüs, Zeus grant it so—he the loud thunderer, husband of Here—that I go home and see my day of coming. Then would I there too, as to any god, give thanks to you forever, all my days; for, maiden, it was you who gave me life."

He spoke, and took his seat by king Alcinoüs. Men were already serving food and mixing wine. The page drew near, leading the honored bard, Demodocus, beloved of all, and seated him among the feasters, backed by a lofty pillar. Then to the page said wise Odysseus, cutting a slice of chine, whereof still more was left, from out a white-toothed boar, the rich fat on its sides:

"Page, set before Demodocus this piece of meat, that he may eat and I may do him homage, sad though I be myself; for at the hands of all on earth bards meet respect and honor, because the muse has taught them song and loves the race of bards."

He spoke, and the page bore the food and put it in the hands of lord Demodocus. He took it and was glad, and on the food spread out before them they laid hands. But after they had stayed desire for drink and food, then to Demodocus said wise Odysseus:

"Demodocus, I praise you beyond all mortal men, whether your teacher was the muse, the child of Zeus, or was Apollo. With perfect truth you sing the lot of the Achaeans, all that they did and bore, the whole Achaean struggle, as if yourself were there, or you had heard the tale from one who was. Pass on then now, and sing the building of the wooden horse, made by Epeius with Athene's aid, which royal Odysseus once conveyed into the citadel,—a thing of craft, filled full of men, who by its means sacked Ilios. And if you now relate the tale in its due order, forthwith I will declare to all mankind how bounteously God gave to you a wondrous power of song."

So he spoke. Thereat the other, stirred by the god, began and showed his skill in song: starting the story where some Argives boarding the well-benched ships were setting sail and spreading fire through the camp; while others still, under renowned Odysseus, lay in the assembly of the Trojans all hidden in the horse; for the Trojans themselves had dragged it to their citadel. So there it stood, while long and uncertainly the people argued, seated around it. Three plans were finding favor: either to split the hollow trunk with ruthless axe; or else to drag it to the height and hurl it down the rocks; or still to spare the monstrous image, as a propitiation of the gods. And thus at last it was to end; for it was fated they should perish so soon as their city should inclose the enormous wooden horse, where all the Argive chiefs were lying, bearing to the Trojans death and doom. He sang how they o'erthrew the town, these sons of the Achaeans, issuing from the horse, leaving their hollow ambush. Each for himself, he sang, pillaged the stately city; but Odysseus went like Ares to the palace of Deïphobus with godlike Menelaus; and there, he said, braving the fiercest fight, at last he won the day through resolute Athene.

So sang the famous bard. Odysseus melted into tears, and all below his eyes his cheeks were wet. And as a woman wails and clings to her dear husband, who falls for town and people, seeking to shield his home and children from the ruthless day; seeing him dying, gasping, she flings herself on him with a piercing cry; while men behind, smiting her with their spears on back and shoulder, force her along to bondage to suffer toil and trouble; with pain most pitiful her cheeks are thin; so pitifully fell the tears beneath Odysseus' brows. And yet he hid from all the rest the tears he shed; only Alcinoüs marked him and took heed, for he sat near and heard his deep-drawn sighs; and to the Phaeacians, who delight in oars, he straightway said:

"Hearken, Phaeacian captains and councilors, and let Demodocus hush now the tuneful lyre, because not to the pleasure of us all he sings to-day; for since we supped and since the sacred bard began, this stranger has not ceased from bitter sighs. Surely some grief hovers about his heart. Let then the bard cease singing, that all alike be merry, stranger and entertainers, for that is better far; since for the worthy stranger's sake all things are ready now, escort and friendly gifts, which we grant heartily. Even as a brother is the stranger and the suppliant treated by any man who feels a touch of wisdom.

"And do not you, then, longer cautiously conceal what I will ask; plain speech is better. Tell me the name by which at home your father and mother called you,—they and the other folk, your townsmen and your neighbors; for none of all mankind can lack a name, be he of low degree or high, when once he has been born; since in the very hour of birth parents give names to all. And tell me of your land, your home, and city, that thither our ships may bear you with a discerning aim; for on Phaeacian ships there are no pilots, nor are there rudders such as other vessels carry, but the ships understand the will and mind of man. They know the cities and rich lands of every nation, and swiftly they cross the sea-gulf, shrouded in mist and cloud. On them there is no fear of being harmed or lost. Still, this is what I heard Nausithoüs, my father, tell: he said Poseidon was displeased because we were safe guides for all mankind; and he averred the god one day would wreck a stanch ship of the Phaeacians, returning home from pilotage upon the misty sea, and so would throw a lofty mound about our city. That was the old man's tale, and this God may fulfill, or else it may go unfulfilled, as pleases him. But now declare me this and plainly tell where you have wandered and what countries you have seen. About the men and stately towns, too, let me hear,—what ones were fierce and savage, with no regard for right, what ones were kind to strangers and reverent toward the gods. And tell me why you weep and grieve within your breast on hearing of the lot of Argive Danaäns and of Ilios. This the gods wrought; they spun the thread of death for some, that others in the time to come might have a song. Had you some relative who fell at Ilios? One who was dear? some daughter's husband or wife's father?—they who stand closest to us after our flesh and blood. Or was it perhaps some friend who pleased you well, a gallant comrade? For a friend with an understanding heart is worth no less than a brother."

IX.

THE STORY TOLD TO ALCINOÜS.—THE CYCLOPS

THEN WISE Odysseus answered him and said: "Mighty Alcinoüs, renowned of all, surely it is a pleasant thing to hear a bard like this, one who is even like the gods in voice. For more complete delight I think there cannot be than when good cheer possesses a whole people, and feasting through the houses they listen to a bard, seated in proper order, while beside them stand the tables supplied with bread and meat, and dipping wine from out the mixer the pourer bears it round and fills the cups. That is a sight most pleasing. Nevertheless your heart inclines to learn my grievous woes, and thus to make me weep and sorrow more. What shall I tell you first, then, and what last? For many are the woes the gods of heaven have given me. First, I will tell my name, that you, like all, may know it; and I accordingly, seeking deliverance from my day of doom, may be your guest-friend, though my home is far away. I am Odysseus, son of Laërtes, who for all craft am noted among men, and my renown reaches to heaven. I live in Ithaca, a land far seen; for on it is the lofty height of Neriton, covered with waving woods. Around lie many islands, very close to one another,—Doulichion, Same, and woody Zacynthus. Ithaca itself lies low along the sea, far to the west,— the others stretching eastward, toward the dawn,—a rugged land, and yet a kindly nurse. A sweeter spot than my own land I shall not see. Calypso, a heavenly goddess, sought to keep me by her side within her hollow grotto, desiring me to be her husband; so too Aeaean Circe, full of craft, detained me in her palace, desiring me to be her husband; but they never beguiled the heart within my breast. Nothing more sweet than home and parents can there be, however rich one's dwelling far in a foreign land, cut off from parents. But let me tell you of the grievous journey home which Zeus ordained me on my setting forth from Troy.

"The wind took me from Ilios and bore me to the Ciconians, to Ismarus. There I destroyed the town and slew its men; but from the town we took the women and great stores of treasure, and parted all, that none might go lacking his proper share. This done, I warned our men swiftly to fly; but they, in utter folly, did not heed. Much wine was drunk, and they slaughtered on the shore a multitude of sheep and swing-paced, crook-horned oxen. Meanwhile, escaped Ciconians began to call for aid on those Ciconians who were their neighbors and more numerous and brave than they,—a people dwelling inland, skillful at fighting in chariot or on foot, as need might be. Accordingly at dawn they gathered, thick as leaves and flowers appear in spring. And now an evil fate from Zeus beset our luckless men, causing us many sorrows; for setting the battle in array by the swift ships, all fought and hurled their brazen spears at one another. While it was morning and the day grew stronger, we steadily kept them off and held our ground, though they were more than we; but as the sun declined, toward stalling-time, then the Ciconians turned our men and routed the Achaeans. Six of the crew of every ship fell in their harness there; the rest fled death and doom.

"Thence we sailed on with aching hearts, glad to be clear of death, though missing our dear comrades; yet the curved ships did not pass on till we had called three times to each poor comrade who died upon the plain, cut off by the Ciconians. But now cloud-gathering Zeus sent the north wind against our ships in a fierce tempest, and covered with his clouds both land and sea; night broke from heaven. The ships drove headlong onward, their sails torn into tatters by the fury of the wind. These sails we lowered, in terror for our lives, and rowed the ships themselves hurriedly toward the land. There for two nights and days continuously we lay, gnawing our hearts because of toil and trouble. But when the fair-haired dawn brought the third day, we set our masts, and hoisting the white sails we sat us down, while wind and helmsmen kept us steady. And now I should have come unharmed to my own native land, but that the swell and current, in doubling Maleia, and the north wind turned me aside and drove me past Cythera.

"Thence for nine days I drifted before the deadly winds along the swarming sea; but on the tenth we touched the land of Lotus-eaters, men who make food of flowers. So here we went ashore and drew us water, and soon by the swift ships my men prepared their dinner. Then after we had tasted food and drink, I sent some sailors forth to go and learn what men who live by bread dwelt in the land,—selecting two, and joining with them a herald as a third. These straightway went and mingled with the Lotus-eaters, and yet the Lotus-eaters had no thought of harm against our men; indeed, they gave them lotus to taste; but whosoever of them ate the lotus' honeyed fruit wished to bring tidings back no more and never to leave the place, but with the Lotus-eaters there desired to stay, to feed on lotus and forget his going home. These men I brought back weeping to the ships by very force, and dragging them under the benches of our hollow ships I bound them fast, and bade my other trusty men to hasten and embark on the swift ships, that none of them might eat the lotus and forget his going home. Quickly they came aboard, took places at the pins, and sitting in order smote the foaming water with their oars.

"Thence we sailed on with aching hearts, and came to the land of the Cyclops, a rude and lawless folk, who, trusting to the immortal gods, plant with their hands no plant, nor ever plough, but all things spring unsown and without ploughing,—wheat, barley, and grape-vines with wine in their heavy clusters, for rain from Zeus makes the grape grow. Among this people no assemblies meet; they have no stable laws. They live on the tops of lofty hills in hollow caves; each gives the law to his own wife and children, and for each other they have little care.

"Now a rough island stretches along outside the harbor, not close to the Cyclops' coast nor yet far out, covered with trees. On it innumerable wild goats breed; no tread of man disturbs them; none comes here to follow hounds, to toil through woods and climb the crests of hills. The island is not held for flocks or tillage, but all unsown, untilled, it evermore is bare of men and feeds the bleating goats. Among the Cyclops are no red-cheeked ships, nor are there shipwrights who might build the well-benched ships to do them service, sailing to foreign cities; as usually men cross the sea in ships to one another. With ships they might have worked the well-placed island; for it is not at all a worthless spot, but would bear all things duly. For here are meadows on the banks of the gray sea, moist, with soft soil; here vines could never die; here is smooth ploughing-land; a very heavy crop, and always well in season, might be reaped, for the under soil is rich. Here is a quiet harbor, never needing moorings,—throwing out anchor-stones or fastening cables,—but merely to run in and wait awhile till sailor hearts are ready and the winds are blowing. Just at the harbor's head a spring of sparkling water flows from beneath a cave; around it poplars grow. Here we sailed in, some god our guide, through murky night; there was no light to see, for round the ships was a dense fog. No moon looked out from heaven; it was shut in with clouds. So no one saw the island, and the long waves rolling upon the shore we did not see until we beached our well-benched ships. After the ships were beached, we lowered all our sails and forth we went ourselves upon the shore; where falling fast asleep we awaited sacred dawn.

"But when the early rosy-fingered dawn appeared, in wonder at the island we made a circuit round it, and nymphs, daughters of ægis-bearing Zeus, started the mountain goats, to give my men a meal. Forthwith we took our bending bows and our long hunting spears from out the ships, and parted in three bands began to shoot; and soon God granted ample game. Twelve ships were in my train; to each there fell nine goats, while ten they set apart for me alone. Then all throughout the day till setting sun we sat and feasted on abundant meat and pleasant wine. For the ruddy wine of our ships was not yet spent; some still was left, because our crews took a large store in jars the day we seized the sacred citadel of the Ciconians. And now we looked across to the land of the neighboring Cyclops, and marked the smoke, the sounds of men, the bleat of sheep and goats; but when the sun went down and darkness came, we laid us down to sleep upon the beach. Then as the early rosy-fingered dawn appeared, holding a council, I said to all my men:

"'The rest of you, my trusty crews, stay for the present here; but I myself, with my own ship and my own crew, go to discover who these men may be,—if they are fierce and savage, with no regard for right, or kind to strangers and reverent toward the gods.'

"When I had spoken thus, I went on board my ship, and called my crew to come on board and loose the cables. Quickly they came, took places at the pins, and sitting in order smote the foaming water with their oars. But as we reached the neighboring shore, there at the outer point, close to the sea, we saw a cave, high, overhung with laurel. Here many flocks of sheep and goats were nightly housed. Around was built a yard with a high wall of deep-embedded stone, tall pines, and crested oaks. Here a man-monster slept, who shepherded his flock alone and far apart; with others he did not mingle, but quite aloof followed his lawless ways. Thus had he grown to be a marvelous monster; not like a man who lives by bread, but rather like a woody peak of the high hills, seen single, clear of others.

"Now to my other trusty men I gave command to stay there by the ship and guard the ship; but I myself chose the twelve best among my men and sallied forth. I had a goat-skin bottle of the dark sweet wine given me by Maron, son of Evanthes, priest of Apollo, who watches over Ismarus. He gave me this because we guarded him and his son and wife, through holy fear; for he dwelt within the shady grove of Phoebus Apollo. He brought me splendid gifts: of fine-wrought gold he gave me seven talents, gave me a mixing-bowl of solid silver, and afterwards filled me twelve jars with wine, sweet and unmixed, a drink for gods. None knew that wine among the slaves and hand-maids of his house, none but himself, his own dear wife, and one sole house-dame. Whenever they drank the honeyed ruddy wine, he filled a cup and poured it into twenty parts of water, and still from the bowl came a

a surprising strength; then to refrain had been no easy
    a large skin full of this and took it with me, and also took
    a sack; for my stout heart suspected I soon should meet a
    in mighty power, a savage, ignorant of rights and laws.
    we reached the cave, but did not find him there; for he was
tending his fat flock afield. Entering the cave, we looked around. Here
crates were standing, loaded down with cheese, and here pens
thronged with lambs and kids. In separate pens each sort was folded: by
themselves the older, by themselves the later born, and by themselves
the younglings. Swimming with whey were all the vessels, the well-
wrought pails and bowls in which he milked. Here at the very first my
men entreated me to take some cheeses and depart; then quickly to
drive the kids and lambs to our swift ship out of the pens, and sail away
over the briny water. But I refused,—far better had I yielded,—hoping
that I might see him and he might offer gifts. But he was to prove, when
seen, no pleasure to my men.

"Kindling a fire here, we made burnt offering and we ourselves took of
the cheese and ate; and so we sat and waited in the cave until he came
from pasture. He brought a ponderous burden of dry wood to use at
supper time, and tossing it down inside the cave raised a great din. We
hurried off in terror to a corner of the cave. But into the wide-mouthed
cave he drove his sturdy flock, all that he milked; the males, both rams
and goats, he left outside in the high yard. And now he set in place the
huge door-stone, lifting it high in air, a ponderous thing; no two and
twenty carts, stanch and four-wheeled, could start it from the ground;
such was the rugged rock he set against the door. Then sitting down, he
milked the ewes and bleating goats, all in due order, and underneath put
each one's young. Straightway he curdled half of the white milk, and
gathering it in wicker baskets, set it by; half he left standing in the pails,
ready for him to take and drink, and for his supper also. So after he had
busily performed his tasks, he kindled a fire, noticed us, and asked:

"'Ha, strangers, who are you? Where do you come from, sailing
the watery ways? Are you upon some business? Or do you rove at random, as the pirates roam the seas, risking their lives and bringing ill
to strangers?'

"As he thus spoke, our very souls were crushed within us, dismayed by
the heavy voice and by the monster's self; nevertheless I answered thus
and said:

"'We are from Troy, Achaeans, driven by shifting winds out of our
course across the great gulf of the sea; homeward we fared, but through
strange ways and wanderings are come hither; so Zeus was pleased to purpose. Subjects of Agamemnon, son of Atreus, we boast ourselves to be,
whose fame is now the widest under heaven; so great a town he sacked,

so many men he slew. But chancing here, we come before your knees to ask that you will offer hospitality, and in other ways as well will give the gift which is the stranger's due. O mighty one, respect the gods. We are your suppliants, and Zeus is the avenger of the suppliant and the stranger; he is the stranger's friend and waits on worthy strangers.'

"So I spoke, and from a ruthless heart he straightway answered: 'You are simple, stranger, or come from far away, to bid me dread the gods or shrink before them. The Cyclops pay no heed to ægis-bearing Zeus, nor to the blessed gods; because we are much stronger than themselves. To shun the wrath of Zeus, I would not spare you or your comrades, did my heart not bid. But tell me where you left your stanch ship at your coming. At the far shore, or near? Let me but know.'

"He thought to tempt me, but he could not cheat a knowing man like me; and I again replied with words of guile: 'The Earth-shaker, Poseidon, wrecked my ship and cast her on the rocks at the land's end, driving her on a headland; the wind blew from the sea; and I with these men here escaped impending ruin.'

"So I spoke, and from a ruthless heart he answered nothing, but starting up laid hands on my companions. He seized on two and dashed them to the ground as if they had been dogs. Their brains ran out upon the floor, and wet the earth. Tearing them limb from limb, he made his supper, and ate as does a mountain lion, leaving nothing, entrails, or flesh, or marrow bones. We in our tears held up our hands to Zeus, at sight of his reckless deeds; helplessness held our hearts. But when the Cyclops had filled his monstrous maw by eating human flesh and pouring down pure milk, he laid himself in the cave full length among his flock. And I then formed the plan within my daring heart of closing on him, drawing my sharp sword from my thigh, and stabbing him in the breast where the midriff holds the liver, feeling the place out with my hand. Yet second thoughts restrained me, for there we too had met with utter ruin; for we could never with our hands have pushed from the lofty door the enormous stone which he had set against it. Thus then with sighs we awaited sacred dawn.

"But when the early rosy-fingered dawn appeared, he kindled a fire, milked his goodly flock, all in due order, and underneath put each one's young. Then after he had busily performed his tasks, seizing once more two men, he made his morning meal. And when the meal was ended, he drove from the cave his sturdy flock, and easily moved the huge door-stone; but afterwards he put it back as one might put the lid upon a quiver. Then to the hills, with many a call, he turned his sturdy flock, while I was left behind brooding on evil and thinking how I might obtain revenge, would but Athene grant my prayer. And to my mind this seemed the wisest way. There lay beside the pen a great club of the Cyclops, an olive stick still green, which he had cut to be his staff when dried. Inspecting it, we guessed its size, and thought it like the mast of a black ship of twenty oars,—some broad-built merchantman which sails the great gulf of the sea; so huge it looked in length and thickness. I went and cut away a fathom's length of this, laid it before my men, and bade them shape it down; they made it smooth; I then stood by to point the tip and, laying hold, I charred it briskly in the blazing fire. The piece I now put carefully away, hiding it in the dung which lay about the cave in great abundance; and then I bade my comrades fix by lot who the bold men should be to help me raise the stake and grind it in his eye, when pleasant sleep should come. Those drew the lot whom I myself would fain have chosen; four were they, for a fifth I counted in myself. He came toward evening, shepherding the fleecy flock, and forthwith drove his sturdy flock into the wide-mouthed cave, all with much care; he did not leave a sheep in the high yard outside, either through some suspicion, or God bade him so to do. Again he set in place the huge door-stone, lifting it high in air, and, sitting down, he milked the ewes and bleating goats, all in due order, and underneath put each one's young. Then after he had busily performed his tasks, he seized once more two men and made his supper. And now it was that drawing near the Cyclops I thus spoke, holding within my hands an ivy bowl filled with dark wine:

"'Here, Cyclops, drink some wine after your meal of human flesh, and see what sort of liquor our ship held. I brought it as an offering, thinking that you might pity me and send me home. But you are mad past bearing. Reckless! How should a stranger come to you again from any people, when you have done this wicked deed?'

"So I spoke; he took the cup and drank it off, and mightily pleased he was with the taste of the sweet liquor, and thus he asked me for it yet again:

"'Give me some more, kind sir, and straightway tell your name, that I may give a stranger's gift with which you shall be pleased. Ah yes, the Cyclops' fruitful fields bear wine in their heavy clusters, for rain from Zeus makes the grape grow; but this is a bit of ambrosia and nectar.'

"So he spoke, and I again offered the sparkling wine. Three times I brought and gave; three times he drank it in his folly. Then as the wine began to dull the Cyclops' senses, in winning words I said to him:

"'Cyclops, you asked my noble name, and I will tell it; but do you give the stranger's gift, just as you promised. My name is Noman. Noman I am called by mother, father, and by all my comrades.'

"So I spoke, and from a ruthless heart he straightway answered: 'Noman I eat up last, after his comrades; all the rest first; and that shall be the stranger's gift for you.'

"He spoke, and sinking back fell flat; and there he lay, lolling his thick neck over, till sleep, that conquers all, took hold upon him. Out of his throat poured wine and scraps of human flesh; heavy with wine, he spewed it forth. And now it was I drove the stake under a heap of ashes, to bring it to a heat, and with my words emboldened all my men, that none might flinch through fear. Then when the olive stake, green though it was, was ready to take fire, and through and through was all aglow, I snatched it from the fire, while my men stood around and Heaven inspired us with great courage. Seizing the olive stake, sharp at the tip, they plunged it in his eye, and I, perched up above, whirled it around. As when a man bores shipbeams with a drill, and those below keep it in motion with a strap held by the ends, and steadily it runs; even so we seized the fire-pointed stake and whirled it in his eye. Blood bubbled round the heated thing. The vapor singed off all the lids around the eye, and even the brows, as the ball burned and its roots crackled in the flame. As when a smith dips a great axe or adze into cold water, hissing loud, to temper it,—for that is strength to steel,—so hissed his eye about the olive stake. A hideous roar he raised; the rock resounded; we hurried off in terror. He wrenched the stake from out his eye, all dabbled with the blood, and flung it from his hands in frenzy. Then he called loudly on the Cyclops who dwelt about him in the caves, along the windy heights. They heard his cry, and ran from every side, and standing by the cave they asked what ailed him:

"'What has come on you, Polyphemus, that you scream so in the immortal night, and keep us thus from sleeping? Is a man driving off your flocks in spite of you? Is a man murdering you by craft or force?'

"Then in his turn from out the cave big Polyphemus answered: 'Friends, Noman is murdering me by craft. Force there is none.'

"But answering him in winged words they said: 'If no man harms you then when you are left alone, illness which comes from mighty Zeus you cannot fly. But make your prayer to your father, lord Poseidon.'

"This said, they went their way, and in my heart I laughed,—my name, that clever notion, so deceived them. But now the Cyclops, groaning and in agonies of anguish, by groping with his hands took the stone off the door, yet sat himself inside the door with hands out-stretched, to catch whoever ventured forth among the sheep; for he probably hoped in his heart that I should be so silly. But I was planning how it all might best be ordered that I might win escape from death both for my men and me. So many a plot and scheme I framed, as for my life; great danger was at hand. Then to my mind this seemed the wisest way: some rams there were of a good breed, thick in the fleece, handsome and large, which bore a dark blue wool. These I quietly bound together with the twisted willow withes on which the giant Cyclops slept,—the brute,—taking three sheep together. One, in the middle, carried the man; the other two walked by the sides, keeping my comrades safe. Thus three sheep bore each man. Then for myself,—there was a ram, by far the best of all the flock, whose back I grasped, and curled beneath his shaggy belly there I lay, and with my hands twisted in that enormous fleece I steadily held on, with patient heart. Thus then with sighs we awaited sacred dawn.

"Soon as the early rosy-fingered dawn appeared, the rams hastened to pasture, but the ewes bleated unmilked about the pens, for their udders were well-nigh bursting. Their master, racked with grievous pains, felt over the backs of all the sheep as they stood up, but foolishly did not notice how under the breasts of the woolly sheep men had been fastened. Last of the flock, the ram walked to the door, cramped by his fleece and me the crafty plotter; and feeling him over, big Polyphemus said:

"'What, my pet ram! Why do you move across the cave hindmost of all the flock? Till now you never lagged behind, but with your long strides you were always first to crop the tender blooms of grass; you were the first to reach the running streams, and first to wish to turn to the stall at night: yet here you are the last. Ah, but you miss your master's eye, which a villain has put out,—he and his vile companions,—blunting my wits with wine. Noman it was,—not, I assure him, safe from destruction yet. If only you could sympathize and get the power of speech to say where he is skulking from my rage, then should that brain of his be knocked about the cave and dashed upon the ground. So might my heart recover from the ills which miserable Noman brought upon me.'

"So saying, from his hand he let the ram go forth, and after we were come a little distance from the cave and from the yard, first from beneath the ram I freed myself and then set free my comrades. So at quick pace we drove away those long-legged sheep, heavy with fat, many times turning round, until we reached the ship. A welcome sight we seemed to our dear friends, as men escaped from death. Yet for the others they began to weep and wail; but this I did not suffer; by my frowns I checked their tears. Instead, I bade them straightway toss the many fleecy sheep into the ship, and sail away over the briny water. Quickly they came, took places at the pins, and sitting in order smote the foaming water with their oars. But when I was as far away as one can call, I shouted to the Cyclops in derision:

"'Cyclops, no weakling's comrades you were destined to devour in the deep cave, with brutal might. But it was also destined your bad deeds should find you out, audacious wretch, who did not hesitate to eat the guests within your house! For this did Zeus chastise you, Zeus and the other gods.'

"So I spoke, and he was angered in his heart the more; and tearing off the top of a high hill, he flung it at us. It fell before the dark-bowed ship a little space, but failed to reach the rudder's tip. The sea surged underneath the stone as it came down, and swiftly toward the land the wash of water swept us, like a flood-tide from the deep, and forced us back to shore. I seized a setting-pole and shoved the vessel off; then inspiriting my men, I bade them fall to their oars that we might flee from danger,—with my head making signs,—and bending forward, on they rowed. When we had traversed twice the distance on the sea, again to the Cyclops would I call; but my men, gathering round, sought with soft words to stay me, each in his separate wise:

"'O reckless man, why seek to vex this savage, who even now, hurling his missile in the deep, drove the ship back to shore? We verily thought that we were lost. And had he heard a man make but a sound or speak, he would have crushed our heads and our ships' beams, by hurling jagged granite stone; for he can throw so far.'

"So they spoke, but did not move my daring spirit; again I called aloud out of an angry heart: 'Cyclops, if ever mortal man asks you the story of the ugly blinding of your eye, say that Odysseus made you blind, the spoiler of cities, Laërtes' son, whose home is Ithaca.'

"So I spoke, and with a groan he answered: 'Ah, surely now the ancient oracles are come upon me! Here once a prophet lived, a prophet brave and tall, Telemus, son of Eurymus, who by his prophecies obtained renown and in prophetic works grew old among the Cyclops. He told me it should come to pass in aftertime that I should lose my sight by means of one Odysseus; but I was always watching for the coming of some tall and comely person, arrayed in mighty power; and now a little miserable feeble creature blinded me of my eye, overcoming me with wine. Nevertheless, come here, Odysseus, and let me give the stranger's gift, and beg the famous Land-shaker to aid you on your way. His son am I; he calls himself my father. He, if he will, shall heal me; none else can, whether among the blessed gods or mortal men.'

"So he spoke, and answering him said I: 'Ah, would I might as surely strip you of life and being and send you to the house of Hades, as it is sure the Earth-shaker will never heal your eye!'

"So I spoke, whereat he prayed to lord Poseidon, stretching his hands forth toward the starry sky: 'Hear me, thou girder of the land, dark-haired Poseidon! If I am truly thine, and thou art called my father, vouchsafe no coming home to this Odysseus, spoiler of cities, Laërtes' son, whose home is Ithaca. Yet if it be his lot to see his friends once more, and reach his stately house and native land, late let him come, in evil plight, with loss of all his crew, on vessel of a stranger, and may he at his home find trouble.'

"So spoke he in his prayer, and the dark-haired god gave ear. Then once more picking up a stone much larger than before, the Cyclops swung and sent it, putting forth stupendous power. It fell behind the dark-bowed ship a little space, but failed to reach the rudder's tip. The sea surged underneath the stone as it came down, but the wave swept us forward and forced us to the shore.

"Now when we reached the island where our other well-benched ships waited together, while their crews sat round them sorrowing, watching continually for us, as we ran in we beached our ship among the sands, and forth we went ourselves upon the shore. Then taking the Cyclops' sheep out of the hollow ship, we parted all, that none might go lacking his proper share. The ram my mailed companions gave to me alone, a mark of special honor in the division of the flock; and on the shore I offered him to Zeus of the dark cloud, the son of Kronos, who is the lord of all, burning the thighs. He did not heed the sacrifice. Instead, he purposed that my well-benched ships should all be lost, and all my trusty comrades. But all throughout that day till setting sun we sat and feasted on abundant meat and pleasant wine; and when the sun went down and darkness came, we laid us down to sleep upon the beach. Then as the early rosy-fingered dawn appeared, inspiriting my men, I bade them come on board and loose the cables. Quickly they came, took places at the pins, and sitting in order smote the foaming water with their oars.

"Thence we sailed on, with aching hearts, glad to be clear of death, though missing our dear comrades."

Cyclops

Yet for the first time Odysseus gets blown of coarse and ends up on the island of the cyclopes. The cyclopes are Posidens sons. They go (odysseus + crew) to find supplies and get trapped by the cyclops. The cyclop eats most of odysseus crew, but Odysseus comes up with a plan and they end up blinding the biggest cyclope. when other cyclopes come the bigger cyclops. cant ask for help with odysseus phony name. when odysseus leaves. cyclops talks to his father and asks that Odysseus may be punished for whathe'sdone

X.

AEOLUS, THE LAESTRYGONIANS, AND CIRCE

"Soon we drew near the island of Aeolia, where Aeolus, the son of Hippotas, dear to immortal gods, dwelt on a floating island. All round it is a wall of bronze, not to be broken through, and smooth and steep rises the rocky shore. Within the house of Aeolus, twelve children have been born, six daughters and six sturdy sons, and here he gave his daughters to his sons to be their wives. Here too with their loved father and honored mother they hold continual feasting; before them countless viands lie. By day the steaming house resounds even to its court; by night they sleep by their chaste wives under the coverlets on well-bored bedsteads. Their city it was we reached, their goodly dwelling. For a full month he made me welcome, and he questioned me of all, of Ilios, the Argive ships, and the return of the Achaeans. So I related all the tale in its due order. And when I furthermore asked him about my journey and entreated him for aid, he did not say me nay, but made provision for my going. He gave me a sack,—flaying therefor a nine-year ox,—and in it bound the courses of the blustering winds; for the son of Kronos made him steward of the winds, to stay or rouse which one he would. Upon my hollow ship he tied the sack with a bright cord of silver, that not a breath might stir, however little. Then for my aid he sent the west wind forth, to blow and bear along my ships and men. But it was not to be; by our folly we were lost.

"Nine days we sailed, as well by night as day. Upon the tenth our native fields appeared, so close at hand that we could see men tending fires. Then sweet sleep overcame me, wearied as I was; for I had all the time managed the vessel's sheet and yielded it to no one else among the crew, that so we might the sooner reach our native land. Meanwhile my men began to talk with one another, and to tell how I was bringing gold and silver home as gifts from Aeolus, the generous son of Hippotas; and glancing at his neighbor one would say:

"'Lo, how this man is welcomed and esteemed by all mankind, come to whose town and land he may! He brings a store of goodly treasure out of the spoils of Troy, while we, who toiled along the selfsame road, come home with empty hands. Now Aeolus gives him friendly gifts. Come, then, and let us quickly see what there is here, and how much gold and silver the sack holds.'

"Such was their talk, and the ill counsel of the crew prevailed; they loosed the sack, and out rushed all the winds. Straightway a sweeping storm bore off to sea my weeping comrades, far from their native lands. And I, awaking, hesitated in my gallant heart whether to cast myself out of the ship into the sea and perish there, or saying nothing to endure and bide among the living. I forced myself to stay; covering my head, I laid me down, the while the ships were driven by the cruel storm of wind back to the island of Aeolia, my comrades sighing sore.

"So here we went ashore and drew us water, and soon by the swift ships my men prepared a meal. Then after we had tasted food and drink, taking a herald and a comrade with me, I turned me toward the lordly house of Aeolus. I found him at the feast, beside his wife and children. We entered the hall and on the threshold by the doorposts sat us down; and they all marveled in their hearts and questioned:

"'How came you here, Odysseus? What hostile power assailed you? With care we sent you forth, to let you reach your land and home or anywhere you pleased.'

"So they spoke, and with an aching heart I answered: 'A wicked crew betrayed me—they and a cruel sleep. But heal my woes, my friends, for you have power.'

"So I spoke, addressing them in humble words. Then all the rest were silent, but the father answered thus: 'Out of the island instantly, vilest of all that live! I may not aid or send upon his way a man detested by the blessed gods. Begone! for you are here because detested by the immortals.'

"Therewith he turned me loud lamenting from his door. Thence we sailed on, with aching hearts. Worn was the spirit of my men under the heavy rowing, caused by our folly too; aid on our way appeared no more.

"Six days we sailed, as well by night as day, and on the seventh came to the steep citadel of Lamos, Telepylus in Laestrygonia, where one shepherd leading home his flock calls to another, and the other answers as he leads his own flock forth. Here a man who never slept might earn a double wage: this, herding kine; that, tending silvery sheep; so close are the outgoings of the night and day. Now when we reached the splendid harbor,—round which the rock runs steep, continuous all the way, and the projecting cliffs, facing each other, stretch forward at the mouth, and narrow is the entrance,—into the basin all the rest steered their curved ships, and so the ships lay in the hollow harbor close-anchored, side by side; for no wave swelled within it, large or small, but a clear calm was all around. I alone posted my black ship without the harbor, there at the point, lashing my cables to the rock. Then climbing up, I took my stand on a rugged point of outlook. From it no work of man or beast was to be seen, only we saw some smoke ascending from the ground. So I sent sailors forth to go and learn what men who live by bread dwelt in the land,—selecting two, and joining with them a herald as a third. Leaving the ship, they took a beaten road where carts brought timber from the lofty hills down to the town below. Before the town they met a maiden drawing water, the stately daughter of the Laestrygonian Antiphates. She had come down to the clear-flowing fountain of Artacia, from which they used to fetch the water for the town. So my men, drawing near, addressed her and inquired who was the king of the folk here and whom he ruled; whereat she pointed to her father's high-roofed house. But when they entered the lordly hall, they found a woman there huge as a mountain peak; at her they were aghast. Forthwith she called from the assembly noble Antiphates, her husband, who sought to bring upon my men a miserable end. Straight seizing one, he made his meal of him; and the two others, dashing off, came flying to the ships. Thereat he raised a cry throughout the town, and hearing it, the mighty Laestrygonians gathered from here and there, seeming not men but giants. Then from the rocks they hurled down ponderous stones; and soon among the ships arose a dreadful din of dying men and crashing ships. As men spear fish, they gathered in their loathsome meal. But while they slaughtered these in the deep harbor, I drew my sharp sword from my thigh and cut the cables of my dark-bowed ship; and quickly inspiriting my men, I bade them fall to their oars, that we might flee from danger. They all tossed up the water, in terror for their lives, and cheerily to sea, away from the beetling cliff, my ship sped on; but all the other ships went down together there.

"Thence we sailed on with aching hearts, glad to be clear of death, though missing our dear comrades. And now we reached the island of Aeaea, where fair-haired Circe dwelt, a mighty goddess, human of speech. She was own sister of the sorcerer Aeetes; both were the children of the beaming Sun and of a mother Perse, the daughter of Oceanus. Here we bore landward with our ship and ran in silence into a sheltering harbor, God our guide. Landing, we lay two days and nights, gnawing our hearts because of toil and trouble; but when the fair-haired dawn brought the third day, I took my spear and my sharp sword, and from the ship walked briskly up to a place of distant view, hoping to see some work of man or catch some voice. So climbing up, I took my stand on a rugged point of outlook, and smoke appeared rising from open ground at Circe's dwelling, through some oak thickets and a wood. Then for a time I doubted in my mind and heart whether to go and search the matter while I saw the flaring smoke. Reflecting thus, it seemed the better way first to return to the swift ship and to the shore; there give my men their dinner, and send them forth to search.

"But on my way, as I drew near to the curved ship, some god took pity on me all forlorn, and sent a high-horned deer into my very path. From feeding in the wood he came to the stream to drink, for the sun's power oppressed him. As he stepped out, I struck him in the spine midway along the back; the bronze spear pierced him through; down in the dust he fell with a moan, and his life flew away. Setting my foot upon him, I drew from the wound the brazen spear and laid it on the ground; then I plucked twigs and osiers, and wove a rope a fathom long, twisted from end to end, with which I bound together the monstrous creature's legs. So with him upon my back I walked to the black ship leaning upon my spear, because it was not possible to hold him with my hand upon my shoulder; for the beast was very large. Before the ship I threw him down and then with cheering words aroused my men, standing by each in turn:

"'We shall not, friends, however sad, go to the halls of Hades until our destined day. But while there still is food and drink in the swift ship, let us attend to eating and not waste away with hunger.'

"So I spoke, and my words they quickly heeded. Throwing their coverings off upon the shore beside the barren sea, they gazed upon the deer; for the beast was very large. Then after they had satisfied their eyes with gazing, they washed their hands and made a glorious feast. Thus all throughout the day till setting sun we sat and feasted on abundant meat and pleasant wine; and when the sun went down and darkness came, we laid us down to sleep upon the beach. Then as the early rosy-fingered dawn appeared, holding a council, I said to all my men:

"'My suffering comrades, hearken to my words: for since, my friends, we do not know the place of dusk or dawn, the place at which the beaming sun goes under ground nor where he rises, let us at once consider if a wise course is left. I do not think there is; for I saw, on climbing to a rugged outlook, an island which the boundless deep encircles like a crown. Low in the sea it lies; midway across, I saw a smoke through some oak thickets and a wood.'

"As I thus spoke, their very souls were crushed within them, remembering the deeds of Laestrygonian Antiphates and the cruelty of the daring Cyclops, the devourer of men. They cried aloud and let the big tears fall; but no good came to them from their lamenting.

"Now the whole body of my mailed companions I told off in two bands, and to each band assigned a leader: the one I led, godlike Eurylochus the other. Straightway we shook the lots in a bronze helmet, and the lot of bold Eurylochus leapt out the first. So he departed, two and twenty comrades following, all in tears; and us they left in sorrow too behind. Within the glades they found the house of Circe, built of smooth stone upon commanding ground. All round about were mountain wolves and lions, which Circe had charmed by giving them evil drugs. These creatures did not spring upon my men, but stood erect, wagging their long tails, fawning. As hounds fawn round their master when he comes from meat, because he always brings them dainties that they like, so round these men the strong-clawed wolves and lions fawned. Still my men trembled at the sight of the strange beasts. They stood before the door of the fair-haired goddess, and in the house heard Circe singing with sweet voice, while tending her great imperishable loom and weaving webs, fine, beautiful, and lustrous as are the works of gods. Polites was the first to speak, one ever foremost, and one to me the nearest and the dearest of my comrades:

"'Ah, friends, somebody in the house is tending a great loom and singing sweetly; all the pavement rings. It is a god or woman. Then let us quickly call.'

"He spoke, the others lifted up their voice and called; and suddenly coming forth, she opened the shining doors and bade them in. The rest all followed, heedless. Only Eurylochus remained behind, suspicious of a snare. She led them in and seated them on couches and on chairs, and made a potion for them,—cheese, barley, and yellow honey, stirred into Pramnian wine,—but mingled with the food pernicious drugs, to make them quite forget their native land. Now after she had given the cup and they had drunk it off, straight with a wand she smote them and penned them up in sties; and they took on the heads of swine, the voice, the bristles, and even the shape, yet was their reason as sound as heretofore. Thus, weeping, they were penned; and Circe flung them acorns, chestnuts, and cornel-fruit to eat, such things as swine that wallow in the mire are wont to eat.

"Eurylochus, meanwhile, came to the swift black ship to bring me tidings of my men and tell their bitter fate. Strive as he might, he could not speak a word, so stricken was he to the soul with great distress; his eyes were filled with tears, his heart felt anguish. But when we all in great amazement questioned him, then he described the loss of all his men:

"'We went, as you commanded, noble Odysseus, through the thicket and found within the glades a beautiful house, built of smooth stone upon commanding ground. There somebody was tending a great loom and singing loud, some god or woman. The others lifted up their voice and called; and suddenly coming forth, she opened the shining doors and bade them in. The rest all followed, heedless; but I remained behind, suspicious of a snare. They vanished, one and all; not one appeared again, though long I sat and watched.'

"So he spoke; I slung my silver-studded sword about my shoulders,—large it was and made of bronze,—and my bow with it, and bade him lead me back the selfsame way. But he, clasping my knees with both his hands, entreated me, and sorrowfully said in winged words:

"'O heaven-descended man, bring me not there against my will, but leave me here; for well I know you never will return, nor will you bring another of your comrades. Rather, with these now here, let us speed on; for we might even yet escape the evil day.'

"So he spoke, and answering him said I: 'Eurylochus, remain then here yourself, eating and drinking by the black hollow ship; but I will go, for strong necessity is laid on me.'

"Saying this, I passed up from the ship and from the sea. But when, in walking up the solemn glades, I was about to reach the great house of the sorceress Circe, there I was met, as I approached the house, by Hermes of the golden wand, in likeness of a youth, the first down on his lip,—a time of life most winning. He held my hand and spoke, and thus addressed me:

"'Where are you going, hapless man, along the hills alone, ignorant of the land? Your comrades yonder, at the house of Circe, are penned like swine and kept in fast-closed sties. You come to free them? Nay, I am sure you will return no more, but there, like all the rest, you too will stay. Still, I can keep you clear of harm and give you safety. Here, take this potent herb and go to Circe's house; this shall protect your life against the evil day. And I will tell you all the magic arts of Circe: she will prepare for you a potion and cast drugs into your food; but even so, she cannot charm you, because the potent herb which I shall give will not permit it. And let me tell you more: when Circe turns against you her long wand, then draw the sharp sword from your thigh and spring upon Circe as if you meant to slay her; she then will cower and bid you to her bed. And do not you refuse the goddess' bed, that so she may release your men and care for you. But bid her swear the blessed ones' great oath that she is not meaning now to plot you a new woe, nor when she has you stripped to leave you feeble and unmanned.'

"As he thus spoke, the Speedy-comer gave the herb, drawing it from the ground, and pointed out its nature. Black at the root it is, like milk its blossom, and the gods call it moly. Hard is it for a mortal man to dig; with gods all things may be.

"Hermes departed now to high Olympus, along the woody island. I made my way to Circe's house, and as I went my heart grew very dark.

and ends up sleeping with her so that she will realese his friends. They end up staying a year but when its time to go circe tells him to beware

But I stood at the gate of the fair-haired goddess, stood there and called, and the goddess heard my voice. Suddenly coming forth, she opened the shining doors and bade me in; I followed her with aching heart. She led me in and placed me on a silver-studded chair, beautiful, richly wrought,—upon its lower part there was a rest for feet,—and she prepared a potion in a golden cup, for me to drink, but put therein a drug, with wicked purpose in her heart. Now after she had given the drink and I had drunk it off, and yet it had not charmed me, smiting me with her wand, she spoke these words and cried: 'Off to the sty, and lie there with your fellows!'

"She spoke; I drew the sharp blade from my thigh and sprang upon Circe as if I meant to slay her. With a loud cry, she cowered and clasped my knees, and sorrowfully said in winged words:

"'Who are you? Of what people? Where is your town and kindred? I marvel much that drinking of these drugs you were not charmed. None, no man else, ever withstood these drugs who tasted them, so soon as they had passed the barrier of his teeth; but in your breast there is a mind which cannot be beguiled. Surely you are adventurous Odysseus, who the god of the golden wand, the Speedy-comer, always declared would come upon his way from Troy,—he and his swift black ship. Nay, then, put up your blade within its sheath, and let us now approach our bed, that there we two may join in love and learn to trust each other.'

"So she spoke, and answering her said I: 'Circe, why ask me to be gentle toward you when you have turned my comrades into swine within your halls, and here detain me and with treacherous purpose invite me to your chamber and to approach your bed, that you, when I am stripped, may leave me feeble and unmanned? But I will never willingly approach your bed till you consent, goddess, to swear a solemn oath that you are not meaning now to plot me a new woe.'

"So I spoke, and she then took the oath which I required. So after she had sworn and ended all that oath, then I approached the beauteous bed of Circe.

"Meanwhile attendants plied their work about the halls,—four maids, who were the serving-women of the palace. They are the children of the springs and groves and of the sacred streams that run into the sea. One threw upon the chairs beautiful cloths; purple she spread above, linen below. The next placed silver tables by the chairs and set forth golden baskets. A third stirred in a bowl the cheering wine,— sweet wine in silver—and filled the golden cups. A fourth brought water and kindled a large fire under a great kettle, and let the water warm. Then when the water in the glittering copper boiled, she seated me in the bath and bathed me from the kettle about the head and shoulders, tempering the water well, till from my joints she drew the sore fatigue. And after she had bathed me and anointed me with oil and put upon me a goodly coat and tunic, she led me in and placed me on a silver-studded chair, beautiful, richly wrought,—upon its lower part there was a rest for feet,—and water for the hands a servant brought me in a beautiful pitcher made of gold, and poured it out over a silver basin for my washing, and spread a polished table by my side. Then the grave housekeeper brought bread and placed before me, setting out food of many a kind, freely giving of her store, and bade me eat. But that pleased not my heart; I sat with other thoughts; my heart foreboded evil.

"When Circe marked me sitting thus, not laying hands upon my food but cherishing sore sorrow, approaching me she said in winged words: 'Why do you sit, Odysseus, thus, like one struck dumb, gnawing your heart, and touch no food nor drink? Do you suspect some further guile? You have no cause for fear, for even now I swore to you a solemn oath.'

"So she spoke, and answering her said I: 'Ah, Circe, what upright man could bring himself to taste of food or drink before he had released his friends and seen them with his eyes? But if you in sincerity will bid me drink and eat, then set them free; that I with my own eyes may see my trusty comrades.'

"So I spoke, and from the hall went Circe, wand in hand. She opened the sty doors, and forth she drove what seemed like nine-year swine. A while they stood before her, and, passing along the line, Circe anointed each one with a counter-charm. So from their members fell the hair which at the first the accursed drug which potent Circe gave had made to grow; and once more they were men, men younger than before, much fairer too and taller to behold. They knew me, and each grasped my hand, and from them all passionate sobs burst forth, and all the house gave a sad echo. The goddess pitied us, even she, and standing by my side the heavenly goddess said:

"'High-born son of Laërtes, ready Odysseus, go now to your swift ship and to the shore, and first of all draw up your ship upon the land, and store within the caves your goods and all your gear, and then come back yourself and bring your trusty comrades.'

"So she spoke, and my high heart assented. I went to the swift ship and to the shore, and found by the swift ship my trusty comrades in bitter lamentation letting the big tears fall. As the stalled calves skip round a drove of cows returning to the barn-yard when satisfied with grazing; with one accord they all bound forth, the folds no longer hold them, but with continual bleat they frisk about their mothers; so did these men, when they caught sight of me, press weeping round. To them it seemed as if they had already reached their land, their very town of rugged Ithaca where they were bred and born; and through their sobs they said in winged words:

"'Now you have come, O heaven-descended man, we are as glad as if we were approaching Ithaca, our native land. But tell about the loss of all our other comrades.'

"So they spoke; I in soft words made answer: 'Let us now first of all draw up our ship upon the land and store within the caves our goods and all our gear; then hasten all of you to follow me, and see your comrades in the magic house of Circe drinking and eating, holding constant cheer.'

"So I spoke, and my words they quickly heeded. Eurylochus alone tried to hold back my comrades, and speaking in winged words he said: 'Poor fools, where are we going? Why are you so in love with misery that you will go to Circe's hall and let her turn us all to swine and wolves and lions, that we may then keep watch at her great house, per-force? Such deeds the Cyclops did when to his lair our comrades came, and with them went this reckless man, Odysseus; for through his folly those men also perished.'

"As he thus spoke, I hesitated in my heart whether to draw my keen-edged blade from my stout thigh and by a blow bring down his head into the dust, near as he was by tie of marriage; but with soft words my comrades stayed me, each in his separate wise:

"'High-born Odysseus, we will leave him, if you please, here by the ship to guard the ship; but lead us to the magic house of Circe.'

"Saying this, they passed up from the ship and from the sea. Yet did Eurylochus not tarry by the hollow ship; he followed, for he feared my stern rebuke.

"But in the mean while to my other comrades at the palace Circe had given a pleasant bath, anointed them with oil, and put upon them fleecy coats and tunics; merrily feasting in her halls we found them all. When the men saw and recognized each other, they wept aloud and the house rang around; and standing by my side the heavenly goddess said:

"'High-born son of Laërtes, ready Odysseus, let not this swelling grief rise farther now. I myself know what hardships you have borne upon the swarming sea and how fierce men harassed you on the land. Come, then, eat food, drink wine, until you find once more that spirit in the breast which once was yours when you first left your native land of rugged Ithaca. Now, worn and spiritless, your thoughts still dwell upon your weary wandering. This many a day your heart has not been glad, for sorely have you suffered.'

"So she spoke, and our high hearts assented. Here, then, day after day, for a full year, we sat and feasted on abundant meat and pleasant wine. But when the year was gone and the round of the seasons rolled, as the months waned and the long days were done, then calling me aside my trusty comrades said:

"'Ah, sir, consider now your native land, if you are destined ever to be saved and reach your stately house and native land.'

"So they spoke, and my high heart assented. Yet all throughout that day till setting sun we sat and feasted on abundant meat and pleasant wine; and when the sun went down and darkness came, my men lay down to sleep throughout the dusky halls. But I, on coming to the beauteous bed of Circe, made supplication to her by her knees, and to my voice the goddess hearkened; and speaking in winged words, I said:

"'Circe, fulfill the promise made to send me home; for now my spirit stirs, with that of all my men, who vex my heart with their complaints when you are gone away.'

"So I spoke, and straight the heavenly goddess answered: 'High-born son of Laërtes, ready Odysseus, stay no longer at my home against your will. But you must first perform a different journey, and go to the halls of Hades and of dread Persephone, there to consult the spirit of Teiresias of Thebes,—the prophet blind, whose mind is steadfast still. To him, though dead, Persephone has granted reason, to him alone sound understanding; the rest are flitting shadows.'

"As she thus spoke, my very soul was crushed within me, and sitting on the bed I fell to weeping; my heart no longer cared to live and see the sunshine. But when of weeping and of writhing I had had my fill, then thus I answered her and said: 'But, Circe, who will be my pilot on this journey? None by black ship has ever reached the land of Hades.'

"So I spoke, and straight the heavenly goddess answered: 'High-born son of Laërtes, ready Odysseus, let not the lack of pilot for your ship disturb you, but set the mast, spread the white sail aloft, and sit you down; the breath of Boreas shall bear her onward. When you have crossed by ship the Ocean-stream to where the shore is rough and the grove of Persephone stands,—tall poplars and seed-shedding willows,—there beach your ship by the deep eddies of the Ocean-stream, but go yourself to the mouldering house of Hades. There is a spot where into Acheron run Pyriphlegethon and Cocytus, a stream which is an offshoot of the waters of the Styx; a rock here forms the meeting-point of the two roaring rivers. To this spot then, hero, draw nigh, even as I bid; and dig a pit, about a cubit either way, and round its edges pour an offering to all the dead,—first honey-mixture, next sweet wine, and thirdly water, and over all strew the white barley-meal. Make many supplications also to the strengthless dead, vowing when you return to Ithaca to take the barren cow that is your best and offer it in your hall, heaping the pyre with treasure; and to Teiresias separately to sacrifice a sheep, for him alone, one wholly black, the very choicest of your flock. So when with vows you have implored the illustrious peoples of the dead, offer a ram and a black ewe, bending their heads toward Erebus, but turn yourself away, facing the river's stream; to you shall gather many spirits of those now dead and gone. Then forthwith call your men, and bid them take the sheep now lying there slain by the ruthless sword, and flay and burn them, and call upon the gods,—on powerful Hades and on dread Persephone,—while you yourself, drawing your sharp sword from your thigh, sit still and do not let the strengthless dead approach the blood till you have made inquiry of Teiresias. Thither the seer will quickly come, O chief of men, and he will tell your course, the stages of your journey, and of your homeward way, how you may pass along the swarming sea.'

"Even as she spoke, the gold-throned morning came. On me she put a coat and tunic for my raiment; and the nymph dressed herself in a long silvery robe, fine spun and graceful; she bound a beautiful golden girdle round her waist, and put a veil upon her head. Then through the house I passed and roused my men with cheering words, standing by each in turn:

"'Sleep no more now, nor drowse in pleasant slumber, but let us go, for potent Circe has at last made known to me the way.'

"So I spoke, and their high hearts assented. Yet even from there I did not bring away my men in safety. There was a certain Elpenor, the youngest of them all, a man not very stanch in fight nor sound of understanding, who, parted from his mates, lay down to sleep upon the magic house of Circe, seeking for coolness when overcome with wine. As his companions stirred, hearing the noise and tumult, he suddenly sprang up and quite forgot how to come down again by the long ladder, but he fell headlong from the roof; his neck was broken in its socket, and his soul went down to the house of Hades.

"When my men mustered there, I said to them: 'You think, perhaps, that you are going home to your own native land; but Circe has marked out for us a different journey, even to the halls of Hades and of dread Persephone, there to consult the spirit of Teiresias of Thebes.'

"As I thus spoke, their very souls were crushed within them, and sitting down where each one was they moaned and tore their hair; but no good came to them from their lamenting.

"Now while we walked to the swift ship and to the shore, in sadness, letting the big tears fall, Circe went on before, and there by the black ship tied a black ewe and ram, passing us lightly by. When a god does not will, what man can spy him moving to and fro?"

XI.

THE LAND OF THE DEAD

"NOW WHEN we came down to the ship and to the sea, we in the first place launched our ship into the sacred sea, put mast and sail in the black ship, then took the sheep and drove them in, and we ourselves embarked in sadness, letting the big tears fall. And for our aid behind our dark-bowed ship came a fair wind to fill our sail, a welcome comrade, sent us by fair-haired Circe, the mighty goddess, human of speech. So when we had done our work at the several ropes about the ship we sat us down, while wind and helmsman kept her steady; and all day long the sail of the running ship was stretched. Then the sun sank, and all the ways grew dark.

"And now she reached earth's limits, the deep stream of the Ocean, where the Cimmerian people's land and city lie, wrapt in a fog and cloud. Never on them does the shining sun look down with his beams, as he goes up the starry sky or as again toward earth he turns back from the sky, but deadly night is spread abroad over these hapless men. On coming here, we beached our ship and set the sheep ashore, then walked along the Ocean-stream until we reached the spot foretold by Circe.

"Here Perimedes and Eurylochus held fast the victims, while drawing my sharp blade from my thigh, I dug a pit, about a cubit either way, and round its edges poured an offering to all the dead,—first honey-mixture, next sweet wine, and thirdly water, and over all I strewed white barley-meal; and I made many supplications to the strengthless dead, vowing when I returned to Ithaca to take the barren cow that was my best and offer it in my hall, heaping the pyre with treasure; and to Teiresias separately to sacrifice a sheep, for him alone, one wholly black, the choicest of my flock. So when with prayers and vows I had implored the peoples of the dead, I took the sheep and cut their throats over the pit, and forth the dark blood ran. Then gathered there spirits from out of Erebus of those now dead and gone,—brides, and unwedded youths, and worn old men, delicate maids with hearts but new to sorrow, and many pierced with brazen spears, men slain in fight, wearing their blood-stained armor. In crowds around the pit they flocked from every side, with awful wail. Pale terror seized me. Nevertheless, inspiriting my men, I bade them take the sheep now lying there slain by the ruth-less sword, and flay and burn them, and call upon the gods,—on pow-erful Hades and on dread Persephone,—while I myself, drawing my sharp sword from my thigh, sat still and did not let the strengthless dead approach the blood till I had made inquiry of Teiresias.

"First came the spirit of my man, Elpenor. He had not yet been buried under the broad earth; for we left his body at the hall of Circe, unwept, unburied, since other tasks were urgent. I wept to see him and pitied him from my heart, and speaking in winged words I said:

"'Elpenor, how came you in this murky gloom? Faster you came on foot than I in my black ship.'

"So I spoke, and with a groan he answered: 'High-born son of Laërtes, ready Odysseus, Heaven's cruel doom destroyed me, and excess of wine. After I went to sleep on Circe's house, I did not notice how to go down again by the long ladder, but I fell headlong from the roof; my neck was broken in its socket, and my soul came down to the house of Hades. Now I entreat you by those left behind, not present here, by your wife, and by the father who cared for you when little, and by Telemachus whom you left at home alone,—for I know, as you go hence out of the house of Hades, you will touch with your stanch ship the island of Aeaea,—there then, my master, I charge you, think of me. Do not, in going, leave me behind, unwept, unburied, deserting me, lest I become a cause of anger to the gods against you; but burn me in the armor that was mine, and on the shore of the foaming sea erect the mound of an unhappy man, that future times may know. Do this for me, and fix upon my grave the oar with which in life I rowed among my comrades.'

"So he spoke, and answering him said I: 'Unhappy man, this will I carry out and do for you.'

"In such sad words talking with one another, there we sat,—I on the one side, holding my blade over the blood, while the spectre of my comrade, on the other, told of his many woes.

"Now came the spirit of my dead mother, Anticleia, daughter of brave Autolycus, whom I had left alive on setting forth for sacred Ilios. I wept to see her and pitied her from my heart; but even so, I did not let her—deeply though it grieved me—approach the blood till I had made inquiry of Teiresias.

"Now came the spirit of Teiresias of Thebes, holding his golden sceptre. He knew me, and said to me: 'High-born son of Laërtes, ready
Odysseus, why now, unhappy man, leaving the sunshine, have you
come here to see the dead and this forbidding place? Nay, draw back
from the pit and turn your sharp blade from the blood, that I may drink
and speak what will not fail.'

"So he spoke, and drawing back I thrust my silver-studded sword into
its sheath. And after he had drunk of the dark blood, then thus the
blameless seer addressed me:

"'You are looking for a joyous journey home, glorious Odysseus, but
a god will make it hard; for I do not think you will elude the Land-
shaker, who bears a grudge against you in his heart, angry because you
blinded his dear son. Yet even so, by meeting hardship you may still
reach home, if you will curb the passions of yourself and crew when
once you bring your stanch ship to the Thrinacian island, safe from the
dark blue sea, and find the pasturing kine and sturdy sheep of the Sun,
who all things oversees, all overhears. If you leave these unharmed and
heed your homeward way, you still may come to Ithaca, though you
shall meet with hardship. But if you harm them, then I predict the loss
of ship and crew; and even if you yourself escape, late shall you come,
in evil plight, with loss of all your crew, on the vessel of a stranger. At
home you shall find trouble,—bold men devouring your living, wooing
your matchless wife, and offering bridal gifts. Nevertheless, on your return, you surely shall avenge their crimes. But after you have slain the
suitors in your halls, whether by stratagem or by the sharp sword boldly,
then journey on, bearing a shapely oar, until you reach the men who
know no sea and do not eat food mixed with salt. These therefore have
no knowledge of the red-cheeked ships, nor of the shapely oars which
are the wings of ships. And I will give a sign easy to be observed, which
shall not fail you: when another traveler, meeting you, shall say you
have a winnowing fan on your white shoulder, there fix in the ground
your shapely oar, and make fit offerings to lord Poseidon—a ram, a
bull, and the sow's mate, a boar,—and turning homeward offer sacred
hecatombs to the immortal gods who hold the open sky, all in the order
due. Upon yourself death from the sea shall very gently come and cut
you off bowed down with hale old age. Round you shall be a prosperous people. I speak what shall not fail.'

"So he spoke, and answering him said I: 'Teiresias, these are the threads
of destiny the gods themselves have spun. Nevertheless, declare me this,
and plainly tell: I see the spirit of my dead mother here; silent she sits beside the blood and has not, although I am her son, deigned to look in my
face or speak to me. Tell me, my master, how may she know that it is I?'

"So I spoke, and straightway answering me said he: 'A simple saying

I will tell and fix it in your mind: whomever among those dead and gone you let approach the blood, he shall declare the truth. But whomsoever you refuse, he shall go back again.'

"So saying, into the house of Hades passed the spirit of the great Teiresias, after telling heaven's decrees; but I still held my place until my mother came and drank of the dark blood. She knew me instantly, and sorrowfully said in winged words:

"'My child, how came you in this murky gloom, while still alive? Awful to the living are these sights. Great rivers are between, and fearful floods,—mightiest of all the Ocean-stream, not to be crossed on foot, but only on a strong-built ship. Are you but now come here, upon your way from Troy, wandering a long time with your ship and crew? Have you not been in Ithaca, nor seen your wife at home?'

"So she spoke, and answering her said I: 'My mother, need brought me to the house of Hades, here to consult the spirit of Teiresias of Thebes. I have not yet been near Achaea nor once set foot upon my land, but have been always wandering and meeting sorrow since the first day I followed royal Agamemnon to Ilios, famed for horses, to fight the Trojans there. But now declare me this and plainly tell: what doom of death that lays men low o'erwhelmed you? Some long disease? Or did the huntress Artemis attack and slay you with her gentle arrows? And tell me of my father and the son I left; still in their keeping are my honors? Or does at last an alien hold them, while people say that I shall come no more? Tell me, moreover, of my wedded wife, her purposes and thoughts. Is she abiding by her child and keeping all in safety? Or was she finally married by some chief of the Achaeans?'

"So I spoke, and straight my honored mother answered: 'Indeed she stays with patient heart within your hall, and wearily the nights and days are wasted with her tears. Nobody yet holds your fair honors; in peace Telemachus farms your estate, and sits at equal feasts where it befits the lawgiver to be a guest, for all give him a welcome. Your father stays among the fields, and comes to the town no more. Bed has he none, bedstead, nor robes, nor bright-hued rugs; but through the winter he sleeps in the house where servants sleep, in the dust beside the fire, and wears upon his body sorry clothes. Then when the summer comes and fruitful autumn, wherever he may be about his slope of vineyard-ground a bed is piled of leaves fallen on the earth. There lies he in distress, woe waxing strong within, longing for your return; and hard old age comes on. Even so I also died and met my doom: not that at home the sure-eyed huntress attacked and slew me with her gentle arrows; nor did a sickness come, which oftentimes by sad decay steals from the limbs the life; but longing for you—your wise ways, glorious Odysseus, and your tenderness,—took joyous life away.'

"As she thus spoke, I yearned, though my mind hesitated, to clasp the spirit of my mother, even though dead. Three times the impulse came; my heart urged me to clasp her. Three times out of my arms like a shadow or a dream she flitted, and the sharp pain about my heart grew only more; and speaking in winged words, I said:

"'My mother, why not stay for me who long to clasp you, so that in the very house of Hades, throwing our arms round one another, we two may take our fill of piercing grief? Or is it a phantom high Persephone has sent, to make me weep and sorrow more?'

"So I spoke, and straight my honored mother answered: 'Ah, my own child, beyond all men ill-fated! In no wise is Persephone, daughter of Zeus, beguiling you, but this is the way with mortals when they die: the sinews then no longer hold the flesh and bones together; for these the strong force of the blazing fire destroys, when once the life leaves the white bones, and like a dream the spirit flies away. Nay now, press quickly on into the light, and of all this take heed, to tell your wife hereafter.'

"So we held converse there; but now the women came—for high Persephone had sent them,—who were great men's wives and daughters. Round the dark blood in throngs they gathered, and I considered how to question each. Then to my mind this seemed the wisest way: I drew my keen-edged blade from my stout thigh and did not let them all at once drink the dark blood, but one by one they came, and each declared her lineage, and I questioned all.

"There I saw Tyro first, of noble ancestry, who told of being sprung from gentle Salmoneus; told how she was the wife of Cretheus, son of Aeolus. She loved a river-god, divine Enipeus, who flows the fairest of all streams on earth. So she would walk by the fair currents of Enipeus, and in his guise the Land-shaker, who girds the land, lay with her at the outpouring of the eddying stream. The upheaving water compassed them, high as a hill and arching, and hid the god and mortal woman. He loosed the maiden's girdle and cast on her a sleep. Then when the god had done the deeds of love, he held her hand and spoke and thus addressed her:

"'Be happy, lady, in my love! In the revolving year you shall bear noble children; for the embraces of immortals are not barren. Rear them yourself, and cherish them. And now go home. Hold fast, and speak it not: I am Poseidon, the shaker of the earth.'

"Saying this, he plunged into the surging sea. She then, conceiving, bore Pelias and Neleus, who both became strong ministers of mighty Zeus. Pelias dwelt in the open country of Iolcus, rich in flocks; the other at sandy Pylos. And sons to Cretheus also this queen of women bore,—Aeson, and Pheres, and Amythaon the charioteer.

"And after her I saw Antiope, Asopus' daughter, who boasted she had been embraced by Zeus himself. And so she bore two sons, Amphion and Zethus, who first laid the foundations of seven-gated Thebes, and fortified it; because unfortified, they could not dwell in open Thebes, for all their power.

"And after her I saw Alcmene, wife of Amphitryon, her who bore dauntless Hercules, the lion-hearted, yielding to the embrace of mighty Zeus; and Megara, harsh Creon's daughter, whom the tireless son of Amphitryon took to wife.

"The mother of Oedipus I saw, fair Epicaste, who did a monstrous deed through ignorance of heart, in marrying her son. He, having slain his father, married her; and soon the gods made the thing known to men. In pain at pleasant Thebes he governed the Cadmeians, through the gods' destroying purpose; and she went down to Hades, the strong gaoler, fastening a fatal noose to the high rafter, abandoned to her grief. To him she left the many woes which the Avengers of a mother bring.

"Beautiful Chloris too I saw, whom Neleus once married for her beauty after making countless gifts, the youngest daughter of that Amphion, son of Iasus, who once held powerful sway at Minyan Orchomenus. She was the queen of Pylos, and bore Neleus famous children, Nestor and Chromius and Periclymenus the headstrong. And beside these she bore that stately Pero, the marvel of mankind, whom all her neighbors wooed. But to none would Neleus give her save to him who should drive from Phylace the crook-horned, broad-browed kine of haughty Iphiclus, and dangerous kine were they. A blameless seer alone would undertake to drive them; but cruel doom of God prevented, harsh bonds and clownish herdsmen. Yet after days and months were spent, as the year rolled and other seasons came, then haughty Iphiclus released him on his telling all the oracles. The will of Zeus was done.

"Leda I saw, the wife of Tyndareus, who bore to Tyndareus two stalwart sons: Castor, the horseman, and Polydeuces, good at boxing. These in a kind of life the nourishing earth now holds; and even beneath the ground they have from Zeus the boon that to-day they be alive, to-morrow dead; and they are allotted honors like the gods.

"Iphimedeia I saw, wife of Aloëus, who said that she had lain beside Poseidon. She bore two children, but short-lived they proved,—Otus, the godlike, and the far-famed Ephialtes,—whom the fruitful earth made grow to be the tallest and most beautiful of men, after renowned Orion; for at nine years they were nine cubits broad, and in height they reached nine fathoms. Therefore they even threatened the immortals with raising on Olympus the din of furious war. Ossa they strove to set upon Olympus, and upon Ossa leafy Pelion, that so the heavens might be scaled. And this they would have done, had they but reached the period of their vigor; but the son of Zeus whom fair-haired Leto bore destroyed them both before below their temples the downy hair had sprung and covered their chins with the fresh beard.

"Phaedra and Procris, too, I saw, and beautiful Ariadne, daughter of wizard Minos, whom Theseus tried to bring from Crete to the slopes of sacred Athens. But he gained naught thereby; before she came, Artemis slew her in sea-girt Dia, prompted by the report of Dionysus.

"Maera and Clymene I saw, and odious Eriphyle who took a bribe of gold as the price of her own husband. But all I cannot tell, nor even name the many heroes' wives and daughters whom I saw; ere that, the immortal night would wear away. Already it is time to sleep, at the swift ship among the crew or here. My journey hence rests with the gods and you."

As thus he ended, all were hushed to silence, held by the spell throughout the dusky hall. White-armed Arete was the first to speak: "Phaeacians, how seems to you this man in beauty, height, and balanced mind within? My guest indeed he is, but each one shares the honor. Be not in haste then to dismiss him, nor stint your gifts to one so much in need. By favor of the gods great wealth is in your houses."

Then also spoke the old lord Echeneüs, who was the oldest of Phaeacian men: "My friends, not wide of the mark, nor of her reputation, speaks the wise queen; therefore give heed. Yet word and work rest with Alcinoüs here."

Then answered him Alcinoüs and said: "Even as she speaks that word shall be, if I be now the living lord of oar-loving Phaeacians! But let our guest, however much he longs for home, consent to stay at all events until to-morrow, till I shall make our gift complete. To send him hence shall be the charge of all, especially of me; for power within this land rests here."

Then wise Odysseus answered him and said: "Mighty Alcinoüs, renowned of all, if you should bid me stay a year and then should send me forth, giving me splendid gifts, that is what I would choose; for much more to my profit would it be with fuller hands to reach my native land. Then should I be regarded more and welcomed more by all who saw me coming home to Ithaca."

Then answered him Alcinoüs and said: "Odysseus, we judge you by your looks to be no cheat or thief; though many are the men the dark earth breeds, and scatters far and wide, who fashion falsehoods out of what no man can see. But you have a grace of word and a noble mind within, and you told your tale as skillfully as if you were a bard, relating all the Argives' and your own sore troubles. But now declare me this and plainly tell: did you see any of the godlike comrades who went with you to Ilios and there met doom? The night is very long; yes, vastly long. The hour for sleeping at the hall is not yet come. Tell me the wondrous story. I could be well content till sacred dawn, if you were willing in the hall to tell us of your woes."

Then wise Odysseus answered him and said: "Lord Alcinoüs, renowned of all, there is a time for stories and a time for sleep; yet if you wish to listen longer, I would not shrink from telling tales more pitiful than these, the woes of my companions who died in after-time, men who escaped the grievous war-cry of the Trojans to die on their return through a wicked woman's will.

"When, then, chaste Persephone had scattered here and there those spirits of tender women, there came the spirit of Agamemnon, son of Atreus, sorrowing. Around thronged other spirits of men who by his side had died in the house of Aegisthus and there had met their doom. He knew me as soon as he had drunk of the dark blood; and then he cried aloud and let the big tears fall, and stretched his hands forth eagerly to grasp me. But no, there was no strength or vigor left, such as was once within his supple limbs. I wept to see him, and pitied him from my heart, and speaking in winged words I said:

"'Great son of Atreus, Agamemnon, lord of men, what doom of death that lays men low o'erwhelmed you? Was it on shipboard that Poseidon smote you, raising unwelcome blasts of cruel wind? Or did fierce men destroy you on the land, while you were cutting off their kine or their fair flocks of sheep, or while you fought to win their town and carry off their women?'

"So I spoke, and straightway answering me said he: 'No, high-born son of Laërtes, ready Odysseus, on shipboard Poseidon did not smite me, raising unwelcome blasts of cruel wind, nor did fierce men destroy me on the land; it was Aegisthus, plotting death and doom, who slew me, aided by my accursed wife, when he had bidden me home and had me at the feast, even as one kills the ox before the manger. So thus I died a lamentable death, and all my men, with no escape, were slain around me; like white-toothed swine at some rich, powerful man's wedding, or banquet, or gay festival. You have yourself been present at the death of many men,—men slain in single combat and in the press of war; yet here you would have felt your heart most touched with pity, to see how round the mixing-bowl and by the loaded tables we lay about the hall, and all the pavement ran with blood. Saddest of all, I heard the cry of Priam's daughter, Cassandra, whom crafty Clytaemnestra slew beside me; and I, on the ground, lifted my hands and clutched my sword in dying. But she, the brutal woman, turned away and did not deign, though I was going to the house of Hades, to draw with her hand my eyelids down and press my lips together. Ah, what can be more horrible and brutish than a woman when she admits into her thoughts such deeds as these! And what a shameless deed she plotted to bring about the murder of the husband of her youth! I used to think how glad my coming home would be, even to my children and my slaves; but she, intent on such extremity of crime, brought shame upon herself and all of womankind who shall be born hereafter, even on well-doers too.'

"So he spoke, and answering him said I: 'Alas! The house of Atreus far-seeing Zeus has sorely plagued with women's arts, from the beginning: for Helen's sake how many of us died; and Clytaemnestra devised a plot while you were far away.'

"So I spoke, and straightway answering me said he: 'Never be you, then, gentle to your wife, nor speak out all you really mean; but tell a part and let a part be hid. And yet on you, Odysseus, no violent death shall ever fall from your wife's hand; for truly wise and of an understanding heart is the daughter of Icarius, heedful Penelope. As a young bride we left her, on going to the war. A child was at her breast, an infant then, who now perhaps sits in the ranks of men, and happy too; for his dear father, coming home, will see him, and he will meet his father with embrace, as children should. But my wife did not let me feast my eyes upon my son; before he came, she slew me. Nay, this I will say farther; mark it well. By stealth, not openly, bring in your ship to shore, for there is no more faith in woman. But now declare me this and plainly tell if you hear my son is living still—at Orchomenus, perhaps, or sandy Pylos, or at the home of Menelaus in broad Sparta; for surely nowhere on the earth has royal Orestes died.'

"So he spoke, and answering him said I: 'O son of Atreus, why question me of this? Whether he be alive or dead I do not know. To speak vain words is ill.'

"In such sad words talking with one another mournfully we stood, letting the big tears fall. And now there came the spirit of Achilles, son of Peleus, and of Patroclus too, of gallant Antilochus, and of Ajax who was first in beauty and in stature of all the Danaäns after the gallant son of Peleus. But the spirit of swift-footed Aeacides knew me, and sorrowfully said in winged words:

"'High-born son of Laërtes, ready Odysseus, rash as you are, what will you undertake more desperate than this! How dared you come down hither to the house of Hades, where dwell the senseless dead, spectres of toil-worn men?'

"So he spoke, and answering him said I: 'Achilles, son of Peleus, foremost of the Achaeans, I came for consultation with Teiresias, hoping that he might give advice for reaching rugged Ithaca. I have not yet been near Achaea nor once set foot upon my land, but have had constant trouble; while as for you, Achilles, no man was in the past more fortunate, nor in the future shall be; for formerly, during your life, we Argives gave you equal honor with the gods, and now you are a mighty lord among the dead, when here. Then do not grieve at having died, Achilles.'

"So I spoke, and straightway answering me said he: 'Mock not at death, glorious Odysseus. Better to be the hireling of a stranger, and serve a man of mean estate whose living is but small, than be the ruler over all these dead and gone. No, tell me tales of my proud son, whether or not he followed to the war to be a leader; tell what you know of gallant Peleus, whether he still has honor in the cities of the Myrmidons; or do they slight him now in Hellas and in Phthia, because old age has touched his hands and feet? I am myself no longer in the sunlight to defend him, nor like what I once was when on the Trojan plain I routed a brave troop in succoring the Argives. If once like that I could but come, even for a little space, into my father's house, frightful should be my might and my resistless hands to any who are troubling him and keeping him from honor.'

"So he spoke, and answering him said I: 'Indeed, of gallant Peleus I know nothing. But about your dear son Neoptolemus, I will tell you all the truth, as you desire; for it was I, in my trim hollow ship, who brought him from Scyros to the mailed Achaeans. And when encamped at Troy we held a council, he always was the first to speak, and no word missed its mark; godlike Nestor and I alone surpassed him. Moreover, on the Trojan plain, when we Achaeans battled, he never tarried in the throng nor at the rallying-place, but pressed before us all, yielding to none in courage. Many a man he slew in mortal combat. Fully I cannot tell, nor even name the host he slew in fighting for the Argives; but how he vanquished with his sword the son of Telephus, Eurypylus the hero! Many of that Ceteian band fell with their leader, destroyed by woman's bribes. So goodly a man as he I never saw, save kingly Memnon.

"'Then when we entered the horse Epeius made,—we chieftains of the Argives,—and it lay all with me to shut or open our close ambush, other captains and councilors of the Danaäns would wipe away a tear, and their limbs shook beneath them; but watching him, at no time did I see his fair skin pale, nor from his cheeks did he wipe tears away. Often he begged to leave the horse; he fingered his sword-hilt and his bronze-tipped spear, longing to vex the Trojans. Yet after we overthrew the lofty town of Priam, he took his share of spoil and an honorable prize, and went on board unharmed, not hit by brazen point nor wounded in close combat, as for the most part happens in war; haphazard Ares rages.'

"So I spoke, and the spirit of swift-footed Aeacides departed with long strides across the field of asphodel, pleased that I said his son was famous.

"But the other spirits of those dead and gone stood sadly there; each asked for what he loved. Only the spirit of Ajax, son of Telamon, held aloof, still angry at the victory I gained in the contest at the ships for the armor of Achilles. The goddess mother of Achilles offered the prize, and the sons of the Trojans were the judges,—they and Pallas Athene. Would I had never won in such a strife, since thus the earth closed round the head of Ajax, who in beauty and achievement surpassed all other Danaäns save the gallant son of Peleus. To him I spoke in gentle words and said:

"'Ajax, son of gallant Telamon, will you not, even in death, forget your wrath about the accursed armor? To plague the Argives the gods gave it, since such a tower as you were lost thereby. For you as for Achilles, son of Peleus, do we Achaeans mourn unceasingly. None was to blame but Zeus, who, fiercely hating all the host of Danaän spearmen, brought upon you this doom. Nay, king, draw near, that you may listen to our voice and hear our words. Abate your pride and haughty spirit.'

"I spoke; he did not answer, but he went his way after the other spirits of those dead and gone, on into Erebus. Yet then, despite his wrath, he should have spoken, or I had spoken to him, but that the heart within my breast wished to see other spirits of the dead.

"There I saw Minos, the illustrious son of Zeus, a golden sceptre in his hand, administering justice to the dead from where he sat, while all around men called for judgment from the king, sitting and standing in the wide-doored hall of Hades.

"Next I marked huge Orion drive through the field of asphodel the game that in his life he slew among the lonely hills. He held a club of solid bronze that never can be broken.

"And Tityus I saw, the son of far-famed Gaia, stretched on the plain; across nine roods he stretched. Two vultures sat beside him, one upon either hand, and tore his liver, piercing the caul within. Yet with his hands he did not keep them off; for he did violence to Leto, the honored wife of Zeus, as she was going to Pytho through pleasant Panopeus.

"Tantalus, too, I saw in grievous torment and standing in a pool. It touched his chin. He strained for thirst, but could not take and drink; for as the old man bent, eager to drink, the water always was absorbed and disappeared, and at his feet the dark earth showed. God made it dry. Then leafy-crested trees drooped down their fruit,—pears, pomegranates, apples with shining fruit, sweet figs, and thrifty olives. But when the old man stretched his hand to take, a breeze would toss them toward the dusky clouds.

"And Sisyphus I saw in bitter pains, forcing a monstrous stone along with both his hands. Tugging with hand and foot, he pushed the stone upward along a hill. But when he thought to heave it on clean to the summit, a mighty power would turn it back; and so once more down to the ground the wicked stone would tumble. Again he strained to push it back; sweat ran down from his limbs, and from his head a dust cloud rose.

"And next I marked the might of Hercules,—his phantom form; for he himself is with the immortal gods reveling at their feasts, wed to fair-ankled Hebe, child of great Zeus and golden-sandaled Here. Around him rose a clamor of the dead, like that of birds, fleeing all ways in terror; while he, like gloomy night, with his bare bow and arrow on the string, glared fearfully, as if forever shooting. Terrible was the baldric round about his breast, a golden belt where marvelous devices had been wrought, bears and wild boars and fierce-eyed lions, struggles and fights, murders and blood-sheddings. Let the artificer design no more who once achieved that sword-belt by his art. Soon as he saw, he knew me, and sorrowfully said in winged words:

"'High-born son of Laërtes, ready Odysseus, so you, poor man, work out a cruel task such as I once endured when in the sunlight. I was the son of Kronian Zeus, yet I had pains unnumbered; for to one very far beneath me I was bound, and he imposed hard labors. He even sent me here to carry off the dog, for nothing he supposed could be a harder labor. I brought the dog up hence, and dragged him forth from Hades. Hermes was my guide, he and clear-eyed Athene.'

"So saying, back he went into the house of Hades, while I still held my place, hoping there yet might come some other heroes who died long ago. And more of the men of old I might have seen, as I desired, — Theseus and Peirithoüs, famous children of the gods; but ere they came, myriads of the people of the dead gathered with awful cry. Pale terror seized me; I thought perhaps the Gorgon head of some fell monster high Persephone might send out of the house of Hades. So, turning to my ship, I called my crew to come on board and loose the cables. Quickly they came, took places at the pins, and down the Ocean-stream the flowing current bore us, with oarage first and then a pleasant breeze."

XII.

THE SIRENS, SCYLLA, CHARYBDIS, AND THE KINE OF THE SUN

"After our ship had left the current of the Ocean-stream and come into the waters of the open sea and to the island of Aeaea, where is the dwelling of the early dawn, its dancing-ground and place of rising, as we ran in we beached our ship among the sands, and forth we went ourselves upon the shore; where, falling fast asleep, we awaited sacred dawn.

"But when the early rosy-fingered dawn appeared, I sent men forward to the house of Circe to fetch the body of the dead Elpenor. Then hastily cutting logs, where the coast stood out most boldly we buried him, in sadness, letting the big tears fall. After the dead was burned and the armor of the dead man, we raised a mound, and dragged a stone upon it, and fixed on the mound's highest point his shapely oar.

"With all this we were busied; nevertheless, our coming from the house of Hades was not concealed from Circe, but quickly she arrayed herself and came to meet us. Her maids bore bread and stores of meat and ruddy sparkling wine; and standing in the midst of all, the heavenly goddess said:

"'Madmen! who have gone down alive into the house of Hades, thus twice to meet with death while others die but once, come, eat this food and drink this wine here for to-day, and when to-morrow comes you shall set sail. I will myself point out the way and fully show you all; lest by unhappy lack of skill you be distressed on sea or land and suffer harm.'

"So she spoke, and our high hearts assented. Thus all throughout the day till setting sun we sat and feasted on abundant meat and pleasant wine; and when the sun had set and darkness came, my men lay down to sleep by the ship's cables; but leading me by the hand apart from my good comrades, the goddess bade me sit, herself reclined beside me, and asked me for my story. So I related all the tale in its due order. Then thus spoke potent Circe:

"'All this is ended now; but listen to what I say, and God himself shall help you to remember. First you will meet the Sirens, who cast a spell on every man who goes their way. Whoso draws near unwarned and hears the Sirens' voices, by him no wife nor little child shall ever stand, glad at his coming home; for the Sirens cast a spell of penetrating song, sitting within a meadow. Near by is a great heap of rotting human bones; fragments of skin are shriveling on them. Therefore sail on, and stop your comrades' ears with sweet wax kneaded soft, that none of the rest may hear. If you yourself will listen, see that they bind you hand and foot on the swift ship, upright upon the mast-block,—round it let the rope be wound,—that so with pleasure you may hear the Sirens' song. But if you should entreat your men and bid them set you free, let them with still more fetters bind you fast.

"'After your men have brought the ship past these, what is to be your course I will not fully say; do you yourself ponder it in your heart. I will describe both ways. Along one route stand beetling cliffs, and on them roar the mighty waves of dark-eyed Amphitrite; the blessed gods call them the Wanderers. This way not even winged things can pass,—no, not the gentle doves which bear ambrosia to father Zeus; but one of them the smooth rock always draws away, though the father puts another in to fill the number. No ship of man ever escapes when once come hither, but in one common ruin planks of ships and sailors' bodies are swept by the sea-waves and storms of deadly flame. The only coursing ship that ever passed this way was Argo, famed of all, when voyaging from Aeëtes; and her the waves would soon have dashed on the great rocks, but Here brought her through from love of Jason.

"'By the other way there are two crags, one reaching up to the broad heavens with its sharp peak. Clouds gather about it darkly and never float away; light strikes its peak neither in heat nor harvest. No mortal man could clamber up or down it, though twenty hands and feet were his; for the rock is smooth, as it were polished. About the middle of the crag is a dim cave, facing the west and Erebus, the very way where you must steer your rounded ship, glorious Odysseus; and from that rounded ship no lusty youth could with a bow-shot reach the hollow cave. Here Scylla dwells and utters hideous cries; her voice like that of a young dog, and she herself an evil monster. None can behold her and be glad, be it a god who meets her. Twelve feet she has, and all mis-shapen; six necks, exceeding long; on each a frightful head; in these three rows of teeth, stout and close-set, fraught with dark death. As far as the waist she is drawn down within the hollow cave; but she holds forth her heads outside the awful chasm and fishes there, spying around the crag for dolphins, dogfish, or whatever larger creature she may catch, such things as voiceful Amphitrite breeds by thousands. Never could sailors boast of passing her in safety; for with each head she takes a man, snatching him from the dark-bowed ship.

"'The second crag is lower, you will see, Odysseus, and close beside the first; you well might shoot across. On it a fig-tree stands, tall and in leafy bloom, underneath which divine Charybdis sucks the dark water down. For thrice a day she sends it up, and thrice she sucks it down,—a fearful sight! May you not happen to be there when it goes down, for nobody could save you then from ill, not even the Earth-shaker. But swiftly turn your course toward Scylla's crag, and speed the ship along; for surely it is better to miss six comrades from your ship than all together.'

"So she spoke, and answering her, said I: 'Yet, goddess, tell me this in very truth: might I not possibly escape from fell Charybdis, and then beat off the other when she assails my crew?'

"So I spoke, and straight the heavenly goddess answered: 'Foolhardy man! Still bent on war and struggle! Will you not yield even to immortal gods? This is no mortal being, but an immortal woe,—dire, hard, and fierce, and not to be fought down. Courage is nothing; flight is best. For if you arm and linger by the rock, I fear that, issuing forth once more, she may attack you with her many heads and carry off as many men. Therefore with zeal speed on; and call on Force, the mother of this Scylla, who bore her for a bane to humankind; she will restrain her from a second onset.

"'Next, you will reach the island of Thrinacia, where in great numbers feed the kine and the sturdy flocks of the Sun,—seven droves of kine and just as many beautiful flocks of sheep, fifty in each. Of them, no young are born, nor do they ever die. Goddesses are their shepherds, nymphs of fair hair, Phaëthousa and Lampetia, whom to the exalted Sun divine Neaera bore. These their potent mother bore and reared, and sent them to the island of Thrinacia to dwell afar and keep their father's flocks and crook-horned kine. If you leave these unharmed and heed your homeward way, you still may come to Ithaca, though you shall meet with hardship. But if you harm them, then I predict the loss of ship and crew; and even if you yourself escape, late shall you come, in evil plight, with loss of all your crew.'

"Even as she spoke, the gold-throned morning came, and up the island the heavenly goddess went her way; I turned me toward my ship, and called my crew to come on board and loose the cables. Quickly they came, took places at the pins, and sitting in order smote the foaming water with their oars. And for our aid behind our dark-bowed ship came a fair wind to fill our sail, a welcome comrade, sent us by fair-haired

Circe, the mighty goddess, human of speech. When we had done our work at the several ropes about the ship, we sat us down, while wind and helmsman kept her steady.

"Now to my men, with aching heart, I said: 'My friends, it is not right for only one or two to know the oracles which Circe told, that heavenly goddess. Therefore I speak, that, knowing all, we so may die, or fleeing death and doom, we may escape. She warns us first against the marvelous Sirens, and bids us flee their voice and flowery meadow. Only myself she bade to hear their song; but bind me with galling cords, to hold me firm, upright upon the mast-block,—round it let the rope be wound. And if I should entreat you, and bid you set me free, thereat with still more fetters bind me fast.'

"Thus I, relating all my tale, talked with my comrades. Meanwhile our stanch ship swiftly neared the Sirens' island; a fair wind swept her on. On a sudden the wind ceased; there came a breathless calm; Heaven hushed the waves. My comrades, rising, furled the sail, stowed it on board the hollow ship, then sitting at their oars whitened the water with the polished blades. But I with my sharp sword cut a great cake of wax into small bits, which I then kneaded in my sturdy hands. Soon the wax warmed, forced by the powerful pressure and by the rays of the exalted Sun, the lord of all. Then one by one I stopped the ears of all my crew; and on the deck they bound me hand and foot, upright upon the mast-block, round which they wound the rope; and sitting down they smote the foaming water with their oars. But when we were as far away as one can call and driving swiftly onward, our speeding ship, as it drew near, did not escape the Sirens, and thus they lifted up their penetrating voice:

"'Come hither, come, Odysseus, whom all praise, great glory of the Achaeans! Bring in your ship, and listen to our song. For none has ever passed us in a black-hulled ship till from our lips he heard ecstatic song, then went his way rejoicing and with larger knowledge. For we know all that on the plain of Troy Argives and Trojans suffered at the gods' behest; we know whatever happens on the bounteous earth.'

"So spoke they, sending forth their glorious song, and my heart longed to listen. Knitting my brows, I signed my men to set me free; but bending forward, on they rowed. And straightway Perimedes and Eurylochus arose and laid upon me still more cords and drew them tighter. Then, after passing by, when we could hear no more the Sirens' voice nor any singing, quickly my trusty crew removed the wax with which I stopped their ears, and set me free from bondage.

"Soon after we left the island, I observed a smoke, I saw high waves and heard a plunging sound. From the hands of my frightened men down fell the oars, and splashed against the current. There the ship stayed, for they worked the tapering oars no more. Along the ship I passed, inspiriting my men with cheering words, standing by each in turn:

"'Friends, hitherto we have not been untried in danger. Here is no greater danger than when the Cyclops penned us with brutal might in the deep cave. Yet out of that, through energy of mine, through will and wisdom, we escaped. These dangers, too, I think some day we shall remember. Come then, and what I say let us all follow. You with your oars strike the deep breakers of the sea, while sitting at the pins, and see if Zeus will set us free from present death and let us go in safety. And, helmsman, these are my commands for you; lay them to heart, for you control the rudders of our hollow ship: keep the ship off that smoke and surf and hug the crags, or else, before you know it, she may veer off that way, and you will bring us into danger.'

"So I spoke, and my words they quickly heeded. But Scylla I did not name,—that hopeless horror,—for fear through fright my men might cease to row, and huddle all together in the hold. I disregarded too the hard behest of Circe, when she had said I must by no means arm. Putting on my glittering armor and taking in my hands my two long spears, I went upon the ship's fore-deck, for thence I looked for the first sight of Scylla of the rock, who brought my men disaster. Nowhere could I descry her; I tired my eyes with searching up and down the dusky cliff.

"So up the straight we sailed in sadness; for here lay Scylla, and there divine Charybdis fearfully sucked the salt sea-water down. Whenever she belched it forth, like a kettle in fierce flame all would foam swirling up, and overhead spray fell upon the tops of both the crags. But when she gulped the salt sea-water down, then all within seemed in a whirl; the rock around roared fearfully, and down below the bottom showed, dark with the sand. Pale terror seized my men; on her we looked and feared to die.

"And now it was that Scylla snatched from the hollow ship six of my comrades who were best in skill and strength. Turning my eyes toward my swift ship to seek my men, I saw their feet and hands already in the air as they were carried up. They screamed aloud and called my name for the last time, in agony of heart. As when a fisher, on a jutting rock, with long rod throws a bait to lure the little fishes, casting into the deep the horn of stall-fed ox; then, catching a fish, flings it ashore writhing; even so were these drawn writhing up the rocks. There at her door she ate them, loudly shrieking and stretching forth their hands in mortal pangs toward me. That was the saddest sight my eyes have ever seen, in all my toils, searching the ocean pathways.

"Now after we had passed the rocks of dire Charybdis and of Scylla, straight we drew near the pleasant island of the god. Here were the goodly broad-browed kine and the many sturdy flocks of the exalted

Sun. While still at sea, on the black ship, I heard the lowing of stalled cattle and the bleat of sheep; and on my mind fell words of the blind prophet, Teiresias of Thebes, and of Aeaean Circe, who very strictly charged me to shun the island of the Sun, the cheerer of mankind. So to my men with aching heart I said:

"'My suffering comrades, hearken to my words, that I may tell you of the warnings of Teiresias, and of Aeaean Circe, who very strictly charged me to shun the island of the Sun, the cheerer of mankind; for there our deadliest danger lay, she said. Then past the island speed the black ship on her way.'

"As I spoke thus, their very souls were crushed within them, and instantly Eurylochus, with surly words, made answer: 'Headstrong are you, Odysseus; more than man's is your mettle, and your limbs never tire; and yet you must be made of nothing else than iron not to allow your comrades, worn with fatigue and sleep, to land, though on this sea-girt island we might make once more a savory supper. Instead, just as we are, night falling fast, you bid us journey on and wander from the island over the misty deep. But in the night rough winds arise, fatal to vessels; and how could any one escape from utter ruin if by some chance a sudden storm of wind should come, the south wind or the blustering west, which wreck ships oftentimes, heedless of sovereign gods? No, let us now obey the dark night's bidding, let us prepare our supper and rest by the black ship; to-morrow morning we will embark and sail the open sea.'

"So spoke Eurylochus, the rest assented, and then I knew some god intended ill; and speaking in winged words I said:

"'Eurylochus, plainly you force me, since I am only one. But come, all swear me now a solemn oath that if we find a herd of cattle or great flock of sheep, none in mad willfulness will slay a cow or sheep; but be content, and eat the food immortal Circe gave.'

"So I spoke, and they then took the oath which I required. And after they had sworn and ended all their oath, we moored our stanch ship in the rounded harbor, near a fresh stream, and my companions left the ship and busily got supper. But after they had stayed desire for drink and food, then calling to remembrance their dear comrades, they wept for those whom Scylla ate, those whom she snatched from out the hollow ship; and as they wept, on them there came a pleasant sleep. Now when it was the third watch of the night and the stars crossed the zenith, cloud-gathering Zeus sent forth a furious wind in a fierce tempest, and covered with his clouds both land and sea; night broke from heaven. And when the early rosy-fingered dawn appeared, we beached our ship, hauling her up into a hollow cave where there were pretty dancing-grounds and haunts for nymphs. Then holding a council, I said to all my men:

"'Friends, there is food and drink enough on the swift ship; let us then spare the kine, for fear we come to harm, for these are the herds and sturdy flocks of a dread god, the Sun, who all things oversees, all overhears.'

"So I spoke, and their hearts assented. But all that month incessant south winds blew; there came no wind except from east and south. So long as they had bread and ruddy wine, they spared the kine, because they loved their lives. But when the vessel's stores were now all spent, and roaming perforce they sought for game,—for fish, for fowl, for what might come to hand, caught by their crooked hooks,—and hunger pinched their bellies, then I departed by myself far up the island, to beg the gods to show my homeward way. And when by a walk across the island I had escaped my crew, I washed my hands where there was shelter from the breeze, and offered prayer to all the gods that hold Olympus. But they poured down sweet sleep upon my eyelids, while Eurylochus began his evil counsel to my crew:

"'My suffering comrades, hearken to my words. Hateful is every form of death to wretched mortals; and yet to die by hunger, and so to meet one's doom, is the most pitiful of all. Come then, and let us drive away the best of the Sun's kine, and sacrifice them to the immortals who hold the open sky. And if we ever come to Ithaca, our native land, we will at once build a rich temple to the exalted Sun, and put therein many fair offerings. If then the Sun, wroth for his high-horned kine, seeks to destroy our ship, and other gods consent, for my part I would rather, open-mouthed in the sea, give up my life at once than slowly let it wear away here in this desert island.'

"So spoke Eurylochus; the rest assented. Forthwith they drove away the best of the Sun's kine out of the field close by; for not far from the dark-bowed ship the kine were grazing, crook-horned and beautiful and broad of brow. Round them they stood and prayed the gods, stripping the tender leaves from off a lofty oak; for they had no white barley on the well-benched ship. Then after prayer, when they had cut the throats and flayed the kine, they cut away the thighs, wrapped them in fat in double layers, and placed raw flesh thereon. They had no wine to pour upon the blazing victims, but using water for libation they roasted all the entrails. So after the thighs were burned and the inward parts were tasted, they sliced the rest and stuck it on the spits.

"And now the pleasant sleep fled from my eyelids; I hastened to the swift ship and the shore. But on my way, as I drew near to the curved ship, around me came the savory smell of fat. I groaned and called aloud to the immortal gods:

"'O father Zeus, and all you other blessed gods that live forever, verily to my ruin you laid me in ruthless sleep, while my men left behind plotted a monstrous deed.'

"Soon to the exalted Sun came long-robed Lampetia, bearing him word that we had slain his kine; and straightway with an angry heart he thus invoked the immortals:

"'O father Zeus, and all you other blessed gods that live forever, avenge me on the comrades of Laërtes' son, Odysseus, who insolently slew the kine in which I joy as I go forth into the starry sky, or as again toward earth I turn back from the sky. But if they do not make me fit atonement for the kine, I will go down to Hades and shine among the dead.'

"Then answered him cloud-gathering Zeus, and said: 'O Sun, do you shine on among the immortals and on the fruitful fields of mortal men. Soon I will smite their swift ship with a gleaming bolt, and cleave it in pieces in the middle of the wine-dark sea.'

"All this I heard from fair-haired Calypso, who said she heard it from the Guide-god Hermes.

"Now when I came to the ship and to the sea, I chid my men, confronting each in turn. But no help could we find; the kine were dead already. Soon too the gods made prodigies appear: the skins would crawl; the spitted flesh, both roast and raw, would moan; and sounds came forth like those of kine.

"For six days afterwards my trusty comrades feasted, for they had driven away the best of the Sun's kine; but when Zeus, the son of Kronos, brought the seventh day round, then the wind ceased to blow a gale, and we in haste embarking put forth on the open sea, setting our mast and hoisting the white sail.

"Yet when we had left the island and no other land appeared, but only sky and sea, the son of Kronos set a dark cloud over the hollow ship and the deep gloomed below. The ship ran on for no long time; for soon a shrill west wind arose, blowing a heavy gale. The storm of wind snapped both the forestays of the mast. Back the mast fell, and all its gear lay scattered in the hold. At the ship's stern it struck the helmsman on the head and crushed his skull, all in an instant; like a diver from the deck he dropped, and from his frame the strong life fled. Zeus at the same time thundered, hurling his bolt against the ship. She quivered in every part, struck by the bolt of Zeus, and filled with sulphur smoke. Out of the ship my comrades fell and then like sea-fowl were borne by the side of the black ship along the waves; God cut them off from coming home.

"I myself paced the ship until the surge tore her ribs off the keel, which the waves then carried along dismantled. The mast broke at the keel; but to it clung the backstay, made of ox-hide. With this I bound the two together, keel and mast, and getting a seat on these, I drifted before the deadly winds.

"And now the west wind ceased to blow a gale; but soon the south wind came and brought me anguish that I must measure back my way to fell Charybdis. All night I drifted on, and with the sunrise I came to Scylla's crag and dire Charybdis. She at that moment sucked the salt sea-water down; and when to the tall fig-tree I was upward borne, I clutched and clung as a bat clings. Yet could I nowhere set my feet firmly down or climb the tree; for its roots were far away and out of reach its branches, and these were long and large, and overspread Charybdis. But steadily I clung, until she should disgorge my mast and keel; and as I hoped they came, though it was late. But at the hour one rises from the assembly for his supper, after deciding many quarrels of contentious men, then was it that the timbers came to light from out Charybdis. I let go feet and hands, and down I dropped by the long timbers, and getting a seat on these rowed onward with my hands. But the father of men and gods gave me no further sight of Scylla, or else I should not have escaped from utter ruin.

"Thence for nine days I drifted; on the tenth, at night, gods brought me to the island of Ogygia, where dwells Calypso, a fair-haired powerful goddess, human of speech. She welcomed me and gave me care. Why tell the tale? It was but yesterday I told it in the hall to you and your good wife; and it is irksome to tell a plain-told tale a second time."

XIII.

FROM PHAEACIA TO ITHACA

As HE thus ended, all were hushed to silence, held by the spell through-out the dusky hall. At length, Alcinoüs answering said: "Odysseus, having crossed the brazen threshold of my high-roofed house, you shall be aided home with no more wanderings, be sure, long as you now have suffered. And this I say with earnestness to everybody here, to you who in my hall drink of the elders' sparkling wine and listen to the bard: you know that in a polished chest lie garments for the stranger, with rich-wrought gold and all the other gifts which the Phaeacian councilors have brought him hither. But let us also, each man here, give a caldron and large tripod; then gathering the cost among the people, we will repay ourselves. For one to give outright were hard indeed."

So said Alcinoüs, and his saying pleased them; and now desiring rest, they each departed homeward. But when the early rosy-fingered dawn appeared, they hastened to the ship and brought the gladdening bronze. Revered Alcinoüs, going himself aboard the vessel, stowed it all carefully beneath the benches, so that it might not incommode the crew upon the passage while they labored at the oars. Then to Alcinoüs' house they went and turned to feasting.

In their behalf revered Alcinoüs offered an ox to Zeus of the dark cloud, the son of Kronos, who is the lord of all; and having burned the thighs, they held a glorious feast and made them merry. Among them sang the sacred bard, Demodocus, beloved of all. Nevertheless Odysseus would often turn his face toward the still shining sun, eager to see its setting, because he was impatient to be gone. As a man longs for supper whose pair of tawny oxen all day long have dragged the jointed plough through the fresh field; gladly for him the sunlight sinks and sends him home to supper; stiff are his knees for walking; so gladly for Odysseus sank the sun. Straightway he turned to the oar-loving Phaeacians, and speaking to Alcinoüs especially he said:

"Mighty Alcinoüs, renowned of all, pour a libation and send me safely forth. Fare you all well! All that my heart desired is ready—escort and friendly gifts—and may the gods of heaven make them a blessing! My true wife may I find on coming home, and dear ones safe! And you who stay, may you make glad your wedded wives and children! The gods bestow all happiness, and may no ill be found among you!"

He spoke, and all approved and bade send forth the stranger, for rightly had he spoken. Then said revered Alcinoüs to the page: "Pontonoüs, mix a bowl and pass the wine to all within the hall, that with a prayer to father Zeus we may send forth the stranger to his native land."

He spoke; Pontonoüs stirred the cheering wine and served to all in turn; then to the blessed gods who hold the open sky they poured libations where they sat. But royal Odysseus rose, placed in Arete's hand the double cup, and speaking in winged words he said:

"Fare you well, queen, for all the years until old age and death, which visit all, shall come. I go my way; may you within this home enjoy your children, people, and Alcinoüs the king!"

So saying, royal Odysseus crossed the threshold. With him revered Alcinoüs sent a page, to show the way to the swift ship and to the shore. Arete too sent damsels after: one with the spotless robe and tunic, one to accompany the close-packed chest, and one bore bread and ruddy wine.

Now when they came to the ship and to the sea, straight the tall seamen took the stores and laid them by within the hollow ship, even all the food and drink. Then for Odysseus they spread a rug and linen sheet on the hollow vessel's deck, so that he might sleep soundly, there at the stern; and he himself embarked and laid him down in silence. The other men took places at the pins, each one in order, and loosed the cable from the perforated stone. But now when bending to their work they tossed the water with their oars, upon Odysseus' lids deep slumber fell, sound and most pleasant, very like to death. And as upon a plain four harnessed stallions spring forward all together at the crack of whip, and lifting high their feet speed swiftly on their way; even so the ship's stern lifted, while in her wake followed a huge upheaving wave of the resounding sea. Safely and steadily she ran; no circling hawk, swiftest of winged things, could keep beside her. Running thus rapidly she cut the ocean waves, bearing a man of godlike wisdom, a man who had before met many griefs of heart, cleaving his way through wars of men and through the boisterous seas, yet here slept undisturbed, heedless of all he suffered.

As that most brilliant star arose which comes the surest herald of the light of early dawn, the sea-borne ship drew near the island.

Now in the land of Ithaca there is a certain harbor sacred to Phorcys, the old man of the sea. Here two projecting jagged cliffs slope inward toward the harbor and break the heavy waves raised by wild winds without. Inside, without a cable ride the well-benched ships when once they reach the roadstead. Just at the harbor's head a leafy olive stands, and near it a pleasant darksome cave sacred to nymphs, called Naiads. Within the cave are bowls and jars of stone, and here bees hive their honey. Long looms of stone are here, where nymphs weave purple robes, a marvel to behold. Here are ever-flowing springs. The cave has double doors: one to the north, accessible to men; one to the south, for gods. By this, men do not pass; it is the immortals' entrance.

Here they rowed in, knowing the place of old. The ship ran up the shore full half her length, by reason of her speed; so was she driven by her rowers' arms. The men then left the timbered ship and came ashore, and straightway took Odysseus from the hollow ship—him and his linen sheet and bright-hued rug—and set him on the sands, still sunk in sleep. They also brought the treasure out which the Phaeacian chiefs gave him at his departure, prompted by kind Athene, and laid it all together by the olive trunk a little off the road; for fear, before Odysseus woke, some passer-by might come and harm it. Then they departed homeward. Nevertheless the Earth-shaker did not forget the threats with which at first he threatened great Odysseus, but thus he asked the purposes of Zeus:

"O father Zeus, no more shall I be honored among immortal gods if mortal men, the people of Phaeacia, honor me not, though men of my own kin. For I had meant that through much hardship Odysseus should return; I never tried to cut him off from coming altogether, because you gave him once a promise and confirmed it with a nod. Yet these Phaeacians have borne him through the sea on their swift ship asleep, and set him down in Ithaca, and given him glorious gifts—such stores of bronze and gold and woven stuffs as Odysseus never would have won from Troy itself, had he returned unharmed with his due share of spoil."

Then answered him cloud-gathering Zeus and said: "For shame, wide-ruling Land-shaker! What are you saying? The gods do not refuse you honor. Hard would it be to cast dishonor on our oldest and our best. And as to men, if any, led by pride and power, dishonors you, vengeance is yours and shall be ever. Do what you will, even all your heart's desire!"

Then earth-shaking Poseidon answered: "Soon would I do, dark-clouded one, all that you say, but that I ever dread and would avoid your wrath. Even now this shapely ship of the Phaeacians, returning home from pilotage upon the misty sea, I would destroy,—that they henceforth may hold aloof and cease to give men aid,—and I would throw a lofty mound about their city."

Then answered him cloud-gathering Zeus and said: "Friend, this appears to me the better way. When all the people of the town look off and see her sailing, then turn her into stone close to the shore,—yet like a swift ship still,—that all the folk may marvel, and throw a lofty mound about their city."

On hearing this, earth-shaking Poseidon hastened to Scheria, where the Phaeacians live, and waited there. Then as the sea-borne ship drew near, running full swiftly, the Earth-shaker drew near her too, turned her to stone and rooted her to the bottom, forcing her under with his outspread hand, and went away; but in winged words to one another talked the Phaeacian oarsmen, notable men at sea. And glancing at his neighbor a Phaeacian man would say:

"Hah! Who stopped the swift ship on the sea as she was running in? In full sight too she was."

So they would say, but knew not how things were. And now Alcinoüs addressed them thus: "Ah, surely then the ancient oracles are come to pass, told by my father, who said Poseidon was displeased because we were safe guides for all mankind; and he averred the god one day would wreck a shapely ship of the Phaeacians, returning home from pilotage upon the misty sea, and so would throw a lofty mound about our city. That was the old man's tale, and now it all comes true. However, what I say let us all follow: stop piloting the men who come from time to time here to our city; and to Poseidon let us offer twelve choice bulls, that he may have compassion and so not throw a lofty mound about our city."

He spoke, and all the people feared and brought the bulls. And then to lord Poseidon, standing around his altar, the captains and councilors of the Phaeacians offered prayer.

Meanwhile within his native land royal Odysseus woke from sleep, and did not know the land from which he had been gone so long; for a goddess spread a cloud around, even Pallas Athene, daughter of Zeus, that she might render him unknown and herself tell him all, and that his wife, his townsfolk, and his friends might never know him until the suitors paid the price of all their lawless deeds. Thus to its master all the land looked strange,—the footpaths stretching far away, the sheltered coves, steep rocks, and spreading trees. Rising, he stood and gazed upon his land, then groaned and smote his thighs with outspread hands, saying in anguish:

"Alas! To what men's land am I come now? Lawless and savage are they, with no regard for right, or are they kind to strangers and reverent toward the gods? Where shall I leave my many goods, and whither shall

I turn? Would these had staid with the Phaeacians where they were, and I myself had found some other powerful prince who might have entertained me and sent me on my way! Now, where to store my goods I do not know; yet here I must not leave them, to fall a prey to strangers. Not at all wise and just were the Phaeacian captains and councilors in bringing me to this strange shore. They promised they would carry me to far-seen Ithaca, but that they did not do. May Zeus, the god of suppliants, reward them! For over all men watches Zeus, chastising those who sin. However, let me count my goods, and see that the Phaeacians took none away upon their hollow ship."

So saying, he counted the beautiful tripods, the caldrons, gold, and goodly woven stuffs, and none was lacking. Then sighing for his native land he paced the shore of the resounding sea in sadness. Near him Athene drew, in form of a young shepherd, yet delicate as are the sons of kings. Doubled about her shoulders she wore a fine-wrought mantle; under her shining feet her sandals, and in her hand a spear. To see her made Odysseus glad. He went to meet her, and speaking in winged words he said:

"Friend, since you are the first I find within this land, I bid you welcome, and hope you come with no ill-will. Nay, save these goods and save me too! I supplicate you as a god, and I approach your knees. And tell me truly this, that I may know full well, what land is this? What people? What sort of men dwell here? Is it a far-seen island, or a tongue of fertile mainland that stretches out to sea?"

Then said to him the goddess, clear-eyed Athene: "You are simple, stranger, or come from far away, to ask about this land. It is not quite so nameless. Many men know it well, men dwelling toward the east and rising sun, and those behind us also toward the darksome west. It is a rugged land, not fit for driving horses, yet not so very poor though lacking plains. Grain grows abundantly and wine as well; the showers are frequent and the dews refreshing; here is good pasturage for goats and cattle; trees of all kinds are here, and never-failing springs. So, stranger, the name of Ithaca has gone as far as Troy, which is, they say, a long way from Achaea."

She spoke, and glad was long-tried royal Odysseus, filled with delight over his native land through what was said by Pallas Athene, daughter of ægis-bearing Zeus; and speaking in winged words he said,—yet uttered not the truth, but turned his words awry, ever revolving in his breast some gainful purpose:

"In lowland Crete, I heard of Ithaca far off beyond the sea, and now I reach it—I and these goods of mine. I left an equal portion to my children and fled away from home; for I had killed the dear son of Idomeneus, Orsilochus, the runner, who on the plains of Crete beat all us toiling men in speed of foot. The cause was this: he sought to cut me off from all the Trojan spoil to gain which I bore grief of heart, cleaving my way through wars of men and through the boisterous seas; and all because I did not, as he wished, serve with his father in the land of Troy, but led my separate men. With a brazen spear I struck him as he was coming from his farm and I was lying with a comrade near the road. A very dark night screened the sky; no man observed us; secretly I took his life. So after I had slain him with my brazen pointed spear, I straightway sought a ship, asked aid of the proud Phoenicians, and gave them from my booty what they wished. I bade them take me on their ship and set me down at Pylos, or else at sacred Elis where the Epeians rule. But stress of wind turned them aside, though much against their will; they meant no wrong; and missing our course, here we arrived last night. With much ado we rowed into the port, and gave no thought to supper, hungry although we were, but simply disembarking from the ship, we all lay down. Then, weary as I was, sweet sleep came on me; and the Phoenicians, taking my treasure from the hollow ship, laid it upon the sands where I was lying, and they embarked and sailed away to stately Sidon. So I was left behind with aching heart."

As he thus spoke, the goddess, clear-eyed Athene, smiled and patted him with her hand. Her form grew like a woman's,—one fair and tall and skilled in dainty work,—and speaking in winged words she said:

"Prudent and wily must one be to overreach you in craft of any kind, even though it be a god who strives to match you. Bold, shifty, and insatiate of wiles, will you not now within your land cease from the false misleading tales which from the bottom of your heart you love? But let us talk no longer thus, both being versed in wiles; for you are far the best of men in plots and tales, and I of all the gods am famed for craft and wiles. And yet you did not know me, Pallas Athene, daughter of Zeus, me who am ever near to guard you in all toil, me who have made you welcome to all Phaeacian folk! Now I am come to frame with you a scheme to hide the treasure which the Phaeacian chiefs, through my advice and prompting, gave you at your departure; and I will tell you too what griefs you must endure within your stately house. Bear them, because you must. Do not report to man or woman of them all that you are come from wandering; but silently receive all pains and bear men's buffets."

Then wise Odysseus answered her and said: "Hard is it, goddess, for a man, however wise he be, to know when you are near, because you take all forms. I very well remember how kind to me you were when all we young Achaeans were in the war at Troy. But since we overthrew the lofty town of Priam, since we went away in ships and God dispersed the Achaeans, I never once have seen you, daughter of Zeus, nor known you to draw near my ship protecting me from harm. Yet bearing ever in my breast a stricken heart, I wandered till the gods delivered me from ill, when in the rich land of the Phaeacians you cheered me by your words and led me to the city. Now I entreat you by your father's name, for I cannot think that I am come to far-seen Ithaca. No, I have strayed to some strange shore, and you in mockery, I think, have told this tale to cheat me. But tell me, have I really reached my own dear land?"

Then answered him the goddess, clear-eyed Athene: "Such thoughts as these are ever in your breast; therefore I cannot leave you even in misfortune, because you are discreet, wary, and steadfast. For any other man on coming back from wanderings would eagerly have hastened home to see his wife and children; but you have no desire to know or hear of them till you have proved your wife, who as of old sits in your hall and wearily the nights and days are wasted with her tears. But I for my part never doubted. I knew within my heart that you would come, though with the loss of all your men. But I did not wish to quarrel with Poseidon, my father's brother, who bore a grudge against you in his heart, angry because you blinded his dear son. Come then, and let me point you out the parts of Ithaca, that so you may believe. Here is the port of Phorcys, the old man of the sea; here at the harbor's head the leafy olive; and near at hand the pleasant darksome cave, sacred to nymphs called Naiads; here is the arching cavern too, where oftentimes you made due sacrifices to the nymphs; and this is the wood-clad hill of Neriton."

The goddess, speaking thus, scattered the cloud, and plain the land appeared. Then glad was long-tried royal Odysseus, and he exulted in his land and kissed the bounteous earth, and straightway prayed the nymphs with outstretched hands:

"O Naiad Nymphs, daughters of Zeus, I said I should not see you any more, yet now with loving prayers I give you greeting. Gifts will we also give, even as of old, if the daughter of Zeus, the Plunderer, graciously grants me life and prospers my dear son."

Then said to him the goddess, clear-eyed Athene: "Be of good courage! Let not these things vex your mind! But in a corner of the monstrous cave let us lay by the goods, instantly, now, here to remain in safety; then let us plan how all may turn out well."

So saying, the goddess entered the darksome cave, and searched about the cave for hiding-places. Odysseus too brought hither all he had, gold and enduring bronze and fair-wrought raiment, things given by the Phaeacians. All these were laid away with care, and at the entrance a stone was set by Pallas Athene, daughter of ægis-bearing Zeus. Then sitting down at the foot of the sacred olive, they planned the death of the audacious suitors; and thus began the goddess, clear-eyed Athene:

"High-born son of Laërtes, ready Odysseus, consider how to lay hands on the shameless suitors, who for three years have held dominion in your hall, wooing your matchless wife and offering bridal gifts; while she, continually mourning at heart over your coming, gives hopes to all, has promises for each, and sends each messages; but her mind has a different purpose."

Then wise Odysseus answered her and said: "Certainly here at home I too had met the evil fate of Agamemnon, the son of Atreus, had you not, goddess, duly told me all. Come then, and frame a plot for me to win revenge. And do you stand beside me, inspiring hardy courage, even so as when we tore the shining crown from Troy. If you would stand as stoutly by me, clear-eyed one, then I would face three hundred men, mated with you, dread goddess, with you for my strong aid."

Then answered him the goddess, clear-eyed Athene: "I surely will be with you; you shall never be forgot when we begin the work. Some too, I think, shall spatter with their blood and brains the spacious floor, some of these suitors who devour your living. But let me make you strange to all men's view. I will shrivel the fair flesh on your supple limbs, pluck from your head the yellow locks, and clothe you in such rags that they who see shall loathe the wearer. And I will blear your eyes, so beautiful before, that you may seem repulsive to all the suitors here, and even to your wife and the son you left at home. But first seek out the swineherd, the keeper of your swine; for he is loyal, loving your son and steadfast Penelope. You will find him sitting by his swine. They feed along the Raven Crag by the spring of Arethusa, eating the pleasant acorns and drinking the shaded water, a food which breeds abundant fat in swine. There wait, and sitting by his side question him fully; while I go on to Sparta, the land of lovely women, to summon thence Telemachus, your son, Odysseus. He went to spacious Lacedaemon to visit Menelaus, hoping to learn if you were still alive."

Then wise Odysseus answered her and said: "Why, knowing all, did you yourself not tell him? Must he too meet with sorrow, roaming the barren sea, while others eat his substance?"

Then answered him the goddess, clear-eyed Athene: "Nay, let him not too much oppress your heart. I was myself his guide, and helped him win a noble name by going thither. He meets no hardship there, but sits at ease within the palace of the son of Atreus, with plenty all around. Young men, indeed, now lie in wait on their black ship and seek to cut him off before he gains his native land. Yet this I think shall never be; rather the earth shall cover some of the suitors who devour your living."

So having said, Athene touched him with her wand, shriveled the fair flesh on his supple limbs, plucked from his head the yellow locks, and made the skin of all his limbs the skin of an old man. Likewise she bleared his eyes, so beautiful before, and gave him for his clothing a wretched frock and tunic, tattered and foul and grimed with filthy smoke. Then over all she threw a swift deer's ample hide, stripped of its hair; and gave him a staff and miserable wallet, full of holes, which hung upon a cord.

So having formed their plans, they parted; and thereupon the goddess went to sacred Lacedaemon, seeking Odysseus' son.

XIV.

THE STAY WITH EUMAEUS

BUT FROM the harbor, up the rock path, along the woody country on the hills, Odysseus went to where Athene bade him seek the noble swineherd, who guarded his estate more carefully than any man royal Odysseus owned.

He found him sitting in his porch, by which was built a high-walled yard upon commanding ground, a handsome yard and large, with space around. With his own hands the swineherd built it for the swine after his lord was gone, without assistance from the queen or old Laërtes, constructing it with blocks of stone and coping it with thorn. Outside the yard he drove down stakes the whole way round, stout and close-set, of split black oak. Inside the yard he made twelve sties alongside one another, as bedding places for the swine; and fifty swine that wallow in the mire were penned in each, all of them sows for breeding; the boars, much fewer, lay outside. On these the gallant suitors feasted and kept their number small; for daily the swineherd sent away the best fat hog he had. Three hundred and sixty they were now. Hard by, four dogs, like wild beasts, always lay, dogs which the swineherd bred, the overseer. He was himself now fitting sandals to his feet, cutting therefor a well-tanned hide. The other men were gone their several ways: three with the swine to pasture; a fourth sent to the town to take to the audacious suitors, as was ordered, a hog to slay and sate their souls with meat.

But now the ever-barking dogs suddenly spied Odysseus, and baying rushed upon him; whereat Odysseus calmly sat down and from his hand let fall his staff. Yet here at his own farm he would have come to cruel grief, had not the swineherd, springing swiftly after, dashed from the door and from his hand let fall the leather. Scolding the dogs, he drove them off this way and that with showers of stones, and thus addressed his master:

"Old man, my dogs had nearly torn you to pieces here all of a sudden, and so you would have brought reproach on me. Ah well! The gods have given me other griefs and sorrows; for over my matchless master I sit and sigh and groan, and tend fat hogs for other men to eat; while he, perhaps longing for food, wanders about the lands and towns of men of alien speech,—if he still lives and sees the sunshine. But follow me, old man, into the lodge; so that you too, when satisfied with food and drink, may tell where you are come from and what troubles you have borne."

So saying, to the lodge the noble swineherd led the way, and bringing Odysseus in made him a seat. Beneath, he laid thick brushwood, and on the top he spread a shaggy wild goat's great soft skin, his usual bed. Odysseus was pleased that he received him so, and spoke and thus addressed him:

"Stranger, may Zeus and the other deathless gods grant all you most desire for treating me so kindly!"

And, swineherd Eumaeus, you answered him and said: "Stranger, it is not right for me to slight a stranger, not even one in poorer plight than you; for in the charge of Zeus all strangers and beggars stand, and our small gift is welcome. But so it is with servants, continually afraid when new men are their masters! Surely the gods kept him from coming who would have loved me well and given me for my own the things a generous master always allows his man—a house, a plot of ground, and a fair wife—at least when one has labored long, and God has made his work prosper, as he makes prosper all the work I undertake. So would my master have well rewarded me, had he but grown old here. But he is gone! Would all the tribe of Helen had gone too, down on their knees! for she has made the knees of many men grow weak. Yes, he too went for Agamemnon's honor to Ilios, famed for horses, to fight the Trojans there."

So saying, he hurriedly girt his tunic with his belt, and went to the sties where droves of pigs were penned. Selecting two, he brought them in and killed them both, singed them and sliced them and stuck them on the spits, and roasting carried all the meat to offer to Odysseus, hot on the spits themselves. He sprinkled it with white barley. Then in an ivy bowl he mixed some honeyed wine, and taking a seat over against Odysseus thus cheerily began:

"Now, stranger, eat what servants have, this young pig's flesh. The fatted hogs are eaten by the suitors, who heed not in their hearts the wrath of Heaven, nor even pity. Yet reckless deeds the blessed gods love not; they honor justice and man's upright deeds. Why, evil-minded

cruel men who land on a foreign shore, and Zeus allows them plunder
so that they sail back home with well-filled ships, — even on the hearts
of such falls a great fear of heavenly wrath. But these men know of
something, having heard the utterance of some god about his mournful end, and therefore they are minded to woo so lawlessly, never
departing to their homes, but at their ease wasting this wealth with recklessness and sparing naught. For every day and night sent us by Zeus,
they slay their victims, no mere one or two; and wine they also waste
with reckless draughts. Odysseus' means were vast. No noble has so
much on the dark mainland or in Ithaca itself. No twenty men together
have such revenues as he. I will reckon up the sum. Twelve herds upon
the mainland; as many flocks of sheep; as many droves of swine; as
many roving bands of goats; all shepherded by foreigners and herdsmen
of his own. Then here in Ithaca graze roving bands of goats, eleven in
all, along the farther shore, and trusty herdsmen watch them. Of these
the herdsman every day drives up the fatted goat that seems the best.
My task it is to guard and keep these swine, and picking carefully the
best to send it to the suitors."

So spoke the swineherd, while his companion hungrily ate his meat
and drank with eagerness his wine in silence, sowing the seeds of evil
for the suitors. But after he had dined and stayed his heart with food,
Eumaeus, filling for his guest the cup from which he drank, gave it
brimful of wine. Odysseus took it and was glad at heart, and speaking
in winged words he said:

"My friend, who was the man that bought you with his wealth and
was so very rich and powerful as you say? You said he died for
Agamemnon's honor. Tell me. I may have known some such as he.
Zeus and the other deathless gods must know if I have seen him and
can give you news; but I have traveled far."

Then said to him the swineherd, the overseer: "Old man, no traveler
coming here to tell of him could win his wife or son to trust the story.
Lightly do vagrants seeking hospitality tell lies, and never care to speak
the truth. So when a vagabond reaches the land of Ithaca, he comes
and chatters cheating stories to my queen. And she receives him well
and, giving entertainment, questions him closely, while from her weeping eyelids trickle tears; for that is the way with wives when husbands
die afar. You too, old man, would soon be patching up a story if somebody would give you clothes, a coat and tunic. But probably already
dogs and swift birds have plucked the flesh from off his bones and life
has left him; or fishes devoured him in the deep, and on the land his
bones are lying wrapped in a heap of sand. So he died, far away, and for
his friends sorrow is left behind — for all of them, and most of all for me;
for never another such kind master shall I find, go where I may, not

even if I return to my father's and mother's house, where I was born and where my parents reared me. Yet nowadays for them I do not greatly grieve, much as I wish to see them and to be in my own land; but longing possesses me for lost Odysseus. Why, stranger, though he is not here I speak his name with awe; for he was very kind and loved me from his heart, and worshipful I call him even when he is away."

Then long-tried royal Odysseus answered thus: "Friend, though you wholly contradict and say he will not come, and ever unbelieving is your heart, yet I declare, not with mere words but with an oath, Odysseus will return. Give me the fee for welcome news when he arrives at home. Then clothe me in a coat and tunic, goodly garments. Before that time, however great my need, I will take nothing; for hateful as the gates of hell is he who pressed by poverty tells cheating tales. First then of all the gods be witness Zeus, and let this hospitable table and the hearth of good Odysseus whereto I come be witness: all this shall be accomplished exactly as I say. This very year Odysseus comes. As this moon wanes and as the next appears, he shall return and punish all who wrong his wife and gallant son."

And, swineherd Eumaeus, you answered him and said: "Old man, I never then shall give that fee for welcome news, nor will Odysseus reach his home. Nay, drink in peace. Let us turn to other thoughts, and do not bring such matters to remembrance. Ah, my heart aches within when one recalls my honored master! As for the oath, why let it be; yet may Odysseus come, as I desire!—I and Penelope, Laërtes the old man, and prince Telemachus. But now I have unceasing grief about Odysseus' child, Telemachus; whom when the gods had made to grow like a young sapling, and I would often say that he would stand in men's esteem no whit behind his father, glorious in form and beauty, some god or man upset the balanced mind within, and off he went for tidings of his father to hallowed Pylos. And now the lordly suitors watch for his coming home, hoping to have the race of prince Arceisius blotted from Ithaca and left without a name. However, let us leave him too, whether he falls or flies, or whether the son of Kronos holds over him his arm. But come, old man, relate to me your troubles; and tell me truly this, that I may know full well: Who are you? Of what people? Where is your town and kindred? On what ship did you come? And how did sailors bring you to Ithaca? Whom did they call themselves? For I am sure you did not come on foot."

Then wise Odysseus answered him and said: "Well, I will very plainly tell you this. But had we in the lodge food and sweet wine for long, and should we feast in quiet, letting others do our work, then might I easily not finish in a year the tale of all the toils I bore by the gods' bidding.

"Of a family in lowland Crete I boast that I was born, a rich man's son. There were many sons besides, born and brought up within that hall, sons of a lawful wife. Me a bought mother bore, a concubine; yet he gave me equal honor with his true-begotten sons, this Castor, son of Hylax, whose child I say I am. Among the Cretans he was at this time honored throughout the land as if he were a god, because of his prosperity, his wealth, and famous sons; but death's doom bore him to the house of Hades, and his disdainful sons divided up his living, casting lots. Me they assigned a very meagre share, besides my dwelling. Nevertheless, I took to wife the daughter of a wealthy house, winning her by my merit; because I was no weakling and not afraid of war. Now all is gone. Yet still, when you see stubble I think you know the grain; hardships innumerable have pressed me sore. In those days Ares and Athene gave me courage, and strength to break the line; and when I picked our bravest for an ambush, sowing the seeds of evil for our foes, my swelling heart cast not a look on death; but charging ever foremost, I would catch upon my spear whatever foeman showed less speed than I. Such was I once in war; labor I never liked, nor household thrift, which breeds good children. But ships equipped with oars were ever my delight, battles and polished javelins and arrows—appalling things, which are to others hateful. Whatever God put in my heart I liked; for different men delight in different deeds. Before the young Achaeans went to Troy, nine times I led forth men and sea-bound ships to plunder foreign tribes; and much I gained. Out of the spoil I picked what pleased me and then obtained much afterwards by lot. Thus rapidly my household grew, and I became a man of weight and honor with the Cretans. But when far-seeing Zeus ordained the unhappy journey which made the knees of many men grow weak, they called on me and famed Idomeneus to lead the ships to Ilios. We had no power to say them nay, the people's voice was stern. There for nine years we young Achaeans battled, and in the tenth, destroying the town of Priam, turned homewards with our ships. But God dispersed the Achaeans; especially for hapless me wise Zeus intended ill. Only a month I stayed at home, glad in my children, in my wedded wife and in my goods; and then my heart impelled me to make a voyage to Egypt with gallant comrades and with ships well fitted out. Nine ships I fitted, and my force was gathered soon.

"For six days afterwards my trusty comrades feasted, and I provided many victims to offer to the gods and make my men a feast. Embarking on the seventh, we sailed from lowland Crete, the north wind fresh and fair, and moved off easily as if down stream. No ship met harm; but safe and sound we sat, while wind and helmsmen kept us steady. In five days we arrived at Egypt's flowing stream, and in the Egyptian river I

anchored my curved ships. Then to my trusty men I gave the command to stay there by the ships and guard the ships, while I sent scouts
to points of observation; but giving way to lawlessness and following
their own bent, they presently began to pillage the fair fields of the
Egyptians, carrying off wives and infant children and slaughtering the
men. Soon the din reached the city. The people there, hearing the
shouts, came forth at early dawn, and all the plain was filled with footmen and with horsemen and with the gleam of bronze. Then Zeus, the
thunderer, brought on my men a cruel panic, and none dared stand
and face the foe. Danger encountered us on every side. So the
Egyptians slew many of our men with the sharp sword, and carried others off alive to work for them in bondage. But Zeus himself put in my
heart this plan. Would I had rather died, and met my doom there by
the stream of Egypt! For since that day sorrow has held me fast.
Straightway I took the well-made helmet from my head and shield
from off my shoulders, and flinging away my spear, I ran to meet the
horses of the king. I clasped and kissed his knees; he spared and pitied
me, and seating me in his chariot bore me weeping home. A multitude
with spears rushed after, intent on killing me, for they were much enraged. He held them back, dreading the wrath of Zeus, the stranger's
friend, who ever visits evil deeds with his displeasure. Here I stayed
seven years, and I amassed much wealth among the Egyptians; for they
all gave me gifts. But when the eighth revolving year was come, a certain Phoenician came, full of deceiving arts, a greedy knave, one who
had wrought much harm to men already. He now prevailed upon me
by his wiles, and took me with him till we reached Phoenicia, where
was his home and substance. Here at his house I stayed throughout the
year. But after days and months were spent, as the year rolled and other
seasons came, he set me on a sea-bound ship sailing for Libya, falsely
professing I should share his gains; but purposing to sell me there and
reap a large reward. I followed him on board, suspecting him, but helpless. And now the ship sped on, with north wind fresh and fair, through
the mid sea past Crete, Zeus purposing our ruin.

"For when we had left Crete and no other land appeared, but only
sky and sea, the son of Kronos set a dark cloud over the hollow ship,
and the deep gloomed below. Zeus at the same time thundered, hurling his bolt against the ship. She quivered in every part, struck by the
bolt of Zeus, and filled with sulphur smoke. Out of the ship my comrades fell, and then like sea-fowl were borne by the side of the black
ship along the waves; God cut them off from coming home. But helping me, whose heart was filled with anguish, Zeus put the long mast of
the dark-bowed ship into my hands, so that I might once more escape
from death. To this I clung and drifted before the deadly winds. Nine

days I drifted; on the tenth, in the dark night, the vast and rolling waters cast me on the coast of the Thesprotians. Here the king of the Thesprotians, lord Pheidon, entertained me, and freely too; it was his son who found me, overcome with cold and toil, and took me home, with his own hand supporting me until we reached his father's palace. He gave me also a coat and tunic for my clothing.

"Here, then, I heard about Odysseus; for Pheidon said he had him as his guest and friend upon his homeward voyage. He showed me all the treasure that Odysseus had obtained, the bronze and gold and well-wrought iron; and really it would support man after man ten generations long, so large a stock was stored in the king's palace. Odysseus himself, he said, was gone at that time to Dodona, to learn from the sacred lofty oak the will of Zeus, and how he might return, whether openly or by stealth, to the rich land of Ithaca, when now so long away. Moreover, in my presence, as he offered a libation in his house, he swore the ship was launched and sailors waiting to bring him home to his own native land. But he sent me off before, for a ship of the Thesprotians happened to be starting for the Doulichian grain-fields. He bade her men conduct me carefully to king Acastus; but in their hearts a wicked scheme found favor, to bring me yet once more into the depths of woe. For when the sea-bound ship was far from shore, they planned a life of slavery for me. They stripped me of my clothes, my coat and tunic, and gave instead the wretched frock and the tunic full of holes which you yourself now see. Toward night they reached the fields of far-seen Ithaca. Here with a twisted rope they bound me fast upon the well-benched ship, and disembarking they hastily took supper on the shore. Meanwhile the gods themselves lightly untied my cords; and I, wrapping my frock about my head and sliding down the slippery rudder, brought my breast into the sea, where swimming hard I oared my way with my two hands, and very soon was out of the water, clear of them. Climbing the bank where there were thickets of leafy trees, I laid me down and hid. With loud cries ran the others here and there; but as there seemed no profit in any further search, they entered their hollow ship once more. So the gods with ease concealed me and brought me to this farm of a sagacious man; because it was my lot to live still longer."

Then, swineherd Eumaeus, you answered him and said: "Alas, poor stranger! You have deeply stirred my heart by telling me this tale of all your woes and wanderings. Yet here I think you err: you never can persuade me with talk about Odysseus. Why should a man like you tell lies for nothing? I understand about my master's coming; he has been hated utterly by all the gods, who did not let him die among the Trojans nor in the arms of friends when the skein of war was wound. Then would the whole Achaean host have made his grave, and for his son in after days a great name had been gained. Now, silently the robber winds have swept him off. I, meanwhile, dwell apart among the swine. To the town I never go, unless sometimes heedful Penelope commands my going, when any tidings come. Ah, then the people sit around and closely question, some grieving for their long-gone master, some glad to eat his substance and make him no amends. But as for me, I have no mind to search and question since an Aetolian fellow cheated me with his tale. He killed a man, and wandering far and wide came to my farmstead here, and I received him kindly. He told me how in Crete he saw Odysseus with Idomeneus, mending the ships which storms had shattered. He said he would be here by summer or by harvest, bringing a store of wealth and all his gallant crew. You too, old woe-worn man, now Heaven has brought you here, do not by lying tales attempt to please or win me; since out of no such cause I show respect and kindness, but out of reverence for Zeus the stranger's friend, and pity for yourself."

Then wise Odysseus answered him and said: "Surely in you there is a heart so unbelieving that by an oath I did not move it nor win you to believe. But let us make a covenant now, and for us both hereafter our witnesses shall be the gods who hold Olympus: if ever to this house your master comes, clothe me in coat and tunic and send me to Doulichion, where I desire to be. But if your master does not come, as I declare he will, send out your men and throw me down the lofty cliff, that other beggars may beware of telling lying tales."

Then answering said the noble swineherd: "Stranger, fine fame and fortune would be mine among mankind, both now and evermore, if after I had brought you to the lodge and given you welcome I turned about and slew you and took away your life! With a clear heart thereafter I should pray to Zeus, the son of Kronos! Well, it is supper-time; and may my comrades soon be here to get at the lodge a savory supper!"

So they conversed together. Presently came the swine and those who kept them. They shut them up to sleep in their accustomed sties, and a prodigious noise arose from the penned swine. Then to his comrades called the noble swineherd:—

"Fetch me the best hog hither, to slaughter for the stranger who comes from far away. We too will have some cheer, who for a long time now have plagued ourselves over the white-toothed swine. Others devour our labor and make us no amends."

So saying, with the ruthless axe he cleft some wood. The others brought a boar, well fatted, five years old, and stood him on the hearth; and now the swineherd, being of upright heart, did not forget the immortal gods. At the beginning he cast into the fire hairs from the head of the white-toothed boar, and prayed to all the gods that wise Odysseus might return to his own home. Next raising high a billet of oak, saved when he split the wood, he dealt a blow and the boar's life departed. The others cut the throat and singed the boar, and quickly laid him open. The swineherd then put the raw meat, selected from each joint, into rich fat. Some parts of this, sprinkled with barley meal, they cast into the fire; the rest they sliced and stuck on spits, roasted with care, drew it all off, and tossed it all together on the trenchers. And now the swineherd rose to carve,—for well he knew his duties,—and as he carved divided all in seven messes. The first mess for the Nymphs and Hermes, Maia's son, he set aside with prayer, passing the rest to each. Odysseus he honored with the whole length of the chine, cut from the white-toothed boar, and so rejoiced his master's heart. Addressing him, said wise Odysseus:

"Eumaeus, may you be as dear to father Zeus as now to me, for honoring with kindness such as I."

And, swineherd Eumaeus, you answered him and said: "Good stranger, eat; enjoy what lies before you! God gives and God withholds, as is his pleasure. His power is over all."

He spoke and burned the consecrated pieces to the ever-living gods; then pouring sparkling wine, he put the cup into the hands of city-sacking Odysseus, and took his seat by his own portion. Mesaulius passed them bread, a man the swineherd had acquired after his lord was gone, without assistance from the queen or lord Laërtes; with his own means he bought him of the Taphians. So on the food spread out before them they laid hands. Then after they had stayed desire for drink and food, Mesaulius took away the bread; and so to sleep, sated with bread and meat, they hastened.

And now the night came on, moonless and foul. Zeus rained all night; and strong the west wind blew, a wet wind always. To his companions spoke Odysseus, making trial of the swineherd to see if he would pull his own coat off and offer him, or order one of the men to give a coat, through love of him.

"Hearken, Eumaeus, and all you other men, and I will boast a bit and tell a story; for crazy wine so bids, which sets a man, even if wise, to singing loud and laughing lightly, and makes him dance and brings out stories really better left untold. But since I have begun to croak, I'll not be silent. Would I were in my prime, my vigor firm, as in the days when we went under Troy and set an ambush. Odysseus was our captain, and Atreides Menelaus, and with them I was third; for so they ordered. Now when we reached the city and the lofty wall, in the thick bushes by the citadel, among some reeds and marsh-grass, curled up beneath our armor, we laid us down to sleep. An ugly night came on, although the north wind fell, and bleak it was. From overhead came snow, like hoar-frost, cold; and ice formed on the edges of our shields. Then all the other men had coats and tunics, and slept in comfort with their shields snug round their shoulders. But I at starting foolishly left my coat with my companions, because I did not think I should be cold at all; so off I came with nothing but my shield and colored doublet. But when it was the third watch of the night and the stars crossed the zenith, I spoke to Odysseus who was near, nudging him with my elbow, and readily he listened:

"'High-born son of Laërtes, ready Odysseus, I shall not be among the living long. This cold is killing me, because I have no coat. Some god beguiled me into wearing nothing but my tunic. Now there is no escape.'

"So said I, and he at once had an idea in mind,—so ready was he both to plan and fight,—and speaking in an undertone he said: 'Keep quiet for the present, lest some other Achaean hear.'

"Then raising his head and resting on his elbow, thus he spoke: 'Hark, friends! A dream from heaven came to me in my sleep. Yes, we have come a long way from the ships. Would there were some one here to tell Atreides Agamemnon, the shepherd of the people, to send us more men hither from the fleet.'

"As he thus spoke, up Thoas sprung, Andraemon's son, who, quickly casting off his purple coat, went running to the ships. I, in his garment, lay comfortably down till gold-throned morning dawned.

"So would I now were in my prime, my vigor firm; then one of the swineherds of the farm might give a coat, through kindness and respect for a deserving man. Now they despise me for the sorry clothes I wear."

Then, swineherd Eumaeus, you answered him and said: "Old man, the boastings you have uttered are not ill. You have not spoken an improper or a silly word. Therefore you shall not lack for clothes nor anything besides which it is fit a hard-pressed suppliant should find,—at least for now; to-morrow you shall wrap yourself in your own rags. There are not many coats and extra tunics here to wear, but simply one apiece. But when Odysseus' son returns, he will give a coat and tunic for your clothing and send you where your heart and soul may bid you go."

So saying, he rose and placed a bed beside the fire, and threw upon it skins of sheep and goats. On this Odysseus laid him down, and over him Eumaeus threw a great shaggy coat which lay at hand as extra clothing, to put on when there came a bitter storm.

So here Odysseus slept, and by his side the young men slept, but not the swineherd. A bed here pleased him not, thus parted from his swine, but he prepared to venture forth. Glad was Odysseus that Eumaeus took such care of his estate while he was gone. And first Eumaeus slung a sharp-edged sword about his sturdy shoulders, put on his storm-proof shaggy coat, picked up the fleece of a large full-grown goat, took a sharp spear to keep off dogs and men, and went away to rest where lay the white-toothed swine under a hollow rock, sheltered from Boreas.

XV.

TELEMACHUS AND EUMAEUS

NOW TO spacious Lacedaemon went Pallas Athene to seek the noble son of resolute Odysseus, wishing to call his home to mind and bid him hasten. She found Telemachus and the worthy son of Nestor lying within the porch of famous Menelaus. The son of Nestor was still wrapped in gentle sleep; but to Telemachus came no welcome sleep, for through the immortal night thoughts in his heart about his father kept him awake. So clear-eyed Athene, drawing near, addressed him thus:

"Telemachus, it is not well to wander longer far from home, leaving your wealth behind and persons in your house so insolent as these; for they may swallow all your wealth, sharing with one another, while you are gone a fruitless journey. Nay, with all haste urge Menelaus, good at the war-cry, to send you forth, that you may find your blameless mother still at home. Already her father and her brothers press her to wed Eurymachus; for he excels all suitors in his gifts and overtops their dowry. But let her not against your will take treasure from your home. You know a woman's way: she strives to enrich his house who marries her, while of her former children and the husband of her youth when he is dead she thinks not, and she talks of him no more. Go then and put your household in the charge of her among the maids who seems the best, until the gods grant you an honored wife. And let me tell you more; lay it to heart; by a deliberate plan the leaders of the suitors now guard the strait twixt Ithaca and rugged Samos, and seek to cut you off before you gain your native land. Yet this I think shall never be; rather the earth shall cover some of the suitors who devour your living. Still, keep your stanch ship off the islands and sail both night and day; and one of the immortals who guards and keeps you safe shall send a favoring breeze. When then you reach the nearest shore of Ithaca, send forward to the city your ship and all her crew, and go yourself before all else straight to the swineherd, who is the keeper of your swine and ever loyal. There rest a night, but send the swineherd to the city to bear the news to heedful Penelope how you are safe and how you have returned from Pylos."

So saying, Athene passed away to high Olympus. But from sweet sleep Telemachus waked Nestor's son, touching him with his heel, and thus addressed him: "Wake, Nestor's son, Peisistratus! Bring out the strong-hoofed horses and yoke them to the car, that we may make our journey."

Then Nestor's son, Peisistratus, made answer: "Telemachus, we cannot, eager for the journey though we are, drive in the dusky night. It will be morning soon. Wait then awhile until the royal son of Atreus, the spear-man Menelaus, brings his gifts, places them in the chariot, and sends us forth with cheering words upon our way. For a guest remembers all his days the hospitable man who showed him kindness."

He spoke, and soon the gold-throned morning came; and Menelaus, good at the war-cry, now drew near, just risen from bed by fair-haired Helen. When the son of Odysseus spied him, in haste he girt his glossy tunic round his body, and threw a great cloak round his sturdy shoulders. So forth he went and drawing near thus spoke Telemachus, the son of princely Odysseus:

"O son of Atreus, heaven-descended Menelaus, leader of hosts, now at last let me go to my own native land; for my heart longs for home."

Then answered Menelaus, good at the war-cry: "Telemachus, I will not keep you longer if you desire to go. I blame a host if over-kind, or over-rude. Better, good sense in all things. It is an equal fault to thrust away the guest who does not care to go, and to detain the impatient. Best make the stranger welcome while he stays, and speed him when he wishes. But wait until I bring you gifts and place them in your chariot, beautiful gifts, as you yourself shall see. And let me bid the maids prepare a meal here in the hall from our abundant stores. It brings dignity and honor and benefit besides to feast before you travel along the boundless earth. Then if you choose to make a tour through Hellas and mid-Argos, so far I will attend you; for I will yoke my horses and guide you through the towns. No one will send us empty off, but each will give some single thing to bear away, a brazen tripod, caldron, pair of mules or golden goblet."

Then again answered him discreet Telemachus: "O son of Atreus, heaven-descended Menelaus, leader of hosts, at present I had rather go to my own home, for I left behind at starting no guardian of my goods; so while I seek my godlike father, I may myself be lost, or else may lose out of my house some valued treasure."

When Menelaus, good at the war-cry, heard his words, he straightway bade his wife and maids prepare a meal there in the hall from his abundant stores. And now the son of Boëthoüs, Eteoneus, entered, just risen from his bed; for he lived not far away. Menelaus, good at the war-cry, told him to light the fire and roast the meat; and when he heard, he did not disobey. Menelaus himself, meanwhile, went down to a fragrant chamber; yet not alone, for Helen went and Megapenthes. And when they came where lay his treasure, the son of Atreus took a double cup and ordered Megapenthes to bring a silver bowl, while Helen lingered by the chests where were the embroidered robes which she herself had wrought. Out of these robes the royal lady, Helen, drew forth one to bear away, one handsomest in work and largest, which sparkled like a star; it lay beneath the others. Then forth they hastened through the palace till they found Telemachus, whom light-haired Menelaus thus addressed:

"Telemachus, as your heart hopes, may Zeus, the thunderer, husband of Here, grant you a safe return! And out of all the gifts stored in my house as treasures, I will give you that which is most beautiful and precious: I will give a well-wrought bowl. It is of solid silver, its rim finished with gold, the work of Hephaestus. Lord Phaedimus, the king of the Sidonians, gave it to me, when his house sheltered me upon my homeward way. And now to you I gladly give it."

So saying, the lordly son of Atreus put in his hands the double cup. Then the bright silver bowl strong Megapenthes brought and set before him, while at his side stood fair-cheeked Helen, holding the robe, and thus she spoke and said:

"I too, dear child, will give a gift, this keepsake from the hands of Helen against the wished-for wedding time, for your wife then to wear. Meanwhile, in your good mother's charge lay it away at home: and may you with rejoicing reach your stately house and native land."

So saying, she laid it in his hands; he took it and was glad. Then lord Peisistratus put in the chariot box the gifts as he received them, viewing them all with wonder. Light-haired Menelaus led them to the house, where they took seats on benches and on chairs. Now water for the hands a servant brought in a beautiful pitcher, made of gold, and poured it out over a silver basin for their washing, and spread a polished table by their side. And the grave housekeeper brought bread and placed before them, setting out food of many a kind, freely giving of her store. The son of Boëthoüs, too, carved meat and passed them portions, and the son of famous Menelaus poured their wine: and on the food spread out before them they laid hands. Then after they had stayed desire for drink and food, Telemachus and Nestor's gallant son harnessed the horses, mounted the gay chariot, and off they drove from porch and echoing portico. After them came the son of Atreus, light-haired Menelaus, in his right hand a golden cup of cheering wine, for them to pour at starting. He stopped before the horses and pledging them he said:

"A health to you, young men! And say the same to Nestor, the shepherd of the people; for he was kind to me as any father those days we young Achaeans were in the war at Troy."

Then answered him discreet Telemachus: "Even as you say, O heaven-descended prince, when we arrive we will report all these your words. And would that coming home to Ithaca, I there might find Odysseus in my home, and so might say how after meeting every kindness here with you I went my way and carried many precious treasures with me!"

On his right, as he was speaking, flew an eagle bearing in his claws a large white goose, a tame fowl from the yard. People ran shouting after, men and women. But as the bird drew near, he darted to the right before the horses. All saw it and were glad, and in their breasts their hearts grew warm. And thus began Peisistratus, the son of Nestor:

"Think, heaven-descended Menelaus, leader of hosts! Is it we to whom God shows this sign, or is it you?"

He spoke and valiant Menelaus pondered, doubting what he should think and rightly answer. But long-robed Helen, taking up the word, spoke thus: "Hearken and I will prophesy such things as the immortals bring to mind, things which I think will happen. As the eagle caught the goose,—she, fattened in the house; he, coming from the hills where he was born and bred,—so shall Odysseus, through many woes and wanderings, come home and take revenge. Even now, perhaps, he is at home, sowing the seeds of ill for all the suitors."

Then answered her discreet Telemachus: "Zeus grant it so, he the loud thunderer, husband of Here! Then would I there too, as to any god, give thanks to you."

He spoke and laid the lash upon the horses, and very quickly they started toward the plain, hastening through the city; and all day long they shook the yoke they bore between them.

Now the sun sank and all the ways grew dark; and the men arrived at Pherae, before the house of Diocles, the son of Orsilochus, whose father was Alpheius. There for the night they rested; he gave them entertainment. Then as the early rosy-fingered dawn appeared, they harnessed the horses, mounted the gay chariot, and off they drove from porch and echoing portico. Telemachus cracked the whip to start, and not unwillingly the pair flew off, and by and by they came to the steep citadel of Pylos. Then said Telemachus to Nestor's son:

"O son of Nestor, could you give and perform the promise I shall ask? Friends from of old we call ourselves, because of our fathers' friendship. Besides, we are alike in years, and this our journey will make the tie more close. Do not then, heaven-descended prince, take me beyond my ship, but leave me there; for fear old Nestor, eager for kindness, detain me at his house against my will, when I should hasten on."

So he spoke, and the son of Nestor doubted within his heart if he could rightly give and perform the promise. Yet on reflecting thus, it seemed the better way. He turned his horses toward the swift ship and shore, took out and set by the ship's stern the goodly gifts,—the clothing and the gold which Menelaus gave,—and hastening Telemachus, spoke thus in winged words:

"Quickly embark and summon all your crew before I reach my home and tell old Nestor; for in my mind and heart full well I know how stern his temper is. He will not let me go; he will himself come here and call you. I tell you, too, go back he will not empty-handed; for he will be very angry, notwithstanding what you say."

So saying, he drove his full-maned horses to the town of Pylos, and quickly reached the palace. But Telemachus, inspiriting his crew, called to them thus: "Put all the gear in order, friends, on the black ship; and come aboard yourselves and let us make our journey."

So he spoke, and willingly they heeded and obeyed; quickly they came on board and took their places at the pins.

With these things he was busied, and now by the ship's stern was making prayers and offerings to Athene, when up there came a wanderer, exiled from Argos through having killed a man. He was a seer, and of the lineage of Melampus. In former times Melampus lived at Pylos, the mother-land of flocks, and had a very wealthy home among the Pylians. Then he went to a land of strangers and departed from his country, flying from high-souled Neleus, lordliest of living men, who for a full year held by force his great possessions. He meanwhile in the halls of Phylacus was kept in bitter bondage and suffered great distress, because of the daughter of Neleus and the delusion deep which the divine sharp-scourging fury brought his mind. But he escaped his doom and drove the bellowing oxen from Phylace to Pylos; and punishing matchless Neleus for his disgraceful deed, he brought the maiden home to be his brother's wife. So he came to a land of strangers, grazing Argos, where afterwards he was to live, sovereign of many Argives. And here he took a wife and built a high-roofed house, and he begot two sturdy sons, Antiphates and Mantius. Antiphates again begot brave Oicles, and Oicles Amphiaraüs, the summoner of hosts, whom Zeus the ægis-bearer and Apollo tenderly loved, and showed him every favor; and yet he did not reach the threshold of old age, but died at Thebes, destroyed by woman's bribes. To him were born two sons, Alcmaeon and Amphilochus. Now Mantius begot Cleitus and Polypheides; but gold-throned dawn took Cleitus, by reason of his beauty, to dwell with the immortals. Of eager Polypheides Apollo made a seer, the best among mankind when Amphiaraüs died. Quarrelling with his father, he withdrew to Hyperesia; and there he dwelt and prophesied for all men.

It was his son drew near, named Theoclymenus, and stood before Telemachus. He found him making offerings and prayers beside the swift black ship: and speaking in winged words he said:

"Friend, since I find you offering burnt-offerings here, by these offerings and the god I will entreat you, and by your own life too, and that of those who follow: tell truly all I ask. Hold nothing back. Who are you? Of what people? Where is your town and kindred?"

Then answered him discreet Telemachus: "Well, stranger, I will plainly tell you all. By birth I am of Ithaca. My father is Odysseus—if ever such there were! But long ago he died, a mournful death; so I, with men and a black ship, am come to gather news of my long-absent father."

Then answered godlike Theoclymenus: "Like you, I too am far from home, because I killed a kinsman. He has many relatives and friends in grazing Argos, and with the Achaeans their influence is large. To shun the death and the dark doom which they would deal, I flee; for I must be a wanderer now from tribe to tribe. Set me upon your ship, a fugitive and suppliant. Let them not kill me; for I know they will pursue."

Then answered him discreet Telemachus: "I shall not thrust you forth from the trim ship against your will. Nay, follow! In our land you shall receive what we can give."

So saying he took the brazen spear from Theoclymenus and laid it on the deck of the curved ship. Telemachus himself came on the sea-bound ship and sat him in the stern, while by his side sat Theoclymenus. The others loosed the cables. And now Telemachus, inspiriting his men, bade them lay hold upon the tackling, and they busily obeyed. Raising the pine-wood mast, they set it in the hollow socket, binding it firm with forestays, and tightened the white sail with twisted ox-hide thongs. And a favorable wind clear-eyed Athene sent, which swept with violence along the sky, so that the scudding ship might swiftly make her way through the salt ocean water. Thus on they ran, past Crouni and the pleasant streams of Chalcis. The sun was setting and the ways were growing dark as the ship drew near to Pheae, driven by the breeze of Zeus; then on past sacred Elis where the Epeians rule. From here Telemachus steered for the Pointed Isles, uncertain if he should escape from death or fall a prey.

Meanwhile at the lodge Odysseus and the noble swineherd were eating supper, and with them supped the others. And after they had stayed desire for drink and food, thus spoke Odysseus,—making trial of the swineherd, to see if he would longer give him a hearty welcome and urge his staying at the farm, or if he would send him straightway to the town:

"Hearken, Eumaeus and all you other men! I want to go to-morrow to beg about the town, for fear I burden you and these your men. Only direct me well, and give me a trusty guide to show the way. Once in the city, I must wander by myself, and hope some man will give a cup and crust. And if I come to the house of princely Odysseus, there I will tell my tale to heedful Penelope and join the audacious suitors, who might perhaps give me a meal; since they have great abundance. Soon I could serve them well in all they want. For let me tell you this, and do you mark and listen: by favor of the Guide-god, Hermes, who lends the grace and dignity to all the deeds of men, in servants' work I have no equal,—in laying a fire well, splitting dry wood, carving and roasting meat, and pouring wine,—indeed, in all the ways that poor men serve their betters."

Then deeply moved said you, swineherd Eumaeus: "Why, stranger, how came such a notion in your mind? You certainly must long to die that very instant when you consent to plunge into the throng of suitors, whose arrogance and outrage reach to the iron heavens. Their servants are not such as you; but younger men, well dressed in coats and tunics, ever with glossy heads and handsome faces, are they who do them service. Their polished tables are laden with bread and meat and wine. No, stay with us! Nobody is disturbed that you are here, not I myself, nor any one of these my men. And when Odysseus' son returns, he will give a coat and tunic for your clothing and send you where your heart and soul may bid you go."

Then answered him long-tried royal Odysseus: "May you, Eumaeus, be as dear to father Zeus as now to me, for having stopped my wandering and saved me bitter woe. Nothing is harder for a man than restless roaming. 'Tis for the cursed belly's sake that men meet cruel ills when wandering, misfortune, and distresses come. Yet while you keep me here, bidding me wait your master, pray tell me of the mother of princely Odysseus, and of his father, whom when he went away he left behind on the threshold of old age. Are they still living in the sunshine, or are they now already dead and in the house of Hades?"

Then said to him the swineherd, the overseer: "Well, stranger, I will plainly tell you all. Laërtes is still living, but ever prays to Zeus to let life leave his limbs here at his home; for he mourns exceedingly his absent son and the early-wedded trusty wife whose death distressed him sorely and brought him into premature old age. In sorrow for her famous son, she pined away—a piteous death! May none die so who dwells with me, who is my friend and does me kindness. While she still lived, much as she suffered, pleasant it was to ask for her and make inquiries; for it was she who brought me up with long-robed Ctimene, her stately daughter, the youngest child she bore. With her I was brought up and I was honored little less. Then when we reached together the longed-for days of youth, they sent Ctimene to Same and obtained large wedding gifts, while me my lady dressed in coat and tunic, goodly garments, and giving sandals for my feet she sent me to the farm; yet in her heart she loved me more and more. Now all that love I lack, though the good gods bless all I undertake. By work I get my meat and drink, and give to the deserving, but from the queen I cannot win one cheering word or deed; trouble has fallen on the house through overbearing men. Yet servants long to speak with their mistress face to face, from her to learn of all, with her to eat and drink, and then take something also to the fields. Such things make servants' hearts grow warm."

Then answering said wise Odysseus: "Swineherd Eumaeus, certainly when you were small you must have wandered far from home and kindred. Tell me about it; tell me plainly too. Was the wide-wayed city of your people sacked, the city where your father and honored mother dwelt? Or when you were alone among your sheep and cattle, did foemen take you on their ships and bring you across the sea to the palace of a man who paid a proper price?"

Then said to him the swineherd, the overseer: "Stranger, since now you ask of this and question me, quietly listen; take your ease, and sit and drink your wine. These nights are vastly long. There is time enough to sleep, and time to cheer ourselves with hearing stories. You must not go to bed till bed-time; too much sleeping harms. As for the others here, if anybody's heart and liking bids, let him go off and sleep; then early in the morning after eating, let him attend his master's swine. But let us drink and feast within the lodge and please ourselves with telling one another tales of piteous ill; for afterwards a man finds pleasure in his pains, when he has suffered long and wandered long. So I will tell you what you ask and seek to know.

"There is an island, Syria it is called,—you may have heard its name,—above Ortygia, where the sun's course turns; not very thickly settled, good however, with excellent flocks and herds and full of corn and wine. Into this land dearth never comes, nor any foul disease attacks unhappy men; but when the families throughout the town grow old, Apollo and Artemis come with silver bow and slay them with their gentle arrows. Here are two towns and all the land is shared between them. Over them both my father ruled, Ctesius, son of Ormenus, a man like the immortals.

"Thither Phoenicians came, notable men at sea, but greedy knaves, with countless trinkets in their black-hulled ship. Now in my father's house lived a Phoenician woman, handsome and tall and skilled in dainty work; and her the wily Phoenicians led astray. In the first days, when she was washing clothes beside the hollow ship, a man seduced her by love and kindness; for these things turn the heads of womankind, even the upright too. Then he asked her who she was and whence she came; whereat she pointed straightway to my father's high-roofed house.

"'I boast of being born in Sidon, rich in bronze, and am the daughter of Arybas, a man of abounding wealth. But Taphian pirates seized me as I wandered through the fields, and brought me here across the sea to the palace of a man who paid a proper price.'

"Then said the man who secretly seduced her: 'Return then home again with us, to see your father's and your mother's high-roofed house, and see them too; for they are living still and still accounted rich.'

"Then answered him the woman thus and said: 'It may be, if you sailors pledge yourselves by oath to take me home unharmed.'

"So she spoke, and they all took the oath which she required. Then after they had sworn and ended all their oath, once more the woman answered them and said: 'Be quiet for the present! Let none among your crew utter a word to me, in meetings on the street or at the well, or some one coming to the old king's house may tell; and he, if he understands, will bind me in bitter bonds and plot your ruin. So bear in mind my words, and press the purchase of your cargo; then when the ship is filled with freight, let a messenger come quickly to the palace, and I will bring whatever gold I find at hand. Another kind of passage-money I would gladly give. At home I tend a child,—so bright a boy!—who runs beside me out of doors. Him I might bring on board, and he would fetch a mighty sum from any foreign folk you visit.'

"So saying, she departed to the stately palace. And they continued with us all the year, and by their trading gathered in their hollow ship large stores. But when the hollow ship was freighted to set sail, they sent a messenger to tell the woman. This crafty man came to my father's house, bringing a golden necklace strung with amber beads. The maids about the house and my good mother kept fingering the chain, and eyeing it, and offering a price. The man meanwhile signed to the woman silently, and having given his sign departed to the hollow ship. The woman, then, taking me by the hand, led me off out of doors. In the fore part of the house she found some cups and tables, where people had been feasting who waited on my father. They were now gone to a public gathering and debate. Quickly she hid three goblets in her breast and bore them off. I innocently followed. The sun was setting and the roads were growing dark; but we walked swiftly on and came to the well-known harbor where the Phoenicians' sea-bound ship was lying. Embarking there, the men set sail upon their watery way, mak-ing us too embark. Zeus sent us wind. Six days we sailed, as well by night as day; but when Zeus, the son of Kronos, brought the seventh day round, the huntress Artemis struck down the woman, and, like a sea-coot, in the hold she dropped. They threw her overboard, a prey to seals and fishes, and I was left behind with aching heart. But wind and water bore us thence and brought us here to Ithaca, and here Laërtes bought me with his substance. This is the way I came to see this land."

Then thus replied high-born Odysseus: "Eumaeus, you have deeply stirred the heart within my breast, telling these tales of all the troubles you have borne. Yet side by side with evil Zeus surely gave you good, since at the end of all your toils you reached the house of a kind man who furnishes you food and drink in plenty. A comfortable life you lead; but I come here a wanderer through many cities."

So they conversed together, then lay and slept a little while, not long; for soon came bright-throned dawn.

Meantime, approaching shore, the comrades of Telemachus slackened their sail, hastily lowered the mast, and with their oars rowed the vessel to her moorings. Here they cast anchor and made fast the cables; and going forth themselves upon the shore, prepared their dinner and mixed the sparkling wine. Then after they had stayed desire for food and drink, discreet Telemachus thus began:

"Sail the black-hulled ship, my men, straight to the town; I go to the fields and herdsmen. At evening, after looking at the farm, I too will come to town. To-morrow I will make you payment for your voyage by a bounteous feast of meat and pleasant wine."

Then up spoke godlike Theoclymenus: "Where shall I go, my child? To whose house come, of all the men who rule in rocky Ithaca? Or shall I go directly to your mother's house and yours?"

Then answered him discreet Telemachus: "At any other time I would bid you come to us, because we have no lack of means of welcome. But for yourself it would be somewhat dreary now. I shall be gone, and my mother will not see you; for she is not often seen in the same room with the suitors, but in an upper chamber far away she tends her loom. But I will name another man to whom you well might go: Eurymachus, the illustrious son of skillful Polybus, whom nowadays the men of Ithaca look upon as a god; for he is certainly the chief man here. He much desires to wed my mother and obtain the honors of Odysseus. Nevertheless, Olympian Zeus, who dwells in the clear sky, knows whether before the wedding he will set a day of ill."

Even as he spoke, upon his right there flew a bird, a hawk, Apollo's speedy messenger. With his claws he tore the dove he held and scattered down its feathers to the ground, midway between the ship and Telemachus himself. Then Theoclymenus, calling Telemachus aside from his companions, held fast his hand and spoke and thus addressed him:

"Telemachus, not without God's warrant flew this bird upon our right. I knew him at a glance to be a bird of omen. There is no house in Ithaca more kingly than your own; and you shall always be the rulers here."

Then answered him discreet Telemachus: "Ah stranger, would these words of yours might be fulfilled! Soon should you know my kindness and many a gift from me, and every man you met would call you blessed."

Then turning to Peiraeus, his good comrade: "Peiraeus, son of Clytius, you always do my bidding best of all the men who followed me to Pylos; so take this stranger to your home and treat him kindly, and show him honor till the time that I shall come."

Then answered him Peiraeus, the famous spearman: "Telemachus, though you stay long, I still will entertain him; no lack of welcome shall there be."

So saying, Peiraeus went aboard the ship and called the crew to come on board and loose the cables. Quickly they came and took their places at the pins. Telemachus bound to his feet his beautiful sandals and took his ponderous spear, tipped with sharp bronze, from the ship's deck. The sailors loosed the cables and thrusting off the ship sailed to the town, as they were ordered by Telemachus, the son of princely Odysseus. But him, meanwhile, his feet bore swiftly onward until he reached the court where were the countless swine with whom the trusty swineherd lodged, still faithful to his master.

Suitors have been in Odysseus's house for 10 yr.

since Odysseus has left for battle he had not set foot on his homeland for 20 years.

How long war?

XVI.

THE RECOGNITION BY TELEMACHUS

MEANWHILE AT the lodge Odysseus and the noble swineherd prepared their breakfast in the early dawn, before the lighted fire, having already sent the herdsmen with the droves of swine forth to the fields. As Telemachus drew near, the dogs that love to bark began to wag their tails, but did not bark. Royal Odysseus noticed the dogs wagging their tails, and the sound of footsteps reached him; and straightway to Eumaeus he spoke these winged words:

"Eumaeus, certainly a friend is coming, at least a man you know; for the dogs here do not bark, but wag their tails, and I hear the tramp of feet."

The words were hardly uttered when his own son stood in the doorway. In surprise up sprang the swineherd, and from his hands the vessels fell with which he had been busied, mixing sparkling wine. He went to meet his master, and kissed his face, each of his beautiful eyes, and both his hands, letting the big tears fall. And as a loving father greets the son who comes from foreign lands, ten years away, his only child, now grown a man, for whom he long has sorrowed; even so the noble swineherd took princely Telemachus in his arms and kissed him o'er and o'er, as one escaped from death, and sobbing said to him in winged words:

"So you are here, Telemachus, my own sweet light! I said I should not see you any more after you went away by ship to Pylos. Come in then, child, and let me cheer my heart with looking at you, just come from far away. You do not often visit the farm and herdsmen. You tarry in the town; for nowadays you want to watch the wasteful throng of suitors."

Then answered him discreet Telemachus: "So be it, father! 'Tis for your sake I am here, to see you with my eyes, and hear you tell if my mother still is staying at the hall, or if at last some stranger won her,

153

and so Odysseus' bed, empty of occupants, stands covered with foul cobwebs."

Then answered him the swineherd, the overseer: "Indeed she stays with patient heart within your hall, and wearily the nights and days are wasted with her tears."

So saying, Eumaeus took Telemachus' brazen spear, and Telemachus went in and over the stone threshold. As he drew near, his father, Odysseus, yielded him his seat; but Telemachus on his part checked him, saying:

"Be seated, stranger. Elsewhere we shall find a seat at this our farm. Here is a man will give one."

He spoke, and his father turned and sat once more; but the swineherd threw green brushwood down and on its top a fleece, on which the dear son of Odysseus took his seat. And now the swineherd brought platters of roasted meat, which those who ate the day before had left. Bustling about he heaped bread in the baskets, and in an ivy bowl mixed honeyed wine, then took a seat himself over against princely Odysseus, and on the food spread out before them they laid hands. So after they had stayed desire for drink and food, to the noble swineherd said Telemachus:

"Father, whence came this stranger? How did his sailors bring him to Ithaca? Whom did they call themselves? For I am sure he did not come on foot."

Then, swineherd Eumaeus, you answered him and said: "Well, I will tell you all the truth, my child. He calls himself by birth of lowland Crete, but says he has come to many cities in his wanderings; so Heaven ordained his lot. Lately he ran away from a ship of the Thesprotians and came to my farm here. I place him in your charge. Do what you will. He calls himself your suppliant."

Then answered him discreet Telemachus: "Eumaeus, truly these are bitter words which you have said. How can I take a stranger home? I am myself but young and cannot trust my arm to right me with the man who wrongs me first. Moreover my mother's feeling wavers, whether to bide beside me here and keep the house, and thus revere her husband's bed and heed the public voice, or finally to follow some chief of the Achaeans who woos her in the hall with largest gifts. However, since the stranger has reached your lodging here, I will clothe him in a coat and tunic, goodly garments, give him a two-edged sword and sandals for his feet, and I will send him where his heart and soul may bid him go. Or, if you like, serve him yourself and keep him at the farm; and I will send him clothing and all his food to eat, so that he may not burden you and yours. Yonder among the suitors I would not have him go; for they are full of wanton pride. So they might mock him,—a cruel grief to me. Hard is it even for a powerful man to act against a crowd; because together they are far too strong."

Then said to him long-tried royal Odysseus: "Friend,—for surely I too have a right to answer,—my heart is sore at hearing what you say, that suitors work abomination at the palace against a man like you. But tell me, do you willingly submit, or are the people of your land adverse to you, led by some voice of God? Or have you any cause to blame your brothers, on whom a man relies for aid when bitter strifes arise? Would that, to match my spirit, I were young as you, and were the son of good Odysseus, or even Odysseus' self, come from his wanderings, as there still is room for hope; then quickly should my foe strike off my head, or I would prove the bane of all these suitors when I should cross the hall of Laërtes' son Odysseus. And should they by their number crush me, all single and alone, far rather would I die, cut down within my hall, than constantly behold disgraceful deeds, strangers abused, and damsels dragged to shame through the fair palace, wine running waste, men eating up my bread, all idly, uselessly, to win what cannot be!"

Then answered him discreet Telemachus: "Well, stranger, I will plainly tell you all. My people as a whole bear me no grudge or hate; nor yet can I blame brothers, on whom a man relies for aid when bitter strifes arise; for the son of Kronos made our race run in a single line. Arceisius begot a single son Laërtes; and he, the single son Odysseus; Odysseus left me here at home, the single son of his begetting, and of me had no joy. But bands of evil-minded men now fill my house; for all the nobles who bear sway among the islands—Doulichion, Same, and woody Zacynthus—and they who have the power in rocky Ithaca, all woo my mother and despoil my home. She neither declines the hated suit nor has she power to end it, while they with feasting impoverish my home and soon will bring me also to destruction. However, in the lap of the gods these matters lie. But, father, quickly go and say to steadfast Penelope that I am safe and have returned from Pylos. I will stay here; do you come hither too; and tell your tidings to her only. Let none of the rest of the Achaeans hear; for many are they that plot against me."

Then, swineherd Eumaeus, you answered him and said: "I see, I understand; you speak to one who knows. But now declare me this and plainly say, shall I go tell Laërtes on my way, wretched Laërtes, who for a time, though grieving greatly for Odysseus, still oversaw his fields and with his men at home would drink and eat as appetite inclined; but from the day you went by ship to Pylos did never eat nor drink the same, they say, nor oversaw his fields, but full of moans and sighs sits sorrowing, while the flesh wastes upon his bones."

Then answered him discreet Telemachus: "'Tis hard, but though it grieves us, we will let him be; if all that men desire were in their power, the first thing we should choose would be the coming of my father. No, give your message and return, and do not wander through the fields to find Laërtes. But tell my mother to send forthwith her housemaid thither, yet privately; for to the old man she might bear the news."

So saying, he dispatched the swineherd, who took his sandals, bound them to his feet, and went to town. Yet not unnoticed by Athene swineherd Eumaeus left the farm; but she herself drew near in likeness of a woman, one fair and tall and skilled in dainty work. By the lodge door she stood, visible to Odysseus. Telemachus did not glance her way nor notice her; for not to every one do gods appear. Odysseus saw her, and the dogs; yet the dogs did not bark, but whining slunk away across the place. With her brows she made a sign; royal Odysseus understood, came forth from the hall past the great courtyard wall, and stood before her, and Athene said:

"High-born son of Laërtes, ready Odysseus, tell now your story to your son. Hide it no longer. Then having planned the suitors' death and doom, go forward both of you into the famous city. And I myself will not be far away, for I am eager for the combat."

She spoke and with a golden wand Athene touched Odysseus. And first she laid a spotless robe and tunic on his body, and then increased his bulk and bloom. Again he grew dark-hued; his cheeks were rounded, and dark the beard became about his chin. This done, she went away; and now Odysseus entered the lodge. His son was awestruck and reverently turned his eyes aside, fearing it was a god. Then speaking in winged words he said:

"Stranger, you seem a different person now and a while ago. Your clothes are different and your flesh is not the same. You surely are one of the gods who hold the open sky. Nay, then, be gracious! So will we give you grateful offerings and fine-wrought gifts of gold. Have mercy on us!"

Then long-tried royal Odysseus answered: "I am no god. Why liken me to the immortals? I am your father, him for whom you sighed and suffered long, enduring outrage at the hands of men."

So saying, he kissed his son and down his cheeks upon the ground let fall a tear, which always hitherto he sternly had suppressed. But Telemachus—for he did not yet believe it was his father,—finding his words once more made answer thus:

"No, you are not Odysseus, not my father! Some god beguiles me, to make me weep and sorrow more. No mortal man by his own wit could work such wonders, unless a god came to his aid and by his will made him with ease a young man or an old. For lately you were old and meanly clad; now you are like the gods who hold the open sky."

Then wise Odysseus answered him and said: "Telemachus, it is not right when here your father stands, to marvel overmuch and to be so amazed. Be sure no other Odysseus ever will appear; but as you see me, it is I, I who have suffered long and wandered long, and now in the twentieth year come to my native land. This is the work of the Plunderer, Athene, who makes me what she will,—for she has power,—now like a beggar, now again a youth in fair attire. Easily can the gods who hold the open sky give glory to a mortal man or give him shame."

So saying, he sat down; whereat Telemachus, throwing his arms round his good father, began to sob and pour forth tears, and in them both arose a longing of lament. Loud were their cries and more unceasing than those of birds, ospreys or crook-clawed vultures, when farmers take away their young before the wings are grown: so pitifully fell the tears beneath their brows. And daylight had gone down upon their weeping, had not Telemachus suddenly addressed his father thus:

"Why, father, by what ship did sailors bring you to Ithaca? Whom did they call themselves? For I am sure you did not come on foot."

Then said to him long-tried royal Odysseus: "Well, I will tell you, child, the very truth. The Phaeacians brought me here, notable men at sea, who pilot others too who come their way. They brought me across the sea on a swift ship asleep, landed me here in Ithaca and gave me glorious gifts, much bronze and gold and woven stuff; which treasures by the gods' command are laid away in caves. Here I now am by bidding of Athene, that we may plan together the slaughter of our foes. Come tell me then the number of the suitors, that I may know how many and what sort of men they are; and so, weighing the matter in my gallant heart, I may decide if we can meet them quite alone, without allies, or whether we shall seek the aid of others."

Then answered him discreet Telemachus: "Verily, father, I have ever heard your great renown, what a warrior you are in arm and what a sage in council. But now you speak of something far too vast; I am astonished. Two could not fight a troop of valiant men. The suitors number no mere ten, nor twice ten either; many more. You shall soon learn their number. From Doulichion, two and fifty chosen youths and six attendants; four and twenty men from Same; from Zacynthus twenty young Achaeans; twelve out of Ithaca itself, all men of mark, with whom are also the page Medon and the sacred bard, besides two followers skilled in table service. If we confront all these within the hall, bitter and grievous may the vengeance be, gained by your coming. So if you possibly can think of aid, consider who will aid us now whole-heartedly."

Then said to him long-tried royal Odysseus: "Nay, let me speak, and do you mark and listen. Consider if Athene, joined with father Zeus, suffice for us, or shall I seek for other aid?"

Then answered him discreet Telemachus: "Excellent helpers are the two you name, who sit among the clouds on high. All else they govern, all mankind and the immortal gods."

Then said to him long-tried royal Odysseus: "Not long will they be absent from the mighty fray when in my hall betwixt the suitors and ourselves the tug of war is tried. But go at early morning straightway home, and join the audacious suitors. Thereafter the swineherd shall bring me to the city, like an old and wretched beggar. And if they treat me rudely in my home, let the faithful heart within your breast endure what I must bear; yes, though they drag me through the palace by the heels and out of door, or hurl their missiles at me, see and be patient still. Bid them, however, cease their folly, and with gentle words dissuade. They will not heed you, for their day of doom draws near. But this I will say farther; mark it well. When wise Athene puts it in my mind, then I will nod my head, and you take note. And all the fighting gear that lies about the hall do you collect and lay in a corner of the lofty chamber, carefully, every piece. Then with soft words beguile the suitors when they, because they miss it, question you: 'I put it by out of the smoke, for it looks no longer like the armor which Odysseus left behind when he went away to Troy; it is all tarnished, where the scent of fire has come nigh. Besides, the son of Kronos brought this graver fear to mind. You might when full of wine begin a quarrel and give each other wounds, making a scandal of the feast and of your wooing. Steel itself draws men on.' Yet privily reserve two swords, two spears, two leathern shields, for us to seize—to rush and seize. And thereupon shall Pallas Athene and all-wise Zeus confound the suitors. Nay, this I will say farther; mark it well. If you are truly mine, my very blood, then that Odysseus now is here let no man know; let not Laërtes learn it, let not the swineherd, let none of the household, nor Penelope herself. But you and I alone will test the temper of the women. And we might also try the serving-men, and see who honors and respects us in his heart, and who neglects and scorns a man like you."

Then answered him his noble son and said: "My father, you shall know my heart, believe me, by and by. No laggard thoughts are mine; and yet I think your plan will prove for neither of us gain, and so I say: Consider! Long will you vainly go, trying the different men among the farms; while undisturbed within the hall these waste your wealth with recklessness and do not spare. But I advise your finding out the women, and learning who dishonor you and who are guiltless. As to the men about the place, I would not prove them. Let that at any rate be thought of later, when you are really sure of signs from aegis-bearing Zeus."

So they conversed together. But in the mean while on to Ithaca ran the stanch ship which brought Telemachus and all his crew from Pylos.

When they had entered the deep harbor, they hauled the black-hulled ship ashore, and stately squires carried their armor and straightway bore the goodly gifts to Clytius' house. And now they sent a page to the palace of Odysseus, to tell the news to heedful Penelope,—how Telemachus was at the farm, but had ordered that the ship sail to the city—lest the stately queen should be alarmed and shed a tender tear. So the two met, the herald and the noble swineherd, while on the self-same errand, bearing tidings to the queen. And when they reached the palace of the noble king, the page said to Penelope in hearing of her maids: "O queen, your son has come from Pylos." But the swineherd stood beside Penelope and so reported all that her dear son had bade him say. Then when he had delivered all his charge, he departed to his swine, and left the court and hall.

But the suitors grew dismayed and downcast in their hearts, and came forth from the hall past the great courtyard wall and there before the gate sat down to council; and first Eurymachus, the son of Polybus, addressed them:

"Friends, here is a monstrous action impudently brought to pass, this journey of Telemachus. We said it should not be. Come, then, and let us launch the best black ship we have, and get together fishermen for rowers, quickly to carry tidings to our friends, and bid them sail for home with all the speed they may."

The words were hardly uttered when Amphinomus, turning in his place, sighted the ship in the deep harbor, some of her crew furling the sail and some with oars in hand. Then lightly laughing, thus he called to his companions:

"No need to send a message now, for here they are. Some god has told the story; or else they saw the vessel pass and could not catch her."

He spoke, and all arose and hastened to the shore. Swiftly the black-hulled ship was hauled ashore, and stately squires carried their armor. The men themselves went in a body to the assembly and suffered no one, either young or old, to join them there; and thus Antinoüs, Eupeithes' son, addressed them:

"Strange, how the gods help this man out of danger! By day our sentries sat upon the windy heights, posted in close succession; and after sunset, we did not pass the night ashore, but sailed our swift ship on the sea, awaiting sacred dawn, lying in wait to seize and slay Telemachus. Meantime some god has brought him home. Then let us here contrive a miserable ending for Telemachus, not letting him escape; for while he lives, nothing, be sure, will prosper. He is himself shrewd in his thoughts and plans, and people here proffer us no more aid. Come then, before he gathers the Achaeans in a council. Backward he will not be, I know. He will be full of wrath, and rising he will tell to all how we contrived his instant death but could not catch him. And when men hear our evil deeds, they will not praise them; but they may cause us trouble and drive us from our country, and we may have to go away into the land of strangers. Let us be quick, then, and seize him in the fields far from the city, or on the road at least; and let us take possession of his substance and his wealth, sharing all suitably among ourselves; the house, however, we might let his mother keep, or him who marries her. If this plan does not please you, and you will let him live to hold his father's fortune, then let us not devour his store of pleasant things by gathering here; but from his own abode let each man make his wooing, and press his suit with gifts. So may Penelope marry the man who gives her most and comes with fate to favor."

As he thus spoke, the rest were hushed to silence. But Amphinomus addressed them now and said—Amphinomus, the illustrious son of noble Nisus and grandson of Aretias, who from Doulichion, rich in wheat and grass, had led a band of suitors, and more than all the rest found favor with Penelope through what he said, because his heart was upright—he with good will addressed them thus and said:

"Nay, friends, I would not like to kill Telemachus. It is a fearful thing to kill a king. Let us at least first ask the gods for counsel; and if the oracles of mighty Zeus approve, I will myself share in the killing and urge the others too; but if the gods turn from us, I warn you to forbear."

So said Amphinomus, and his saying pleased them. Soon they arose and entered the hall of Odysseus, and went and took their seats on polished chairs.

Heedful Penelope, meanwhile, had planned anew to show herself among the suitors, overweening in their pride. Within the palace she learned of the intended murder of her son, for the page Medon told her, who overheard the plot; so to the hall she went with her attendant women. And when the royal lady reached the suitors, she stood beside a column of the strong-built roof, holding before her face her delicate wimple; and she rebuked Antinoüs and spoke to him and said:

"Antinoüs, full of all insolence and wicked guile, in Ithaca they say you are the foremost person of your years in judgment and in speech. But such you never were. Madman! Why do you seek the death and ruin of Telemachus, and pay no heed to suppliants, though Zeus be witness for them? 'Tis impious plotting crimes against one's fellow men. Do you not know your father once took refuge here, in terror of the people? For they were very angry because he joined with Taphian pirates and troubled the Thesprotians, men who were our allies. So the people would destroy him,—would snatch his life away, and swallow all his large and pleasant living; but Odysseus held them back and stayed their madness. Yet you insultingly devour his house; you woo his wife, murder his child, and make me wholly wretched. Forbear, I charge you, and bid the rest forbear!"

Then answered her Eurymachus, the son of Polybus: "Daughter of Icarius, heedful Penelope; be of good courage! Let not these things vex your mind! The man is not alive, and never will be born, who shall lay hands upon your son, Telemachus, so long as I have life and sight on earth. For this I tell you, and it shall be done: soon the dark blood of such a man shall flow around my spear. Many a time the spoiler of towns, Odysseus, has set me on his knee, put roasted meat into my hands and given me ruddy wine. Therefore I hold Telemachus dearest of all mankind. I bid him have no fear of death, at least not from the suitors. Death from the gods can no man shun."

So he spoke, cheering her, yet was himself plotting the murder. But she, going to her bright upper chamber, bewailed Odysseus, her dear husband, till on her lids clear-eyed Athene caused a sweet sleep to fall.

At evening the noble swineherd joined Odysseus and his son. Busily they prepared their supper, having killed a yearling pig. And Athene, drawing near, touched with her wand Laërtes' son, Odysseus, and made him old once more and clad him in mean clothes; for fear the swineherd looking in his face might know, and go and tell the tale to steadfast Penelope, not holding fast the secret in his heart.

Now Telemachus first addressed the swineherd, saying: "So you are come, noble Eumaeus. What news then in the town? Are the haughty suitors at home again after their ambuscade, or are they watching still for me to pass?"

Then, swineherd Eumaeus, you answered him and said: "I had no mind to search and question while stumbling through the town. My inclination bade me to tell my message with all speed and hasten home. There overtook me, though, an eager newsman of your crew, a page, who told his story to your mother first. Moreover, this I know, because I saw it: I was already on the road above the town, where stands the hill of Hermes, when I saw a swift ship entering our harbor. A crowd of men were on her. Heavy she was with shields and double-pointed spears. 'Twas they, I thought, and yet I do not know."

As he thus spoke, revered Telemachus smiled, and glancing at his father shunned the swineherd's eye.

Now ceasing from their labor of laying out the meal, they fell to feasting. There was no lack of appetite for the impartial feast. And after they had stayed desire for drink and food, they turned toward bed and took the gift of sleep.

XVII.

THE RETURN OF TELEMACHUS TO ITHACA

SOON AS the early rosy-fingered dawn appeared, Telemachus, the son of princely Odysseus, bound to his feet his goodly sandals, took the ponderous spear which fitted well his hand, and setting off to town, addressed his swineherd thus:

"Father, I go to the city to let my mother see me; for I know she will not cease from gloomy grief and crying until she sees my very self. This charge I lay on you: bring the poor stranger to the city, to beg his living there; and whosoever will shall give a cup and crust. I cannot put up all; my heart is full of trouble. And if the stranger chafes at this, so much the worse for him. I like to speak the truth."

But wise Odysseus answered him and said: "Friend, I do not care to tarry here. Better a beggar should beg his living in the town than in the fields; and he who will may give; for I am now too old to stay about a farm and answer all the orders of an overseer. Go then your way; this man shall be my guide, even as you bid, when I have warmed me at the fire and when the sunshine comes. The clothes I wear are miserably bad, and the early frost may harm me; the town is far, they say."

He spoke, and through the farm-stead passed Telemachus, moving with rapid stride and sowing seeds of evil for the suitors. And when he reached his stately dwelling, he took his spear and set it up by a tall pillar, while he himself went farther in and over the stone threshold.

His nurse was first to see him, Eurycleia, now busy spreading fleeces on the carven chairs. With a burst of tears she came straight forward; and other maids of hardy Odysseus gathered round and fondly kissed his face and neck. Then from her chamber came heedful Penelope, like Artemis or golden Aphrodite. Round her dear son, weeping, she threw her arms, and kissed his face and both his beauteous eyes, and sobbing said to him in winged words:

162

"So you are come, Telemachus, my own sweet light! I said I should not see you any more after you went away by ship to Pylos, so secretly, with no consent of mine, to hear about your father. Come then and tell me all you chanced to see."

But wise Telemachus made answer: "My mother, do not stir my tears nor move my heart within, for I am only now escaped from utter ruin. But bathe, and putting on fresh garments, go to your upper chamber with your maids, and vow to pay full hecatombs to all the gods if Zeus some day will grant us deeds of vengeance. But I will go to the market-place to call a stranger who joined me on my journey here from Pylos. I sent him forward with my gallant crew and bade Peiraeus take him home and entertain him well and give him honor till the time that I should come."

Such were his words; unwinged, they rested with her. Bathing, and putting on fresh garments, she vowed to all the gods to pay full hecatombs if Zeus some day would grant her deeds of vengeance.

Presently through the hall forth went Telemachus, his spear in hand, two swift dogs following after; and marvelous was the grace Athene cast about him, that all the people gazed as he drew near. And round him flocked the haughty suitors, kind in their talk but in their hearts brooding on evil. He turned aside from the great company of these and off where Mentor sat with Antiphus and Halitherses, who were of old his father's friends, he went and sat him down; and much they questioned. Peiraeus, the famous spearman, now drew near, leading the stranger through the city to the market-place. Not long then from his guest delayed Telemachus, but came to meet him; though Peiraeus was the first to speak and say:

"Telemachus, quickly send women to my house, and let me send to you what Menelaus gave."

Then answered him discreet Telemachus: "Peiraeus, as yet we do not know how matters here will be. Suppose the haughty suitors at the palace should slay me privily and share my father's goods, I had rather you yourself should keep and enjoy the gifts than any one of these. But if I sow for these men death and doom, when I am merry merrily fetch all here."

So saying, he led the way-worn stranger home. And entering the stately buildings, they threw their coats upon the couches and the chairs, and went to the polished baths and bathed. And when the maids had bathed them and anointed them with oil, and put upon them fleecy coats and tunics, out of the baths they came and sat upon the couches. And water for the hands a servant brought in a beautiful pitcher made of gold, and poured it out over a silver basin for their washing, and spread a polished table by their side. Then the grave housekeeper brought bread and placed before them, setting out food of many a kind, freely giving of her store. The mother of Telemachus sat on the farther side, by a column of the hall, resting upon a couch, spinning fine threads of yarn. So on the food spread out before them they laid hands. And after they had stayed desire for drink and food, then thus began heedful Penelope:

"Telemachus, I go to my upper chamber and lay me on my bed,— which has become for me a bed of sorrows, ever watered with my tears since Odysseus went away to Ilios with the Atreidae,—because you did not deign before the haughty suitors entered, plainly to tell what tidings you have heard about your father's coming."

Then answered her discreet Telemachus: "Nay, mother, I will tell you all the truth. We went to Pylos, to Nestor, the shepherd of the people. And he, receiving me within his lofty palace, gave me such hearty welcome as a father gives his child when lately come from far, after long time away; so heartily he entertained me, he and his noble sons. Of hardy Odysseus, he said he had not heard from any man on earth, if he were alive or dead. But with horses and a strong-built chariot he sent me to the son of Atreus, to the spearman Menelaus. There I saw Argive Helen, her in behalf of whom Argives and Trojans bore so much at the gods' bidding. And Menelaus, good at the war-cry, soon asked me on what errand I came to royal Lacedaemon. I told him all the truth. And then he answered thus and said to me: 'Heavens! In a very brave man's bed they sought to lie, the weaklings! As when in the den of a strong lion a hind has laid asleep her new-born sucking fawns, then roams the slopes and grassy hollows seeking food, and by and by into his lair the lion comes and on both hind and fawns brings ghastly doom; so shall Odysseus bring a ghastly doom on these. Ah father Zeus, Athene, and Apollo! if with the power he showed one day in stately Lesbos, when he rose and wrestled in a match with Philomeleides, and down he threw him heavily while the Achaeans all rejoiced,—if as he was that day Odysseus now might meet the suitors, they all would find quick turns of fate and bitter rites of marriage. But as to what you ask thus urgently, I will not turn to talk of other things and so deceive you; but what the unerring old man of the sea told me, in not a word will I disguise or hide from you. He said he saw Odysseus on an island, in great distress, at the hall of the nymph Calypso, who holds him there by force. No power has he to reach his native land, for he has no ships fitted with oars, nor crews to bear him over the broad ocean-ridges.' So said the son of Atreus, the spearman Menelaus. And this accomplished, back I sailed; the gods gave breezes and brought me swiftly to my native land."

So he spoke, and stirred the heart within her breast. But godlike Theoclymenus addressed them thus: "O honored wife of Laërtes' son Odysseus, certainly Menelaus did not know the truth. Listen instead to words of mine; for I will plainly prophesy and not conceal. First then of all the gods be witness Zeus, and let this hospitable table and the hearth of good Odysseus whereto I come be witness; Odysseus is already within his native land,—biding his time or moving,—and, understanding all these wicked deeds, is sowing seeds of ill for all the suitors. As proof, while on the well-benched ship I marked a bird of omen, and I announced it to Telemachus."

Then said to him heedful Penelope: "Ah stranger, would these words of yours might be fulfilled! Soon should you know my kindness and many a gift from me, and every man you met would call you blessed."

So they conversed together. Meanwhile before the palace of Odysseus the suitors were making merry, throwing the discus and the hunting-spear upon the level pavement, holding riot as of old. But now when it was dinner-time, and from the fields around the flocks returned,—the shepherds leading who were wont to lead,—then Medon spoke; a man most loved of all the pages, one who was ever present at their feasts:

"Now, lads, since all your hearts are cheered with sports, come to the house and let us lay the table. One's dinner at the proper time is no bad thing."

He spoke, and up they sprang and went to heed his words. And entering the stately buildings, they threw their coats upon the couches and chairs, and they began to kill great sheep and fatted goats, to kill sleek pigs and the heifer of the herd, and so to make their meal.

Meanwhile at the farm Odysseus and the noble swineherd were making ready to depart to town. And thus began the swineherd, the overseer: "Stranger, so you desire to go to town to-day, just as my master ordered, though I myself would rather leave you as a watchman for the farm; but of him I stand in fear and awe, lest he hereafter chide me. Hard is a master's censure. Come then and let us go. The day is passing. It will be colder by and by toward night."

Then wise Odysseus answered him and said: "I see, I understand; you speak to one who knows. Let us go on, and all the way be you my guide. But give me a stick, if you have one cut, to lean upon; for you said the road was very rough."

He spoke, and round his shoulders slung his miserable wallet, full of holes, which hung upon a cord. Eumaeus gave the staff desired, and so the two set forth; but dogs and herdsmen stayed behind to keep the farm. On to the town Eumaeus led his lord, like an old and wretched beggar, leaning upon a staff. Upon his back were miserable clothes.

Now as they walked along the rugged road, nearing the city, they reached a stone-built fountain, running clear, from which the towns-folk draw their water, a fountain made by Ithacus, by Neritus and Polyctor. There was a grove of stream-fed poplars, encircling it, and from the rock above ran the cool water, while at the top was built an altar to the nymphs, where all who passed made offerings. Here the son of Dolius, Melanthius, met them, driving the goats that were the best of all the flock, to make the suitors' dinner. Two herdsmen followed after. Seeing Eumaeus and Odysseus, he broke into abuse; and speaking to them, used rude and indecent words, which stirred Odysseus' blood:

"Now sure enough the vile man leads the vile! As ever, god brings like and like together! Where are you carrying that glutton, you good-for-nothing swineherd, that nasty beggar to make mischief at our feasts? A man to stand and rub his back on many doors and tease for scraps of food, but not for swords and caldrons. If you would let me have him for a watchman at my farm, to be a stable-cleaner and fetch fodder to the kids, he might by drinking whey grow a big thigh. But no! For he has learned bad ways and will not turn to work. He will prefer to beg about the town, teasing for stuff to feed his greedy maw. But this I tell you, and it shall be done: if he comes near the house of princely Odysseus, many a footstool from men's hands flying around his head his ribs shall rub, as he is knocked about the house."

He spoke, and as he passed recklessly kicked Odysseus on the hip, but did not force him from the pathway. Fixed he stood. Odysseus doubted whether to spring and with his cudgel take his life, or to lift him in the air and dash his head upon the ground. But he was patient, and by thought restrained himself. And now the swineherd, looking him in the face, rebuked the man and stretching forth his hands prayed thus aloud:

"Nymphs of the fountain, daughters of Zeus, if ever Odysseus burned on thy altars thighs of lambs and kids, and wrapped them in rich fat, grant this my prayer! May he return and Heaven be his guide! Then would he scatter all the smartness you now recklessly assume, roaming continually around the town, while careless herdsmen let the flock decay."

Then answered him Melanthius the goatherd: "So, so! How the cur talks, as if he knew some magic arts! Some day I'll take him on a black and well-benched ship far off from Ithaca, and get me a great fortune. Oh that Apollo of the silver bow would smite Telemachus at home to-day, or let him fall before the suitors, as certainly as for Odysseus, far in foreign lands, the day of coming home is lost!"

So saying, he left them slowly plodding on, and off he went and soon he came to the king's palace. He entered at once and took his seat among the suitors over against Eurymachus, for he liked him best of all. Then those who served passed him a portion of the meat, while the grave housekeeper brought bread and set before him, for him to eat. Meantime Odysseus and the noble swineherd halted as they drew near, while round them came notes of the hollow lyre; for Phemius lifted up his voice to sing before the suitors. And taking the swineherd by the hand, Odysseus said:

"Surely, Eumaeus, this is the goodly palace of Odysseus, easy to notice even among many. Building joins building here. The court is built well with wall and cornice, and a double gate protects. No man may scorn it. I notice too that a great company are banqueting within; for the savory steam mounts up, and in the house resounds the lyre, made by the gods the fellow of the feast."

And, swineherd Eumaeus, you answered him and said: "You notice quickly, dull of thought in nothing. Come then and let us plan what we must do. You enter the stately building first and mingle with the suitors, while I stay here behind; or if you like, wait you, and I will go. But do not linger long, or somebody may spy you at the door and throw a stone or strike you. Take care, I say!"

Then long-tried royal Odysseus answered: "I see, I understand; you speak to one who knows. But go you on before, I will stay here behind: for I am not unused to blows and missiles. Stanch is my soul; for many dangers have I borne from waves and war. To those let this be added. Yet I cannot disregard a gnawing belly, the pest which brings so many ills to men. To ease it, timbered ships are fitted and carry woe to foemen over barren seas."

So they conversed together. But a dog lying near lifted his head and ears. Argos it was, the dog of hardy Odysseus, whom long ago he reared but never used. Before the dog was grown, Odysseus went to sacred Ilios. In the times past young men would take him on the chase, for wild goats, deer, and hares; but now he lay neglected, his master gone away, upon the pile of dung which had been dropped before the door by mules and oxen, and which lay there in a heap for slaves to carry off and dung the broad lands of Odysseus. Here lay the dog, this Argos, full of fleas. Yet even now, seeing Odysseus near, he wagged his tail and dropped both ears, but toward his master he had not strength to move. Odysseus turned aside and wiped away a tear, swiftly concealing from Eumaeus what he did; then straightway thus he questioned:

"Eumaeus, it is strange this dog lies on the dung-hill. His form is good; but I am not sure if he has speed of foot to match his beauty, or if he is merely what the table-dogs become which masters keep for show."

And, swineherd Eumaeus, you answered him and said: "Aye truly, that is the dog of one who died afar. If he were as good in form and action as when Odysseus left him and went away to Troy, you would be much surprised to see his speed and strength. For nothing could escape him in the forest-depths, no creature that he started; he was keen upon the scent. Now he has come to ill. In a strange land his master perished, and the slack women give him no more care; for slaves, when masters lose control, will not attend to duties. Ah, half the value of a man far-seeing Zeus destroys when the slave's lot befalls him!"

So saying, he entered the stately house and went straight down the hall among the lordly suitors. But upon Argos fell the doom of darksome death when he beheld Odysseus, twenty years away.

By far the first to see the swineherd as he walked along the hall was princely Telemachus, and he quickly gave a nod to call him to his side. Glancing around, Eumaeus took a stool which stood at hand, where the carver sat at feasts within the hall when carving for the suitors the many joints of meat; carrying the stool to the table of Telemachus, he placed it on the farther side and there sat down. And then a page took up a dish of meat and passed it, and from the basket gave him also bread.

Close following after, Odysseus entered the palace, like an old and wretched beggar leaning upon a staff. Upon his back were miserable clothes. He sat down on the ash-wood threshold just within the door, leaning against the cypress post which long ago the carpenter had smoothed with skill and leveled to the line. But to the swineherd said Telemachus, calling him to his side and taking a whole loaf from the goodly basket and also all the meat his hands stretched wide would hold:

"Take this and give the stranger, and bid him move about and beg of all the suitors. Shyness is no good comrade for a needy man."

He spoke, and the swineherd went as soon as he heard the order, and standing by Odysseus said in winged words: "Stranger, Telemachus gives this, and bids you move about and beg of all the suitors. Shyness, he says, is no good comrade for a beggar man."

Then answering him, said wise Odysseus: "O Zeus above, may Telemachus be blessed among mankind, and may he get whatever in his heart he longs for!"

He spoke, and took the food with both his hands and laid it down before his feet on his mean wallet, and so ate, the while within the hall the bard was singing. But when the meal was ended and the sacred bard had ceased, the suitors raised an uproar in the hall. And now Athene, drawing near Laërtes' son, Odysseus, urged him to gather crusts among the suitors, and learn who were the righteous ones and who the lawless; though not even thus would she preserve a man of them from ruin. So off he went to beg of all from left to right, stretching his hand around as if he had been long a beggar. They pitied him and gave, and wondering at the man asked one another who he was and whence he came; and Melanthius, the goatherd, said:

"Hear from me, suitors of the illustrious queen, something about the stranger. I saw him a while ago; and certainly it was the swineherd brought him hither. The man himself I do not really know, nor of what tribe he boasts himself to be."

When he had spoken, Antinoüs rebuked the swineherd thus: "Infamous swineherd, why bring this man to town? Have we not here already plenty of vagabonds and nasty beggars to make mischief at our feasts? Do you not mind that men devour the living of their lord by gathering here? And do you ask this fellow too to come?"

Then, swineherd Eumaeus, you answered him and said: "Antinoüs, you speak but ill, noble although you are. Who ever goes and calls a stranger from abroad? Unless indeed the stranger is a master of some craft, a prophet, healer of disease, or builder, or else a wondrous bard who pleases by his song; for these are welcomed by mankind the wide world through. A beggar, who would ask to be a torment to himself? But you are always harsh—more than the other suitors,—to the servants of Odysseus, especially to me. And yet I do not care, so long as heedful Penelope is living in the palace, Penelope and prince Telemachus."

Then said discreet Telemachus: "Hush! Do not make him a long answer. It is Antinoüs' way ever to tease with ugly talk. He stirs up others too."

He spoke, and to Antinoüs in winged words he said: "Antinoüs, finely you care for me, as a father for his son, bidding me drive this stranger forth by a compulsive word! God let that never be! Take of the food and give him. I do not grudge it; indeed I bid you give. Be not disquieted about my mother or any servant of the house of great Odysseus. But in your breast there is no thought of giving. Far better you like to eat than give to others."

Then answering said Antinoüs: "Telemachus, of the lofty tongue and the unbridled temper, what do you mean? If every suitor gave as much as I, for three months' space at least the house would miss him."

So saying, he seized his stool and drew it out from under the table where it lay. On it he used to set his dainty feet while feasting. Now all the rest had given food and filled with bread and meat the beggar's wallet. A moment and Odysseus would go back to the threshold to taste the Achaeans' bounty. Before Antinoüs he paused, and said:

"Give me some food, kind sir! You do not seem the poorest of the Achaeans; rather, the chief; for you are like a king. So you shall give me bread more generously than others, and I will sing your praise the wide world through. For once I lived in luxury among my mates, in a rich house, and often gave to wanderers, careless who they might be or with what needs they came. Servants I had in plenty, and everything besides by which men live at ease and are reputed rich. But Zeus, the son of Kronos, brought me low. His will it was. He sent me with a roving band of plunderers to Egypt, a long voyage, to my ruin. In Egypt's stream I anchored my curved ships; then to my trusty men I gave command to stay there by the ships and guard the ships, while I sent scouts to points of observation. But giving way to lawlessness and following their own bent, they presently began to pillage the fair fields of the Egyptians, carrying off wives and infant children and slaughtering the men. Soon the din reached the city. The people there, hearing the shouts, came forth at early dawn, and all the plain was filled with footmen and with horsemen and with the gleam of bronze. Then Zeus, the Thunderer, brought on my men a cruel panic, and none dared stand and face the foe. Danger encountered us on every side. So the Egyptians slew many of our men with the sharp sword, and carried others off alive to work for them in bondage. They gave me to a friend who chanced to meet them upon his way to Cyprus, to Dmetor son of Iasus, who ruled with power in Cyprus. Thence I am now come hither, sore distressed."

Then answered him Antinoüs and said: "What god has brought to us this pest, this mar-feast here? Stand off there in the middle, back from my table, or you shall find a bitter Egypt and a bitter Cyprus too, brazen and shameless beggar that you are! You go to all in turn, and they give lavishly. No scruple or compunction do they feel at being generous with others' goods, while there remains abundance for themselves."

Then stepping back said wise Odysseus: "Indeed! In you then wisdom does not go with beauty. From your own house you would not give a suppliant salt, if sitting at another's table you will not take and give me bread. Yet here there is abundance."

As he thus spoke, Antinoüs was angered in his heart the more, and looking sternly on him said in winged words: "Now you shall never leave the hall in peace, I think, now you have taunted me."

So saying, he seized his footstool, flung it and struck Odysseus on the back of the right shoulder, near the spine. Firm as a rock he stood; the missile of Antinoüs did not move him. Silent he shook his head, brooding on evil. Then once more walking toward the threshold, down he sat, laid off his well-filled wallet, and thus addressed the suitors:

"Hearken, you suitors of the illustrious queen, and let me tell you what the heart within me bids. One feels no smart or indignation in his mind if struck while fighting for his own possessions, his oxen, say, or white-wooled sheep; but Antinoüs gave this blow because of my poor belly, that wretched part which brings to men so many ills. If then for beggars there be gods and furies, may death's doom seize Antinoüs before his marriage."

Then said Antinoüs, Eupeithes' son: "Stranger, sit still and eat, or go off elsewhere; or for such talk as this young men will drag you through the house by hand and foot, and strip off all your skin."

At these his words all were exceeding wroth, and a rude youth would say: "Antinoüs, 'twas not well done to assault the wretched wanderer. A doomed man you, if he should be a god come down from heaven. And gods in guise of strangers from afar in every form do roam our cities, marking the sin and righteousness of men."

So said the suitors; Antinoüs did not heed their words. But Telemachus nursed in his heart great indignation at the blow, yet let no tear fall from his eyelids to the ground. Silent he shook his head, brooding on evil.

When heedful Penelope heard how in the hall a man was struck, she said to her maids: "May the archer-god Apollo strike you even so!" Whereat Eurynome the housekeeper made answer: "If only prayers of ours might be fulfilled, no one of them should see another bright-throned dawn."

And heedful Penelope replied: "Nurse, hateful are they all; their ways are evil; but Antinoüs is like dark doom itself. Into the house strays some poor stranger, and begs for bread, as need compels; then while all others gave and filled his wallet, Antinoüs struck him with a footstool on the back of the right shoulder."

So talked Penelope with her maids as she sat within a chamber, while royal Odysseus was busied with his meal. Then calling the noble swineherd, thus she spoke: "Go, noble Eumaeus, go bid the stranger come to me. I wish to greet him and to ask if he has heard of hardy Odysseus or with his own eyes seen him. He looks a traveled man."

Then, swineherd Eumaeus, you answered her and said: "Would, queen, the Achaeans would be still! What he can tell would charm your very soul. Three nights I had him; for three days I kept him at the lodge; he came to me at once on escaping from his vessel. Yet all that time he never ended telling me his troubles. And just as when men gaze upon a bard who has been taught by gods to sing them moving lays, and they long to listen endlessly so long as the bard will sing; even so he held me spell-bound as he sat within my room. He calls Odysseus his ancestral friend, and says his home is Crete, where the race of Minos dwell. Thence he is now come hither, sore distressed and onward driven ever. He declares he has heard that Odysseus is near at hand, in the rich land of the Thesprotians, a living man, and that he brings a mass of treasure home."

Then said to him heedful Penelope: "Go call him hither, to tell his story here before my face. Let men make merry, sitting before the door, or here within the house. Their hearts are gay. Untouched at home their goods are lying, their bread and their sweet wine. On these their servants feed. But haunting this house of ours day after day, killing our oxen, sheep, and fatted goats, these suitors hold high revel, drinking sparkling wine with little heed. Much goes to waste; for there is no man here fit, like Odysseus, to keep damage from our doors. But if Odysseus should return, home to his native land, soon with his son's help he would punish these men's crimes."

As she spoke thus, Telemachus sneezed loudly, and all the hall gave a great echo. Penelope laughed, and to Eumaeus straightway said in winged words: "Pray go and call the stranger before me, as I bade. Do you not notice how my son sneezed at my words? Therefore no partial death shall strike the suitors. On all it falls; none shall escape from death and doom. Nay, this I will say farther; mark it well: if I shall find that all the stranger tells is true, I will clothe him in a coat and tunic, goodly garments."

She spoke, and the swineherd went as soon as he heard the order, and standing near the stranger said in winged words: "Here, good old stranger, heedful Penelope is calling, the mother of Telemachus. Her heart inclines her to ask for tidings of her husband, so full of grief is she. And if she finds that all you tell is true, she will clothe you in a coat and tunic, things that you greatly need. Moreover, you shall beg your bread about the land and fill your belly. Whoever will shall give."

Then said to him long-tried royal Odysseus: "Eumaeus, I would straightway tell my whole true story to the daughter of Icarius, heedful Penelope; for well I know about Odysseus. We have borne the self-same sorrows. But I have fears about this crowd of cruel suitors, whose arrogance and outrage reaches the iron heavens; for even now when, as I walked along the hall doing no harm, this person struck and hurt me, neither Telemachus nor others interfered. Bid then Penelope, however eager, wait in the hall till sunset; then let her ask about her husband's coming, after giving me a seat beside the fire; for the clothes I wear are poor. That, you yourself well know; because it was of you I first sought aid."

He spoke, and the swineherd went as soon as he heard the order. But as he crossed the threshold, thus spoke Penelope: "Are you not bringing him, Eumaeus? What does the wanderer mean? Is he afraid of some bad man, or simply shy at being in the palace? To be a homeless man and shy is bad."

Then, swineherd Eumaeus, you answered her and said: "Rightly he speaks, as any man must think, if he would shun the violence of these audacious men. He bids you wait till sunset. And it is better too for you, my queen, to speak to the stranger privately and listen to his tale."

Then said to him heedful Penelope: "Not without wisdom thinks the stranger thus, whoever he may be; for mortal men have never yet so wantonly wrought outrage."

She spoke, and the noble swineherd entered the throng of suitors, when he had told her all; and straightway to Telemachus he spoke these winged words,—his head bent close, that others might not hear:

"My dear, I go to guard the swine and matters there, your livelihood and mine; do you mind all things here. Above all else, keep yourself safe and see that nothing happens. Many of the Achaeans are forming wicked plans, whom Zeus confound before harm falls on us!"

Then answered him discreet Telemachus: "So be it, father! Go when you have supped; and in the morning come and bring us goodly victims. To me and the immortal gods leave all things here."

He spoke, and once more down Eumaeus sat upon a polished bench. Then, after having satisfied desire for food and drink, he departed to his swine, leaving the courts and hall crowded with feasters, who with dance and song were making merry; for evening now drew near.

XVIII.

THE FIGHT OF ODYSSEUS AND IRUS

THERE CAME into the hall a common beggar, who used to beg about the town of Ithaca, and everywhere was noted for his greedy belly, eating and drinking without end. He had no strength nor sinew, but in bulk was large to see. Arnaeus was his name, the name his honored mother gave at his birth; but Irus all the young men called him, because he used to run on errands at anybody's bidding. Coming in now, he tried to drive Odysseus from the house, and jeeringly he spoke these winged words:

"Get up, old man, and leave the door-way, or you will soon be dragged off by the leg. Do you not see how everybody gives the wink and bids me drag you forth? I still hold back. Up, then! Or soon our quarrel comes to blows."

But looking sternly on him wise Odysseus said: "Sir, I am doing you no harm by deed or word, nor do I grudge it when men take and give you much. This door will hold us both. Surely you should not grudge the goods of others. You seem a wanderer, like myself; but the gods may grant us fortune. Yet do not challenge me too far with show of fists, or you may rouse my rage; and old as I am, I still might stain your breast and lips with blood. Then I should have more peace to-morrow than to-day; for a second time, I think, you would not seek the hall of Laërtes' son, Odysseus."

Then angrily replied the beggar Irus: "Pshaw! How glibly the glutton talks, like an old oven-woman! But I will do him an ugly turn, knocking him right and left, and scattering all the teeth out of his jaws upon the ground, as if he were a pig spoiling the corn. Gird yourself then, that all these men may watch our fighting. Yet how could you defend yourself against a younger man?"

Thus on the well-worn threshold before the lofty door they fiercely wrangled. Revered Antinoüs observed them, and gaily laughing he thus addressed the suitors:

"Friends, nothing so good as this has ever happened. What sport God sends this house! The stranger here and Irus are goading one another on to blows. Let us quickly set them on!"

He spoke, and laughing all sprang up and flocked around the tattered beggars, and Antinoüs, Eupeithes' son, called out: "Hearken, you haughty suitors, while I speak. Here are goat-paunches lying by the fire, set there for supper, full of fat and blood. Whichever wins and proves the better man, let him step forth and take what one of these he will; and that man shall hereafter always attend our feasts and we will allow no other beggar to come here asking alms."

So said Antinoüs, and his saying pleased them. But in his subtlety said wise Odysseus: "It is not fair, my friends, a young man should fight an old one, one broken too by trouble. Yet a reckless belly forces me to bear his blows. Come then, all swear a solemn oath that nobody helping Irus will strike with heavy hand an unfair blow, and put me down before the man perforce."

He spoke, and all then took the oath which he required. And after they had sworn and ended all their oath, once more revered Telemachus spoke out among them: "Stranger, if heart and daring spirit tempt you to meet the man, be not afraid of any of the Achaeans; for he shall fight the crowd who strikes at you. I am the host. The princes too assent, Antinoüs and Eurymachus, both honest-minded men."

He spoke, and all approved. Meanwhile Odysseus gathered his rags around his waist and showed his thighs, so far and large, and his broad shoulders came in sight, his breast and sinewy arms. Athene, drawing nigh, filled out the limbs of the shepherd of the people, that all the suitors greatly wondered. And glancing at his neighbor one would say:

"Irus will soon be no more Irus, but catch a plague of his own bringing; so big a thigh the old man shows under his rags."

So they spoke, and Irus' heart was sorely shaken; nevertheless, the serving-men girt him and led him out, forcing him on in spite of fears. The muscles quivered on his limbs. But Antinoüs rebuked him and spoke to him and said:

"Better you were not living, loud-mouthed bully, and never had been born, if you quake and are so mightily afraid at meeting this old man, one broken by the trouble he has had. Nay, this I tell you and it shall be done: if he shall win and prove the better man, I will toss you into a black ship and send you to the mainland, off to king Echetus, the bane of all mankind; and he will cut your nose and ears off with his ruthless sword, and tearing out your bowels give them raw to dogs to eat."

So he spoke, and a trembling greater still fell on the limbs of Irus.

But into the ring they led him, and both men raised their fists. Then long-tried royal Odysseus doubted whether to strike him so that life might leave him as he fell, or to strike lightly and but stretch him on the ground. Reflecting thus, it seemed the better way lightly to strike, for fear the Achaeans might discover it was he. So when they raised their fists, Irus struck the right shoulder of Odysseus; but he struck Irus on the neck below the ear and crushed the bones within. Forthwith from out his mouth the red blood ran, and down in the dust he fell with a moan, gnashing his teeth and kicking on the ground. The lordly suitors raised their hands and almost died with laughter. But Odysseus caught Irus by the foot and dragged him through the door-way, until he reached the courtyard and the opening of the porch. Against the courtyard wall he set him up aslant, then thrust a staff into his hand, and speaking in winged words he said:

"Sit there awhile, and scare off dogs and swine; and do not try to be the lord of strangers and of beggars, while pitiful yourself, or haply some worse fate may fall on you."

He spoke, and round his shoulder slung his miserable wallet, full of holes, which hung upon a cord, then once more walking to the threshold he sat down; meanwhile the others pressed indoors with merry laughter and thus accosted him:

"Stranger, may Zeus and the other immortal gods grant all you wish for most, even all your heart's desire, for stopping this insatiate fellow's begging through the land. Soon we will take him to the mainland, off to king Echetus, the bane of all mankind."

So they spoke, and royal Odysseus was happy in the omen. Antinoüs too set a great paunch before him, full of fat and blood, and Amphinomus took two loaves out of the basket and offered them, and pledged him in a golden cup and said: "Hail, aged stranger! May happiness be yours in time to come, though you are tried by many troubles now!"

Then wise Odysseus answered him and said: "Indeed, Amphinomus, you seem a man of understanding. Such was your father too; for I have heard a good report of Nisus of Doulichion, how he was brave and rich. They say you are his son. You appear kind. So I will speak and do you mark and listen. Earth breeds no creature frailer than a man, of all that breathe and move upon the earth. For he says he never more will meet with trouble, so long as the gods give vigor and make his knees be strong. Then when the blessed gods send sorrow, this too he bears with patient heart, although against his will. Ever the mood of man while on the earth is as the day which the father of men and gods bestows. Once among men I too was counted prosperous; but many wrongs I wrought, led on by pride and sense of power, confident in my father's and my brothers' aid. Wherefore let none in any wise be reckless, but calmly take whatever gifts the gods provide. Yet I behold you suitors working wrong, wasting the wealth and worrying the wife of one who, I can tell you, will not be absent long from friends and native land; for he is very near. May then some heavenly power conduct you to your homes! And may you not encounter him whenever he returns to his own native land! Surely not bloodless will the parting be between the suitors and himself when underneath this roof he comes once more."

He spoke, and pouring a libation drank the honeyed wine, then back in the hands of the guardian of the people placed the cup. Amphinomus walked down the hall heavy at heart, shaking his head; his soul foreboded ill. Yet even so he did not escape his doom; for Athene bound him fast, beneath the hand and spear of Telemachus to be perforce laid low. So back he turned and took the seat from which he first arose.

And now the goddess, clear-eyed Athene, put in the mind of Icarius' daughter, heedful Penelope, to show herself among the suitors; that she might thus open the suitors' hearts most largely, and so become more highly prized by husband and by son than heretofore. Idly she laughed and thus she spoke and said:

"Eurynome, my heart is longing as it never longed before to show myself among the suitors, hateful although they be. I would say to my son a word that may be useful; tell him to mingle not at all with the audacious suitors, for they speak kindly but have evil thoughts behind."

And in her turn Eurynome, the housewife, answered: "Truly, my child, in all this you speak rightly. Go then and tell this saying to your son and do not hide it; only first wash your body and anoint your cheeks. Go not with such a tear-stained face. To grieve incessantly makes matters worse. And now your son is what you often prayed the immortals you might see him, a bearded man already."

Then said to her heedful Penelope: "Eurynome, urge me not, out of kindness, to wash my body and anoint me with the oil. All charm of mine the gods who hold Olympus took away when he departed in the hollow ships. But tell Autonoë and Hippodameia to come hither, to attend me in the hall. Among the men I will not go alone, for very shame."

So she spoke, and through the hall forth the old woman went to give the message to the maids and bid them come with speed.

Then a new plan the goddess formed, clear-eyed Athene. She poured sweet slumber on the daughter of Icarius; and lying back she slept and every joint relaxed, there on her couch. Meanwhile the heavenly goddess gave her immortal gifts, to make the Achaeans marvel. And first she bathed her lovely cheeks with an immortal bloom, like that with which crowned Cytherea anoints herself when going to the

gladsome dance among the Graces. She made her also taller and larger
to behold, and made her whiter than the new-cut ivory. So having
done, the heavenly goddess went her way; and out of the hall the white-
armed damsels came, entering the room with noise. Sweet slumber left
Penelope. She drew her hands across her cheeks and thus she spoke:

"Ah, utterly wretched as I am, soft slumber wrapt me round. Would
that chaste Artemis would send a death so soft,—instantly now,—that,
sad at heart no more, I might not waste my days mourning the many-
sided worth of him, my husband, the best of all Achaeans!"

So saying, down she went from her bright upper chamber, yet not
alone; two damsels followed her. And when the royal lady reached the
suitors, she stood beside a column of the strong-built roof, holding
before her face her delicate wimple, the while a faithful damsel stood
upon either hand. The suitors' knees grew weak; with love their hearts
were tranced. Each prayed to lie beside her. But she addressed
Telemachus, her own dear son:

"Telemachus, your mind and judgment are no longer sound. While
still a boy you managed more discreetly. But now when you are grown
and come to man's estate, and any stranger would call you the son of a
man of worth, if he observed your height and beauty,—now mind and
judgment are not trusty any more. For only see what happened in the
hall: you let this stranger be maltreated there. And what will be thought
if a stranger, seated within our house, should meet with harm through
brutal handling? Shame and disgrace would come on you from all men."

Then answered her discreet Telemachus: "Mother, I do not blame
you for your anger. Yet in my heart I know and fully understand the
right and wrong. Before, I was a child, and I am not always able now to
see what wise ways are; for the suitors disconcert me, coming on every
side with wicked plans, while I have none to help. However, the quarrel of Irus and the stranger turned out in no wise to the suitors' mind.
In strength the stranger proved the better man. Ah father Zeus, Athene,
and Apollo, would that the suitors in our halls might beaten hang their
heads,—some in the yard, some in the house,—and so their limbs be
loosed, as that same Irus at the courtyard gate now sits and hangs his
head, like a man drunk, and cannot stand straight on his feet nor go off
home, wherever that may be, because his limbs are loose."

So they conversed together. But now Eurymachus addressed
Penelope: "Daughter of Icarius, heedful Penelope, if all Achaeans in
Iasian Argos could behold you, more suitors would be feasting in your
halls to-morrow; for you excel all womankind in beauty, height, and
balanced mind within."

Then answered him heedful Penelope: "Eurymachus, all excellence
of mine in face or form the immortals took away the day the Argive host

took ship for Ilios, and with them went my lord Odysseus. If he would come and tend this life of mine, greater would be my fame and fairer then. Now I am in distress, such woes God thrusts upon me. Ah, when he went and left his native land, holding my hand,—my right hand, by the wrist,—he said: 'Wife, I do not think the mailed Achaeans will all come back from Troy safe and unharmed; for they say the Trojans are good fighters,—hurlers of spears, drawers of bows, and riders on swift horses,—such men as soon decide the struggle of uncertain war. Therefore I do not know if God will bring me back, or if I shall be captured there in Troy. On you must rest the care of all things here. Be mindful of my father and my mother here at home, as you are now, and even more when I am gone. And when you see our son a bearded man, then marry whom you will, and leave the house now yours.' Such were his words, and all now nears its end. The night will come when a detested marriage falls on doomed me, whom Zeus has stripped of fortune. One bitter vexation, too, touches my heart and soul: this never was the way with suitors heretofore; they who will woo a lady of rank, a rich man's daughter, rivaling one another, bring oxen and sturdy sheep, to feast the maiden's friends, and give rich gifts besides. They do not, making no amends, devour another's substance."

She spoke, and glad was long-tried royal Odysseus to see her winning gifts and charming the suitors' hearts with pleasing words, while her mind had a different purpose.

Then said Antinoüs, Eupeithes' son: "Daughter of Icarius, heedful Penelope, if any Achaean cares to bring gifts hither, accept them; for it is not gracious to refuse a gift. But we will never go to our estates, nor elsewhere either, till you are married to the best Achaean here."

So said Antinoüs, and his saying pleased them; and for the bringing of the gifts each man sent forth his page. The page of Antinoüs brought a fair large robe of many colors; on it were golden brooches, twelve in all, mounted with twisted clasps. To Eurymachus his page presently brought a chain, wrought curiously in gold and set with amber, bright as the sun. His servants brought Eurydamus a pair of earrings, each brilliant with three drops; from them great beauty sparkled. Out of the house of lord Peisander, son of Polyctor, his servant brought a necklace, a jewel exceeding fair. And other servants brought still other fitting gifts from the Achaeans.

Then went the royal lady to her upper chamber, her damsels carrying the goodly gifts. Meanwhile the suitors to dancing and the gladsome song turned merrily, and waited for the evening to come on. And on their merriment dark evening came. Straightway they set three braziers in the hall, to give them light, and piled upon them sapless logs,—long seasoned, very dry, and freshly split,—with which they mingled brands.

By turns the maids of hardy Odysseus fed the fire; and he, the high-born wise Odysseus, thus addressed them:

"You damsels of Odysseus, a master long away, go to the room where your honored mistress stays. There twirl your spindles by her side and furnish her good cheer, as you sit within her hall, and card with your hands the wool. I will supply the light for all these here. Yes, if they wish to stay till bright-throned dawn, they will not weary me; I am practiced to endure."

At these his words the damsels laughed and glanced at one another, and Melantho rudely reviled Odysseus,—Melantho the fair-faced girl, daughter of Dolius, whom Penelope had reared and treated as her child, granting her every whim. But for all this, she entertained no sorrow for Penelope, but loved Eurymachus and was his paramour. She now reviled Odysseus in these abusive words:

"Why, silly stranger, you are certainly some crack-brained person, unwilling to go to the coppersmith's to sleep, or to the common lodge; but here you prate continually, braving these many lords and unabashed at heart. Surely the wine has touched your wits; or else it is your constant way to chatter idly. Are you beside yourself because you beat that scapegrace Irus? A better man than Irus may by and by arise, to box your pate with doughty blows and pack you out of doors all dabbled with your blood."

But looking sternly on her, wise Odysseus said: "You cur, I go, and at once tell Telemachus what words you use; and he shall tear you limb from limb upon the spot."

So saying, by his words he frightened off the women. They hurried along the hall. The knees of each grew weak with terror, for they thought he spoke in earnest. He, meanwhile, keeping up the fire, stood by the blazing braziers observing all the men. But other thoughts his heart debated, thoughts not to fail of issue.

Yet Athene allowed the haughty suitors not altogether yet to cease from biting scorn. She wished more pain to pierce the heart of Laërtes' son, Odysseus. So Eurymachus the son of Polybus began to speak, and jeering Odysseus raised a laugh among his mates: "Hearken, you suitors of the illustrious queen, and let me tell you what the heart within me bids. Not without guidance of a god this fellow comes to the household of Odysseus. At any rate, a torchlight seems to rise from his very head; for hair upon it there is none, no not the least."

With that he called to the spoiler of towns, Odysseus: "Stranger, if I would take you, would you like to work for hire on the outskirts of my farm,—there will be pay enough,—gathering stones for walls and setting out tall trees? There for a year I would provide you food, furnish you clothing and put sandals on your feet. Still, now that you have learned bad ways you will not care to work, but will prefer to beg about the town, so long as you can find wherewith to stuff your greedy maw."

Then wise Odysseus answered him and said: "Eurymachus, I wish that we might have a match at work, in spring-time when the days are long, upon the grass; and I would take a well-curved scythe and you another like it to test our power of work, fasting right up till dark, with grass still plenty. Or if again the match were driving oxen,—choice, tawny, large ones, both well fed with grass, equal in years and pulling well together, tireless in strength,—and here were a field four acres large, whose soil would take the plow; then you should see if I could cut a straight and even furrow. Or, once more, if the son of Kronos by some means stirred up war, this very day, and I had a shield and pair of spears and a brazen helmet fitted to my brow, then would you see me join the foremost in the fight, and you would no longer jest and talk about my belly. No, you are very proud and your temper is disdainful; no doubt you seem a great man and a mighty, because you mix with few and they of little worth. But should Odysseus come and reach his native land, soon would these doors, however wide, prove all too narrow, as you hurried through the porch."

As he spoke thus, Eurymachus grew angrier still at heart, and looking sternly on Odysseus, he spoke these winged words: "Wretch, I shall do you mischief soon for prating so, braving these many lords and unabashed at heart. Surely the wine has touched your wits; or else it is your constant way to chatter idly. Are you beside yourself because you beat that scapegrace Irus?"

So saying, he seized a footstool; Odysseus crouched by the knees of Amphinomus of Doulichion, fearing Eurymachus, who hit the right hand of the wine-pourer. Down went his beaker clattering to the ground, and he himself fell moaning in the dust. But the suitors broke into uproar up and down the dusky ball, and glancing at his neighbor one would say:

"Would that the vagabond had perished elsewhere before he came in here! He would not then have caused this din. Here we are brawling over beggars. No more delight in jolly feasts; now worse things have their way!"

Then said to them revered Telemachus: "Sirs, you are mad, and do not hide that you have drunk and eaten. Some god excites you. But now that you have feasted well, go home to bed as quickly as you please. Yet I drive none away."

He spoke, and all with teeth set in their lips marveled because Telemachus had spoken boldly. And then Amphinomus, the illustrious son of noble Nisus, and grandson of Aretias, addressed them saying: "Friends, in answering what is fairly said, none should be angry and retort with spiteful words. Let none abuse the stranger nor any of the servants in great Odysseus' hall. Come then and let the wine-pourer give pious portions to our cups, that after a libation we each go home to bed. And let us leave the stranger here within Odysseus' hall, to be cared for by Telemachus; for to his house he came."

He spoke, and to them all his words were pleasing. So a bowl was brewed by the lord Moulius, a Doulichian page and follower of Amphinomus. To all in turn he served; and they, with a libation to the blessed gods, drank of the honeyed wine. Then after they had poured and drunk as their hearts would, desiring rest, they each departed homeward.

XIX.

THE MEETING WITH PENELOPE AND THE RECOGNITION BY EURYCLEIA

So in the hall was royal Odysseus left behind, plotting to slay the suitors with Athene's aid, and straightway to Telemachus he spoke these winged words:

"Telemachus, this fighting gear must all be laid away, and with soft words you must beguile the suitors when they because they miss it question you: 'I put it by out of the smoke, for it looks no longer like the armor which Odysseus left behind when he went away to Troy; it is all tarnished, where the scent of fire has come nigh. Besides, this graver fear some god put in my mind. You might when full of wine begin a quarrel and give each other wounds, making a scandal of the feast and of your wooing. Steel itself draws men on.'"

He spoke, and Telemachus heeded his dear father, and calling aside nurse Eurycleia, said: "Nurse, go and keep the women in their rooms while I place in the chamber my father's goodly armor, which as it lies uncared for round the house smoke stains, while he is gone. I have been foolish. Now I will place it where no scent of fire shall come nigh."

Then said to him his dear nurse Eurycleia: "Ah! Would, my child, you might incline to heedful ways, and mind the house and guard its treasures! But who shall go and bear the light? You will not let the women stir who might have lighted you."

Then answered her discreet Telemachus: "This stranger here; for I will allow no idle man to touch my bread, come he from whence he may."

Such were his words; unwinged, they rested with her. She locked the doors of the stately hall. And now arose Odysseus and his gallant son and bore away the helmets, bulging shields and pointed spears. Before them Pallas Athene, holding a golden lamp, made beauteous light. Thereat Telemachus said to his father quickly:

"Father, my eyes behold a mighty marvel. The palace walls and the fair interspaces, the pine-wood beams and the uprising pillars are all aglow as from a blazing fire. Surely a god is in this house, even such as they who hold the open sky."

But wise Odysseus answered him and said: "Hush, check your thoughts and ask no question. It is indeed an indication of the gods that hold Olympus. Go you to rest. I will continue here, to try these damsels and your mother more; and she shall weep and question me of all."

So he spoke, and through the hall forth went Telemachus with blazing torch, to rest within that chamber where he always lay when pleasant sleep drew near. Here then he laid him down, awaiting sacred dawn; while in the hall royal Odysseus staid behind, plotting to slay the suitors with Athene's aid.

Now from her room came heedful Penelope, like Artemis or golden Aphrodite. Beside the fire where she was wont to sit, they placed a chair fashioned with spiral work of ivory and silver; which Icmalius, the carpenter, had made long time ago, setting upon the lower part a rest for feet, fixed to the chair itself. Over the whole a large fleece had been thrown. Here heedful Penelope now sat down. Soon came the white-armed damsels from their hall, and cleared away the abundant food, the tables, and the cups from which the proud lords had been drinking. The embers from the braziers they threw upon the floor, and in the braziers piled fresh heaps of wood to furnish light and warmth. Then thus Melantho once more chid Odysseus:

"Stranger, are you still here, to plague us all night long, prowling about the house, watching the women? Be off, vile thing, and be content with eating, or you will soon be hit with a brand and go."

But looking sternly on her, wise Odysseus said: "Woman, why rail at me with such an angry heart? Is it that I am foul and wear mean clothes and beg about the land? Necessity constrains me. This is what beggars and what homeless people are. Yet once I lived in luxury among my mates, in a rich house, and often gave to wanderers, careless who they might be or with what need they came. Servants I had in plenty and everything besides by which men live at ease and are reputed rich. But Zeus, the son of Kronos, brought me low. His will it was. And you too, woman, some day yet may lose those charms in which you now excel the other maids. Your mistress may become provoked to anger with you. Odysseus may return; there still is room for hope. But if he is dead, as you suppose, and to return no more, yet by Apollo's grace he has a worthy son, Telemachus, whose eye no woman in the hall escapes in her misdeeds; because he is no longer now the child he was."

Heedful Penelope heard what he was saying, and she rebuked her maid and spoke to her and said: "Not in the least, you bold and shameless creature, have you escaped my eye in doing guilty deeds. Your head shall answer for them. Full well you knew—you heard it from myself—that I intended to ask tidings of this stranger here in my hall about my husband; for I am sore distressed."

She spoke, and to the house-keeper Eurynome she said: "Eurynome, pray bring a bench and a fleece on it, and let the stranger sit and tell his tale, and listen too to me; I wish to question him."

She spoke; the other with all speed brought her a polished bench and placed it there, and on it laid a fleece. Then long-tried royal Odysseus sat him down, and thus began heedful Penelope:

"Stranger, I will myself first ask you this: who are you? Of what people? Where is your town and kindred?"

Then wise Odysseus answered her and said: "Lady, no man upon the boundless earth may speak dispraise of you, because your fame is wide as is the sky. Such is the glory of a blameless king who reverences God and rules a people numerous and mighty, upholding justice. For him the dark-soiled earth produces wheat and barley, trees bend low with fruit, the flock has constant issue, and the sea yields fish, under his righteous sway. Because of him his people prosper. Question me, then, of all things else while I am here; but do not ask my lineage and home, nor fill my heart with still more pains by recollection. I am a man of sorrows; yet must I not in a strange house sit down to weep and wail. To grieve incessantly makes matters worse. One of these maids, or you yourself, might take it ill, and say my flood of tears came with a weight of wine."

Then answered him heedful Penelope: "Stranger, all excellence of mine in face or form the immortals took away the day the Argive host took ship for Ilios, and with them went my lord Odysseus. If he would come and tend this life of mine, greater would be my fame and fairer then. Now I am in distress, such woes God thrusts upon me. For all the nobles who bear sway among the islands—Doulichion, Same, and woody Zacynthus—and they who here in far-seen Ithaca dwell round about, sue for unwilling me and waste my house. Wherefore I pay no heed to strangers or to suppliants, nor even to heralds who ply a public trade; but, longing for Odysseus, I waste my heart away. These men urge on my marriage: I wind my skein of guile. First, Heaven inspired my mind to set up a great loom within the hall and weave a robe, fine and exceeding large; and to the men said I, 'Young men who are my suitors, though royal Odysseus now is dead, forbear to urge my marriage till I complete this robe,—its threads must not be wasted,—a shroud for lord Laërtes, against the time when the fell doom of death that lays men low shall overtake him. Achaean wives about the land I fear might give me blame if he should lie without a shroud, he who had great possessions.' Such were my words, and their high hearts assented. Then in the daytime would I weave at the great web, but in the night unravel, after my torch was set. Thus for three years I hid my craft and cheated the Achaeans. But when the fourth year came, as time rolled on, when the months waned and the long days were done, then through the means of maids—the thankless creatures,—they came and caught me and upbraided me; so then I finished it, against my will, perforce. Now I can neither shun the match nor find a fresh device. My parents too press me to marry, and my son chafes at the men who swallow up his living; noting it now, for now he is a man and fully able to heed his house, and Zeus vouchsafes him honor. Yet what of this! Tell me the lineage of which you come. You are not born of immemorial oak or rock."

Then wise Odysseus answered her and said: "O honored wife of Laërtes' son, Odysseus, will you not cease to question of my lineage? Well, I will tell the tale, though you deliver me to sorrows more than I now bear. But so it ever is when one is absent from his land as long as I, wandering from town to town, he meets with hardship! Still, I will tell you what you ask and seek to know.

"There is a country, Crete, in the midst of the wine-dark sea, a fair land and a rich, begirt with water. The people there are many, innumerable indeed, and they have ninety cities. Their speech is mixed; one language joins another. Here are Achaeans, here brave native Cretans, here Cydonians, crested Dorians, and noble Pelasgians. Of all their towns the capital is Cnosus, where Minos became king when nine years old—Minos, the friend of mighty Zeus and father of my father, bold Deucalion. Deucalion begot me and the prince Idomeneus. Idomeneus, however, went in beaked ships to Ilios, in train of the Atreidae. My own proud name is Aethon, and I am the younger born; he was the older and the better man. Here was it that I saw Odysseus and gave him entertainment; for into Crete a strong wind bore him, and while he steered toward Troy it forced him past Maleia. He anchored at Amnisus, where is Elithyia's cave, in a harbor hard to win, and he scarcely cleared the storm. Straightway he came to town, inquiring for Idomeneus; for he said he was his friend, beloved and honored. But it was now the tenth dawn, or the eleventh, since Idomeneus had gone with the beaked ships to Ilios. And so it happened it was I who brought him to the palace, where I entertained him well and gave him generous welcome from the abundance of my house. To him and all the men who followed I furnished barley-meal and sparkling wine from out the public store, with oxen enough for sacrifice to fill

their heart's desire. Here for twelve days the noble Achaeans tarried;
the strong wind Boreas constrained them and even near the shore let
them not lie at anchor. Some baffling power aroused it. But on the thirteenth day the wind went down, and so they put to sea."

He made the many falsehoods of his tale seem like the truth. So as
she listened, drops ran down; she melted into tears. And as the snow
melts on the lofty mountains, when Eurus melts what Zephyrus has
scattered, and at its melting flowing rivers fill; so did her fair cheeks
melt with flowing tears, as she bewailed the husband who was seated by
her side. Odysseus in his heart pitied his sobbing wife; but his eyes
stood fixed as horn or iron, motionless in their sockets. Through craft
he checked his tears. But when she had had her fill of tears and sighs,
finding her words once more she said to him:

"Now, stranger, I shall put you to the test, I think, and see if at your
hall you really entertained my husband and his gallant comrades, as
you say. Tell me what sort of clothes he wore; what the man himself was
like, and the comrades who were with him."

Then wise Odysseus answered her and said: "O lady, it is hard, with
so long a time between, to tell you that; for twenty years are gone since
he set forth and left my land. Still, I will tell you how my mind makes
him appear. A cloak of purple wool Odysseus wore, made with a double fold. A brooch of gold upon it was fashioned with twin buckles, the
front part ornamented. In his forepaws a dog held down a spotted fawn
and clutched it as it writhed. This all admired and marveled how,
though things of gold, the dog would clutch and choke the fawn, and
how the fawn that struggled to escape would twitch its feet. His tunic
too I noticed, sheeny across the flesh, just like the skin stripped down
from a dried onion; so smooth it was, and glistering like the sun. And
truly many a woman gazed on the man with wonder. But this I will say
farther; mark it well. I do not know if Odysseus wore this dress at home,
or if a comrade gave it when he entered the swift ship, or yet perhaps
some host. Odysseus was beloved by many men; few of the Achaeans
equally. I gave him gifts myself,—a sword of bronze, a beautiful purple
doublet and a bordered tunic; and I sent him off with honor on his
well-benched ship. A herald a little older than himself attended him. I
will describe what manner of man this herald was: bent in the shoulders, swarthy, curly-haired, and named Eurybates. Odysseus honored
him beyond his other comrades, because he had a mind that suited
well his own."

So he spoke, and stirred still more her yearning after tears, as she recognized the tokens which Odysseus exactly told. But when she had had
her fill of tears and sighs, finding her words once more she said to him:

"From this time forth, stranger, you who before were pitied shall in my halls be one beloved and honored. For I it was who gave the clothes which you describe. I folded them in the chamber and fixed the glittering brooch to be his pride. But I shall nevermore receive him homeward returning to his native land. Wherefore through evil fate Odysseus went by hollow ship to see accursed Ilios, name never to be named."

Then wise Odysseus answered her and said: "O honored wife of Laërtes' son Odysseus, mar your fair face no more, nor waste your heart with sorrowing for your husband. And yet I do not blame you; for any woman weeps to lose the husband of her youth, whose children she has borne, whose love she tasted, through he were other than Odysseus, who they say is like the gods. Still, cease your grief and mark my word; for I will speak unerringly and nothing will I hide of what I lately heard about the coming of Odysseus,—how he is near, in the rich country of the Thesprotians, a living man, and bringing with him much good treasure which he has begged throughout the land. His trusty crew and hollow ship he lost on the wine-dark sea, when coming from the island of Thrinacia; for Zeus and the Sun were angry with him, because his crew killed the Sun's kine. So they all perished in the surging sea; but he on his ship's keel was cast by a wave ashore on the coast of the Phaeacians, who are kinsmen of the gods. They honored him exceedingly, as if he were a god, and gave him many gifts and themselves wished to bring him home unharmed. And here in Ithaca Odysseus would have been long time ago, only it seemed a thing of greater profit to gather wealth by roaming far and wide,—so many gainful ways, beyond all mortal men, Odysseus understands; no living man can match him. This is the story which the king of the Thesprotians, Pheidon, told me. Moreover in my presence, as he offered a libation in his house, he swore the ship was launched and sailors waiting to bring him home to his own native land. But he sent me off before, for a ship of the Thesprotians happened to be starting for the Doulichian grainfields. He showed me all the treasure that Odysseus had obtained; and really it would support man after man ten generations long, so large a stock was stored in the king's palace. Odysseus himself, he said, was gone at that time to Dodona, to learn from the sacred lofty oak the will of Zeus, and how he might return, whether openly or by stealth, to his dear native land when now so long away. So he is safe, and soon will come, and now is near at hand, and parted from friends and native land he will not tarry long. Lo, I will add an oath. First then of all the gods be witness Zeus, highest of gods and noblest, and let the hearth of good Odysseus whereto I come be witness; all this shall be accomplished exactly as I say. This very year Odysseus comes, as this moon wanes and as the next appears."

Then said to him heedful Penelope: "Ah, stranger, would these words of yours might be fulfilled! Soon should you know my kindness and many a gift from me, and every man you met would call you blessed. But yet the thought is in my heart how it will really be. Odysseus will return no more, nor you get convoy hence; for there are no more masters in the house, able, as once Odysseus was—if ever he was here,—to speed the worthy stranger forth or kindly to receive. Still, wash the stranger's feet, my women, and prepare his bed, bedstead and robes and bright-hued rugs, that well and warmly he may spend the time till gold-throned dawn; and early in the morning bathe and anoint him well, so that indoors beside Telemachus he may await his meal, seated within the hall. And woe to him who persecutes or frets the man. Henceforth he shall get nothing here, though he be sorely vexed. For how could you think me, stranger, better than other women in will and careful wisdom, if you should sit at table in my hall unkempt and meanly clad? Men are short-lived. And if a man is harsh and thinks harsh thoughts, on him all call down curses while he lives, and when he dies revile him; but he who is gentle and thinks gentle thoughts, his praises strangers carry far and wide to all mankind, and many speak him well."

Then wise Odysseus answered her and said: "O honored wife of Laërtes' son Odysseus, hateful to me are robes and bright-hued rugs, since first I left the snowy hills of Crete on board the long-oared ship. Here I would rest just as I used to lie through sleepless nights; for many a night I spent on a rough bed, awaiting sacred bright-throned dawn. Baths for the feet give me no pleasure, and foot of mine shall not be touched by any of these maids who serve the palace,—unless indeed there be some aged woman, sober-minded, one who has borne as many sorrows as myself. It would not trouble me that such a one should touch my feet."

Then said to him heedful Penelope: "Dear stranger,—and none discreet as you among the traveling strangers has been more welcome at my house, so suitably discreet is all you say,—I have an aged woman of an understanding heart, who gently nursed and tended that unfortunate and took him in her arms the day his mother bore him. She, feeble as she is, shall wash your feet. Come, rise up, heedful Eurycleia, and wash a man old as your master! Perhaps Odysseus is already such as he, in feet and hands; for soon in times of trouble men grow old."

As she spoke thus, the old woman hid her face in her hands and shed hot tears and uttered wailing words:

"Alas for you, my child! Powerless am I. Zeus surely hated you beyond all humankind, godfearing though you were. For no man ever burned to Zeus, the Thunderer, fat thighs so good or such choice hecatombs as you have offered when you prayed to reach a hale old age and rear your gallant son. And yet from you alone he utterly cut off the day of coming home. Even so perhaps women reviled him too at foreign tables, when he reached some lordly house, just as these brutes are all reviling you. To shun their insults and their many taunts, you do not let them wash you; and I, not loath, am bidden to it by the daughter of Icarius, heedful Penelope. So I will wash your feet, both for Penelope's own sake and for your own, because my heart within is stirred by sorrow. Yet mark the words I say! Many a way-worn stranger has come hither; but one so like Odysseus I declare I never saw, as you are like him, form, and voice and feet."

Then wise Odysseus answered her and said: "Yes, woman, so says every one who sees us two, that we are like each other, even as you shrewdly say."

As he spoke thus, the old woman took the glittering basin which she used for washing feet and poured in much cold water, afterwards adding warm. Now Odysseus was sitting by the hearth, but soon turned toward the darkness; for suddenly into his mind there came the thought that in touching him she might detect the scar and thus the facts be known. So she drew near him and began to wash her master; and presently she found the scar which a boar inflicted long ago with his white tusk, when to Parnassus came Odysseus to see Autolycus and his sons. Good Autolycus was the father of the mother of Odysseus, and was famous among men for thievery and oaths. Hermes, the god, had given him skill, because to him Autolycus had burned well-pleasing thighs of lambs and kids; so Hermes gladly served him. Now Autolycus, visiting the fertile land of Ithaca, found there his daughter's son, a child new-born; and after supper Eurycleia laid the child upon his knees, and speaking thus she said:

"Autolycus, choose now a name to give your child's own child. He has been wished for long."

Then answered her Autolycus and said: "My son-in-law and daughter, give him the name I say. Since I come hither odious to many men and women on the bounteous earth, therefore Odysseus be his name. And I, when he is grown and visits the great palace of his mother's kin upon Parnassus, where my possessions lie, will give thereof to him and send him home rejoicing."

On this account Odysseus came to get the glorious gifts. And Autolycus and his sons gave him a welcome with friendly hands and courteous words; and Amphithea, his mother's mother, took Odysseus in her arms and kissed his face and both his beauteous eyes. Then Autolycus bade his famous sons to lay the dinner ready, and they hearkened to his call. They quickly brought an ox, five years old, and flayed and dressed it, laid it asunder, sliced it with skill, stuck it on spits, and roasting it with care served out the portions. Thus all throughout the day till setting sun they held their feast. There was no lack of appetite for the impartial feast. But when the sun had set and darkness came, they laid them down and took the gift of sleep.

When now the early rosy-fingered dawn appeared, they started on the hunt; the dogs went forth, the men themselves,—the sons of Autolycus,—and with them went royal Odysseus too. They climbed the steep and wood-clad mountain of Parnassus and soon they reached its windy ridges. Just then the sun began to touch the fields as he ascended from the calm and brimming stream of Ocean. And now to a glen the prickers came. Before them, following the tracks, the hounds ran on, the sons of Autolycus hastening after. With the sons went royal Odysseus, close on the hounds, wielding his outstretched spear. In a dense thicket here a huge boar lay. It was a spot no force of wind with its chill breath could pierce, no sunbeams smite, nor rain pass through, so dense it was, and a thick fall of leaves was in it. Here round the board there came the tramp of men and dogs, as the prickers pushed along. Facing them from his lair, with bristling back, fire flashing in his eyes, the boar stood close at bay. Odysseus first sprang forward, raising the long spear in his sinewy hand, eager to give the blow; but the boar was quick and struck him on the knee, and by a side-thrust of his tusk tore the flesh deep, but reached no bone. And now Odysseus, by a downward blow, struck the right shoulder of the boar; clean through it the bright spear-point passed. Down in the dust he fell with a moan, and his life flew away. Then the good sons of Autolycus looked to the boar; and the wound of gallant princely Odysseus they bound up skillfully, and with a spell stanched the black blood, and soon they reached their father's house. So Autolycus and his sons when they had fully healed Odysseus and given him glorious gifts,—pleasing by kindness him who pleased them too,— sent him with speed to Ithaca, where his father and honored mother rejoiced at his return and questioned much how he had got the scar. He told them how, while he was hunting, a boar inflicted it with his white tusk when he had gone to Parnassus with Autolycus' sons.

This was the scar the woman felt with her flat hand. She knew it by the touch and dropped the foot. The leg fell in the basin; the copper rang, and tilting sidewise let all the water run upon the ground. Then joy and grief together seized her breast; her two eyes filled with tears, her full voice stayed; and laying her hand upon Odysseus' chin she said:

"You really are Odysseus, my dear child, and I never knew you till I handled my master o'er and o'er!"

She spoke and cast her eyes upon Penelope, meaning to let her know her lord was there. But Penelope could not catch the glance nor understand, because Athene drew away her notice; and Odysseus, feeling for Eurycleia's throat, clutched it with his right hand, then drew her closer toward him with his left and said:

"Why, mother, will you kill me? It was yourself who nursed me at the breast; and now through many hardships I come in the twentieth year to my own native land. Though you have found me out and a god inspired your heart, be silent, lest some other person in the hall may know. Or else,—I tell you, and it shall be done,—if God by me subdues the lordly suitors, I will not spare even you, nurse though you are, when I shall slay the other serving-women in my halls."

Then answered heedful Eurycleia: "My child, what word has passed the barrier of your teeth? You know how steadfast, how inflexible my spirit is. I shall hold fast like stubborn rock or iron. And this I will say farther: mark it well. If God by you subdues the lordly suitors, then I will name the women of the hall and tell you who dishonor you and who are guiltless."

But wise Odysseus answered her and said: "Mother, why talk of them? You have no need. I will myself observe them well and find out each. Be quiet with your story! Leave the matter to the gods!"

So he spoke, and through the hall forth went the aged woman to fetch water for his feet; for all the first was spilled. Now when she had washed him and anointed him with oil, again Odysseus drew his bench closer beside the fire, to warm himself,—but with his tatters hid the scar,—and thus began heedful Penelope:

"Stranger, there is but little more that I will ask; because the season of sweet rest will soon be here, for those to whom kind sleep will come when they are sad. But upon me God sends incessant sorrow. Day after day my joys are tears and sighs, as I watch my household tasks and watch my women. Then when night comes and slumber visits all, I lie in bed, and crowding on my heavy heart sharp cares sting me to weeping. As when Pandareos' daughter, the russet nightingale, sings sweetly at the coming in of spring, perched in the thick-leaved trees, and to and fro pours out her thrilling voice, in lamentation for her dear child, Itylus, whom with the sword she one day blindly slew, her son by royal Zethus; so does my doubtful heart toss to and fro whether to bide beside my son and keep all here in safety,—my goods, my maids, and my great high-roofed house,—and thus revere my husband's bed and heed the public voice, or finally to follow some chief of the Achaeans who woos me in my hall with countless gifts. My son, while but a child and slack of understanding, did not permit my marrying and departing from my husband's home; but now that he is grown and come to man's estate, he prays me to go home again and leave the hall, so troubled is he for that substance which the Achaeans waste. But come, interpret now and hear this dream of mine. I have twenty geese about the place who pick up corn out of the water, and I amuse myself with watching them. But from the mountain came a great hook-beaked eagle and broke the necks of all and killed my geese. In heaps they lay, scattered about the buildings, while he was borne aloft into the sacred sky. So I began to weep and wail,—still in my dream,—and fair-haired Achaean damsels gathered round and found me sadly sobbing that the eagle killed my geese. Then down again he came, lit on a jutting rafter, and with a human voice he checked my tears and said: 'Courage, O daughter of renowned Icarius! This is no dream, but true reality, which yet shall come to pass. The geese are suitors; and I, the eagle, was at the first a bird, but now, this second time, am come your husband to bring a ghastly doom on all the suitors.' At these his words sweet slumber left me, and opening my eyes I saw the geese about the buildings devouring corn beside the trough just as they used to do."

Then wise Odysseus answered her and said: "Lady, the dream cannot be understood by wresting it to other meanings; Odysseus surely has himself revealed what yet shall be. The suitors' overthrow is plain: on all it falls; none shall escape from death and doom."

But heedful Penelope said to him once more: "Stranger, in truth dreams do arise perplexed and hard to tell, dreams which come not, in men's experience, to their full issue. Two gates there are for unsubstantial dreams, one made of horn and one of ivory. The dreams that pass through the carved ivory delude and bring us tales that turn to naught; those that come forth through polished horn accomplish real things, whenever seen. Yet through this gate came not I think my own strange dream. Ah, welcome, were it so, to me and to my child! But this I will say farther; mark it well. This is the fatal dawn which parts me from Odysseus' home; for now I shall propose a contest with the axes which when at home he used to set in line, like trestles, twelve in all; then he would stand a great way off and send an arrow through. This contest I shall now propose to all the suitors. And whoever with his hands shall lightliest bend the bow and shoot through all twelve axes, him I will follow and forsake this home, this bridal home, so very beautiful and full of wealth, a place I think I ever shall remember even in my dreams."

Then wise Odysseus answered her and said: "O honored wife of Laërtes' son, Odysseus, delay no longer this contest at the hall; for wise Odysseus will be here before the suitors, handling the polished bow, can stretch the string and shoot an arrow through the iron."

Then said to him heedful Penelope: "Stranger, if you were willing to sit beside me here and entertain me, no sleep should ever fall upon my eyes. And yet one cannot be forever without sleep; for to each thing the immortals fix a season, to be ordained for men upon the fruitful earth. So I will go to my upper chamber and lay me on my bed, which has become for me a bed of sorrows, ever watered with my tears since

Odysseus went away to see accursed Ilios,—name never to be named. There I must lie. Do you lie in the hall. Make a bed upon the floor, or the maids shall bring you bedding."

So saying, she went to her bright upper chamber, yet not alone; beside her went her waiting-women too. And coming to the chamber with the maids, she there bewailed Odysseus, her dear husband, till on her lids clear-eyed Athene caused a sweet sleep to fall.

XX.

BEFORE THE SLAUGHTER

ROYAL ODYSSEUS made his bed within the porch. Upon the floor he spread an untanned hide, and on it many fleeces of the sheep which the Achaeans had been slaying; and when he had laid him down, Eurynome threw over him a cloak. So, meditating in his heart how he might harm the suitors, here lay Odysseus sleepless. Forth from the hall came women who had long been paramours of the suitors, now making jest and merriment among themselves. The heart of Odysseus stirred within, and in his mind and heart he doubted much whether to hasten after and deal out death to each, or to allow to the audacious suitors one last and latest night. Within him growled his spirit. Even as a dog walks round her tender young, growling at any man she does not know and resolute to fight him; so within growled his spirit, wroth at these evil deeds. But he smote upon his breast and thus reproved his heart:

"Bear up, my heart! A thing more hideous than this you once endured with patience, that day the Cyclops, unrestrained in fury, devoured your sturdy comrades. Then you bore up till crafty planning brought from the cave you who had thought to die."

So he spoke, chiding the very spirit in his breast; and therefore in obedience his heart held firm and steadfast, yet he himself kept tossing to and fro. As when a man near a great glowing fire turns to and fro a sausage, full of fat and blood, anxious to have it quickly roast; so to and fro Odysseus tossed, and pondered how to lay hands upon the shameless suitors,—he being alone, and they so many. Near him Athene drew, descending out of heaven. In a woman's form she stood beside his head, and thus addressed him:

"Why wakeful still, unhappiest of men? This is your home, and in this home your wife and child, even such a son as others pray for."

But wise Odysseus answered her and said: "In all this, goddess, you speak rightly; and yet my heart within is pondering how to lay hands upon the shameless suitors,—I being alone, while they are always here together. A graver fear besides I ponder in my mind; suppose I slay them, by the aid of Zeus and you, where shall I flee then? Tell me this, I pray."

Then said to him the goddess, clear-eyed Athene: "O doubter! Men trust weaker friends, friends who are mortal and not wise as I. I am a god and will protect you to the end, through all your toils. And let me tell you plainly: should fifty troops of mortal men stand round about us, eager in the fight to slay, you still might drive away from them their oxen and sturdy sheep. Nay! Nay! Let slumber come! Evil it is to watch and wake all the night long. You shall come forth from peril yet."

So spoke she, and poured sleep upon his eyelids; and then the heavenly goddess departed to Olympus. But as the slumber seized him, freeing his heart from care, easing his members, his faithful wife awoke, and sitting up in her soft bed began to weep. When she had satisfied her heart with weeping, the royal lady prayed, and first to Artemis:

"O honored goddess Artemis, daughter of Zeus, strike now I pray an arrow in my breast and take away my life this very instant; or let a sweeping storm bear me its windy way and cast me in the streams of restless Ocean! As when storms seized Pandareos' daughters, whose parents gods had slain and they were left at home as orphans, then goddess Aphrodite brought them cheese, sweet honey and pleasant wine; Here endowed them, beyond all other women, with beauty and understanding; chaste Artemis gave stature; Athene taught them skill in honorable work. But while heavenly Aphrodite went to high Olympus, to win the maids the final boon of happy marriage,—a boon from Zeus, the Thunderer, who understands all well, all fortunes good or ill of mortal men,—the Harpies swept away the maids and gave them over to be servants to the dread Avengers. Even so may those who have their dwellings on Olympus blot out me, or else may I receive a shaft from fair-haired Artemis, that I may go to my dread grave seeing Odysseus still, and never gladden heart of meaner husband! Yet ills like these are bearable if, with a burdened heart, one weeps by day and then by night has sleep. For such an one forgets all good and ill when once the eyelids close. But as for me, Heaven sends me cruel dreams. Again to-night there lay beside me one like him, such as he was when he departed with the army. My heart was glad. I said it was no dream, but truth at last."

While she was speaking gold-throned morning came. And as she wept, royal Odysseus heard her voice and mused awhile. In his heart she seemed to know him and to stand beside his head. Gathering up the cloak and fleece in which he slept, he laid them in the hall upon a chair, carried the ox-hide out of doors and spread it down, and with up-lifted hands prayed thus to Zeus:

"O father Zeus, if of good will ye gods have led me over field and flood to my own land,—though ill ye brought me also,—let some one now awake speak a good word indoors, and another sign from Zeus be given outside the house!"

So spoke he in his prayer, and wise Zeus heard him and straightway thundered out of bright Olympus, out of the clouds above. Royal Odysseus was made glad. Moreover a woman grinding corn sent forth an ominous cry out of the house hard by, where stood the mills of the shepherd of the people. Twelve women in all worked here, preparing barley-meal and corn, men's marrows. The rest were sleeping, having ground their wheat; one only had not ended, for she was very weak. She, stopping at last her mill, uttered these words, an omen for her master:

"O father Zeus, who rulest over gods and men, loud hast thou thun-dered from the starry sky, and no cloud anywhere. Surely in this thou givest man a sign. Then bring to pass for miserable me the words I speak. May the suitors to-day for the last and latest time hold their glad feast within Odysseus' hall! They who with galling labor made my knees grow weak, while I prepared them meal, may they now feast their last!"

She spoke, and royal Odysseus was gladdened by her cry and by the thunder of Zeus. He said that woe was come upon the guilty.

And now the other handmaids of the goodly palace of Odysseus came together and kindled on the hearth a steady fire. Telemachus also, a mortal like a god, rose from his bed, put on his clothes, slung his sharp sword about his shoulder, under his shining feet bound his fair sandals, then took his ponderous spear, tipped with sharp bronze, and went and stood upon the threshold, saying to Eurycleia:

"Good nurse, have you provided for the stranger in the house com-fort in bed and food? Or does he lie neglected? That is my mother's way, wise though she is. Blindly she honors one of the meaner sort, and sends the better man away unhonored."

Then heedful Eurycleia answered: "Now do not blame a blameless person, child! He sat and drank his wine as long as he inclined, and he said he wanted no more bread; she asked him that. And as soon as he began to think of rest and sleep, she bade her damsels spread his bed. Then he, like a man quite mean and miserable, refused to sleep upon a bed and under blankets, but on an undressed hide and fleecy sheep-skins lay down within the porch. We put a cloak upon him."

So she spoke; and through the hall forth went Telemachus, his spear in hand, two swift dogs following after. He hastened to the assembly to join the mailed Achaeans. But noble Eurycleia, daughter of Ops, Peisenor's son, called to the women:

"Come, stir about and sweep the house and sprinkle it, and beat the purple coverings on the shapely chairs. And others, take your sponges and wipe off all the tables, and clean the mixing-bowls and well-wrought double cups. And others still, go to the well for water, and fetch it quickly here. It is not long the suitors will be absent from the hall. They will be here right early. To-day is for them all a holiday."

She spoke, and very willingly they heeded and obeyed. Twenty went to the dark well; the others plied their tasks with skill about the house. Soon came the Achaean's laboring men, who neatly and skillfully split logs of wood; there came the women also, returning from the well. After them came the swineherd, driving three fat hogs, the best of all his herds. He let them feed about the pleasant yard, and said to Odysseus kindly:

"Stranger, do the Achaeans look after you any better, or do they still insult you in the hall, as at the first?"

Then wise Odysseus answered him and said: "Eumaeus, may the gods requite the wrongs which these in their abominable pride work in a house not theirs! They have no touch of shame."

So they conversed together. Melanthius now drew near, the goatherd, driving the goats that were the best of all his flock, to make the suitors' dinner. Two shepherds followed after. He tied his goats under the echoing portico and said to Odysseus rudely:

"Stranger, will you still be a nuisance in the house and beg of people? Will you not quit our doors? We never shall quite settle things, I think, until you taste my fists. Beyond all decency you keep on begging. Surely there are Achaean feasts elsewhere."

He spoke, but not a word did wise Odysseus answer. Silent he shook his head, brooding on evil.

A third now joined them, Philoetius, ever foremost, and brought the suitors a barren cow and fatted goats. The ferrymen brought them over, they who bring people too, whenever anybody comes their way. He tied the cattle carefully under the echoing portico and drawing near the swineherd asked:

"Who is this stranger, swineherd, lately come, and staying at the hall? Out of what tribe does he profess to be? Where are his kinsmen and his native fields? Poor man! He seems in bearing like a lordly king. The gods may well send homeless people troubles when even for kings they weave a web of grief."

He spoke, and turning to Odysseus gave his right hand in welcome, and speaking in winged words he said: "Hail, good old stranger! May happiness be yours in time to come! Now you are bound by many ills. O father Zeus, none of the gods is crueler than thou! Thou carest not that men, when thou hast given them birth, be plunged in misery and sharp distress. A sweat came over me in looking at the man; my eyes were filled with tears for memory of Odysseus; for he also, I suppose, in just such tatters, is a wanderer among men,—if he indeed yet lives and sees the sunshine. But if he is already dead and in the house of Hades, then woe is me for good Odysseus, who gave me charge of cattle when I was but a boy in the land of the Cephallenians. And now the herds have grown enormously. No breed of broad-browed cattle ever bladed better. But strangers bid me drive these now for them to eat. For the son of the house they do not care, nor do they tremble at the wrath of gods; but they are bent on parting out their long-gone master's goods. And as for me, around one point my heart within keeps turning: 'tis very bad while the son lives to go to the land of strangers, cattle and all, to foreigners; worse still to stay with strangers' herds and sit about and suffer. Certainly long ago I would have fled and found some other mighty king,—life here cannot be borne,—but still I think of that unfortunate, how he may come from somewhere, and make a scattering of the suitors up and down the house."

Then wise Odysseus answered him and said: "Herdsman, because you do not seem a common, senseless person, but I perceive wisdom is in your heart, I will speak out and swear a solemn oath on what I say: so first of all the gods be witness Zeus, and let this hospitable table and the hearth of good Odysseus whereto I come be witness; while you are here Odysseus shall return, and you with your own eyes shall see him, if you will, slaying the suitors who now lord it here."

Then answered him the herdsman of the cattle: "Ah stranger, may the son of Kronos fulfill these words of yours! Then shall you know what might is mine and how my hands obey."

So also did Eumaeus pray to all the gods that wise Odysseus might return to his own home. So they conversed together.

Now for Telemachus the suitors had been plotting death and doom. But toward them, on the left, a bird came flying, a soaring eagle, clutching a timid dove; whereat Amphinomus called to them thus and said:

"Ah friends, this plan of ours will not run well, this murder of Telemachus. Let us rather turn to feasting."

So said Amphinomus, and his saying pleased them. Entering the house of princely Odysseus, they threw their coats upon the couches and the chairs, and they began to kill great sheep and fatted goats, to kill sleek pigs and the heifer of the herd. They roasted the inward parts and passed them round, and mixed wine in the mixers. The swineherd passed the cups; Philoetius, ever foremost, handed them bread in goodly baskets; Melantheus poured the wine. So on the food spread out before them they laid hands.

And now Telemachus, with crafty purpose, seated Odysseus within the stately hall by the stone threshold, providing him a common bench and little table. He gave him portions of the inward parts and, pouring him wine into a golden cup, he thus addressed him:

"Sit here among the men and sip your wine, and I will keep you from the taunts and blows of all the suitors. This is no public house. It is Odysseus' own, acquired for me. Therefore you suitors check your taste for insult and abuse, or else there may be strife and quarrel here."

He spoke, and all with teeth set in their lips marveled because Telemachus had spoken boldly. Then said Antinoüs, Eupeithes' son: "Harsh as it is, Achaeans, let us take the bidding of Telemachus. He speaks with lofty threatening. Zeus, son of Kronos, hindered, or long ago we in the hall had stopped him, shrill talker though he be."

So said Antinoüs; Telemachus did not heed his words. For pages came, leading along the town a hecatomb of cattle sacred to the gods. Long-haired Achaeans, too, assembled in the shady grove of the archer-king Apollo.

But when the rest had roasted the outer flesh and drawn it off, dividing up the portions they held a famous feast. And those who served set for Odysseus a portion quite as large as that they took themselves; for this was the bidding of Telemachus, the son of princely Odysseus.

Yet Athene allowed the haughty suitors not altogether yet to cease from biting scorn. She wished more pain to pierce the heart of Laërtes' son, Odysseus. There was among the suitors a man of lawless life; Ctesippus was his name; he lived in Same. Proud of vast wealth, he wooed the wife of Odysseus, long away. He it was now who thus addressed the audacious suitors:

"Hearken, you haughty suitors, while I speak. This stranger here awhile ago received a portion, and, as was proper, one as large as ours; for it is neither honorable nor fitting to worry strangers who may reach this palace of Telemachus. Come then and let me also give a hospitable gift, and he shall have wherewith to give a present to the bath-keeper or to some servant of the house of great Odysseus."

So saying, he flung with his strong hand an ox-hoof which lay near, taking it from the basket. Odysseus with a quick turning of the head avoided it, and in his heart smiled grimly. It struck the massive wall. But Telemachus rebuked Ctesippus thus:

"Surely, Ctesippus, that was lucky for your life. You missed our guest. He shunned your missile. Else I had run you through the middle with my pointed spear, and in the place of wedding-feast your father had been busied with a funeral here. Let no man in this house henceforth show rudeness; for I now mark and understand each deed, good deeds as well as bad. Before, I was a child. And even yet we bear what nevertheless we see,—sheep slain, wine drunk, bread wasted,—for hard it is for one to cope with many. Nay then, do me no more deliberate wrong. But if you seek to slay me with the sword, that I would choose; and better far were death than constantly behold disgraceful deeds, strangers abused, and damsels dragged to shame through the fair palace."

So he spoke and all were hushed to silence; but by and by said Agelaüs, son of Damastor: "Friends, in answering what is fairly said, none should be angry and retort with spiteful words. Let none abuse the stranger nor any of the servants in great Odysseus' hall. But to Telemachus and his mother I would say one friendly word; perhaps it may find favor in the mind of each. So long as your hearts hoped wise Odysseus would return to his own home, it was no harm to wait and hold the suitors at the palace. That was the better way, if but Odysseus had returned and reached his home once more. Now it is plain that he will never come. Go then, sit down beside your mother and plainly tell her this, to marry the man who is the best and offers most. So shall you keep in peace all that your father left, to eat and drink your fill, and she shall guide the household of another."

Then answered him discreet Telemachus: "Nay, Agelaüs, by Zeus I swear and by the sufferings of my father, who far away from Ithaca is dead or lost, it is not I delay my mother's marriage; indeed I urge her to marry whom she will, I will give countless gifts. But I hesitate to drive her forth, against her will, by a compulsive word. God let that never be!"

So spoke Telemachus, but Pallas Athene woke uncontrollable laughter in the suitors. She turned their wits awry. Now they would laugh as if with others' faces, and blood-bedabbled was the flesh they ate. Their eyes were filled with tears, their heart felt anguish; and godlike Theoclymenus addressed them thus:

"Ah wretched men, what woe befalls you? Night shrouds your heads, your faces, and lower still, your knees. Wild cries are kindled; cheeks are wet with tears; walls and the fair mid-spaces drip with blood. The porch is full, the court is full, of shapes that haste to Erebus, down into darkness. The sun is blotted from the heavens; a foul fog covers all."

He spoke, and all burst into merry laughter; and thus began Eurymachus, the son of Polybus: "A crazy stranger this, new come from foreign lands! Quick then, young men, and guide him out of doors, off to the market, since he finds it here like night!"

Then godlike Theoclymenus made answer: "Eurymachus, I do not ask a guide; I have my eyes and ears, and my two feet, and in my breast a steadfast mind of no mean sort. By their aid I go forth, for I perceive an evil approaching you which none shall shun or flee,—nay, not a man among these suitors who in the house of great Odysseus work wantonly abominations to mankind."

So saying, forth he went out of the stately palace and found Peiraeus, who received him kindly. Then all the suitors, glancing at one another, began to tease Telemachus by laughing at his guests, and a rude youth would say:

"Telemachus, no man is more unfortunate in guests than you. For instance, what a filthy vagabond is this you keep, one always wanting bread and wine, incapable of work or deeds of strength, simply a cumberer of the ground! And now this other fellow stands up and plays the prophet. But if you would heed me, the better way were this; to toss your guests into a ship of many oars and pack them off to Sicily, where they would fetch their price."

So said the suitors; Telemachus did not heed their words. Silent he watched his father, waiting ever till he should lay hands on the shameless suitors.

Now having set her goodly seat just opposite the door, the daughter of Icarius, heedful Penelope, attended to the talk of all within the hall. With laughter they prepared their dinner,—a pleasant meal, such as they liked,—and many a beast was slaughtered. But how could feast be more unwelcome than the supper which a goddess and a valiant man were soon to set before them? For from the first they had wrought deeds of shame.

XXI.

THE TRIAL OF THE BOW

AND NOW the goddess, clear-eyed Athene, put in the mind of Icarius'
daughter, heedful Penelope, to offer to the suitors in the hall the bow
and the gray steel, as means of sport and harbingers of death. She
mounted the long stairway of her house, holding a crooked key in her
firm hand,—a goodly key of bronze, having an ivory handle,—and
hastened with her damsels to a far-off room where her lord's treasure
lay, bronze, gold, and well-wrought steel. Here also lay his curved bow
and the quiver for his arrows,—and many grievous shafts were in it
still,—gifts which a friend had given Odysseus when he met him once
in Lacedaemon,—Iphitus, son of Eurytus, a man like the immortals. At
Messene the two met, in the house of wise Orsilochus. Odysseus had
come hither to claim a debt which the whole district owed him; for
upon ships of many oars Messenians carried off from Ithaca three hundred sheep together with their herdsmen. In the long quest for these,
Odysseus took the journey when he was but a youth; for his father and
the other elders sent him forth. Iphitus, on the other hand, was seeking
horses; for twelve mares had been lost, which had as foals twelve hardy
mules. These afterwards became the death and doom of Iphitus when
he met the stalwart son of Zeus, the hero Hercules, who well knew
deeds of daring; for Hercules slew Iphitus in his own house, although
his guest, and recklessly did not regard the anger of the gods nor yet the
proffered table, but slew the man and kept at his own hall the strong-
hoofed mares. It was when seeking these that Iphitus had met Odysseus
and given the bow which in old days great Eurytus was wont to bear,
and which on dying in his lofty hall he left his son. To Iphitus,
Odysseus gave a sharp-edged sword and a stout spear, as the beginning
of a loving friendship. They never sat, however, at one another's table;

ere that could be, the son of Zeus slew godlike Iphitus, the son of Eurytus, who gave the bow. Royal Odysseus when going off to war in the black ships would never take this bow. It always stood in its own place at home, as a memorial of his honored friend. In his own land he bore it.

Now when the royal lady reached this room and stood on the oaken threshold,—which long ago the carpenter had smoothed with skill and leveled to the line, fitting the posts thereto and setting the shining doors,—then quickly from its ring she loosed the strap, thrust in the key, and with a careful aim shot back the door-bolts. As a bull roars when feeding in the field, so roared the goodly door touched by the key, and open flew before her. She stepped to a raised dais where stood some chests in which lay fragrant garments. Thence reaching up, she took from its peg the bow in the glittering case which held it. And now she sat her down and laid the case upon her lap and loudly weeping drew her lord's bow forth. But when she had had her fill of tears and sighs, she hastened to the hall to meet the lordly suitors, bearing in hand the curved bow and the quiver for the arrows, and many grievous shafts were in it still. Beside her, damsels bore a box in which lay many a piece of steel and bronze, implements of her lord's for games like these. And when the royal lady reached the suitors, she stood beside a column of the strong-built roof, holding before her face her delicate wimple, the while a faithful damsel stood upon either hand. And straightway she addressed the suitors, speaking thus:

"Hearken, you haughty suitors who beset this house, eating and drinking ever, now my husband is long gone; no word of excuse can you suggest except your wish to marry me and win me for your wife. Well then, my suitors,—since before you stands your prize,—I offer you the mighty bow of prince Odysseus; and whoever with his hands shall lightliest bend the bow and shoot through all twelve axes, him I will follow and forsake this home, this bridal home, so very beautiful and full of wealth, a place I think I ever shall remember, even in my dreams."

So saying, she bade Eumaeus, the noble swineherd, deliver to the suitors the bow and the gray steel. With tears Eumaeus took the arms and laid them down before them. Near by, the neatherd also wept to see his master's bow. But Antinoüs rebuked them, and spoke to them and said:

"You stupid boors, who only mind the passing minute, wretched pair, what do you mean by shedding tears, troubling this lady's heart, when already her heart is prostrated with grief at losing her dear husband? Sit down and eat in silence, or else go forth and weep, but leave the bow behind, a dread ordeal for the suitors; for I am sure this polished bow will not be bent with ease. There is not a man of all now here so powerful as Odysseus. I saw him once myself and well recall him, though I was then a child."

He spoke, but in his breast his heart was hoping to draw the string and send an arrow through the steel; yet he was to be the first to taste the shaft of good Odysseus, whom he now wronged though seated in his hall, while to like outrage he encouraged all his comrades. To these now spoke revered Telemachus:

"Ha! Zeus the son of Kronos has made me play the fool! My mother,—and wise she is,—says she will follow some strange man and quit this house; and I but laugh and in my silly soul am glad. Come then, you suitors, since before you stands your prize, a lady whose like cannot be found throughout Achaean land, in sacred Pylos, Argos, or Mycenae, in Ithaca itself, or the dark mainland, as you yourselves well know,—what needs my mother praise?—come then, delay not with excuse nor longer hesitate to bend the bow, but let us learn what is to be. I too might try the bow. And if I stretch it and send an arrow through the steel, then with no shame to me my honored mother may forsake this house and follow some one else, leaving me here behind; for I shall then be able to wield my father's arms."

He spoke, and flung his red cloak from his shoulders, rising full height, and put away the sharp sword also from his shoulder. First then he set the axes, marking one long furrow for them all, aligned by cord. The earth on the two sides he stamped down flat. Surprise filled all beholders to see how properly he set them, though he had never seen the game before. Then he went and stood upon the threshold and began to try the bow. Three times he made it tremble as he sought to make it bend. Three times he slacked his strain, still hoping in his heart to draw the string and send an arrow through the steel. And now he might have drawn it by force of a fourth tug, had not Odysseus shook his head and stayed the eager boy. So to the suitors once more spoke revered Telemachus:

"Fie! Shall I ever be a coward and a weakling, or am I still but young and cannot trust my arm to right me with the man who wrongs me first? But come, you who are stronger men than I, come try the bow and end the contest."

So saying, he laid by the bow and stood it on the ground, leaning it on the firm-set polished door. The swift shaft, too, he likewise leaned against the bow's fair knob, and once more took the seat from which he first arose. Then said to them Antinoüs, Eupeithes' son:

"Rise up in order all, from left to right, beginning where the cup-bearer begins to pour the wine."

So said Antinoüs, and his saying pleased them. Then first arose Leiodes, son of Oenops, who was their soothsayer and had his place beside the goodly mixer, farthest along the hall. To him alone their lawlessness was hateful; he abhorred the suitor crowd. He it was now who first took up the bow and the swift shaft; and going to the threshold, he stood and tried the bow. He could not bend it. Tugging the string wearied his hands, his soft, unhorny hands; and to the suitors thus he spoke: "No, friends, I cannot bend it. Let some other take the bow. Ah, many chiefs this bow shall rob of life and breath! Yet better far to die than live and still to fail in that for which we constantly are gathered, waiting expectantly from day to day! Now each man hopes and purposes at heart to win Penelope, Odysseus' wife. But when he shall have tried the bow and seen his failure, then to some other fair-robed woman of Achaea let each go, and offer her his suit and woo her with his gifts. So may Penelope marry the man who gives her most and comes with fate to favor!"

When he had spoken, he laid by the bow, leaning it on the firm-set polished door. The swift shaft, too, he likewise leaned against the bow's fair knob, and once more took the seat from which he first arose. But Antinoüs rebuked him, and spoke to him, and said:

"Leiodes, what words have passed the barrier of your teeth? Strange words and harsh! Vexatious words to hear! As if this bow must rob our chiefs of life and breath because you cannot bend it! Why, your good mother did not bear you for a brandisher of bows and arrows. But others among the lordly suitors will bend it by and by."

So saying, he gave an order to Melanthius, the goatherd: "Hasten, Melantheus, and light a fire in the hall and set a long bench near, with fleeces on it; then bring me the large cake of fat which lies inside the door, that after we have warmed the bow and greased it well, we young men try the bow and end the contest."

He spoke, and straightway Melanthius kindled a steady fire, and set a bench beside it with a fleece thereon, and brought out the large cake of fat which lay inside the door, and so the young men warmed the bow and made their trial. But yet they could not bend it; they fell far short of power. Antinoüs, however, still held back, and prince Eurymachus, who were the suitors' leaders; for they in manly excellence were quite the best of all.

Meanwhile out of the house at the same moment came two men, princely Odysseus' herdsmen of the oxen and the swine; and after them came royal Odysseus also from the house. And when they were outside the gate, beyond the yard, speaking in gentle words Odysseus said:

"Neatherd, and you too, swineherd, may I tell a certain tale, or shall I hide it still? My heart bids speak. How ready would you be to aid Odysseus if he should come from somewhere, thus, on a sudden, and a god should bring him home? Would you support the suitors or Odysseus? Speak freely, as your heart and spirit bid you speak."

Then said to him the herdsman of the cattle: "O father Zeus, grant this my prayer! May he return and Heaven be his guide! Then shall you know what might is mine and how my hands obey."

So prayed Eumaeus too to all the gods, that wise Odysseus might return to his own home. So when he knew with certainty the heart of each, finding his words once more Odysseus said:

"Lo, it is I, through many grievous toils now in the twentieth year come to my native land! And yet I know that of my servants none but you desires my coming. From all the rest I have not heard one prayer that I return. To you then I will truly tell what shall hereafter be. If God by me subdues the lordly suitors, I will obtain you wives and give you wealth and homes established near my own; and henceforth in my eyes you shall be friends and brethren of Telemachus. Come then and I will show you too a very trusty sign, — that you may know me certainly and be assured in heart, — the scar the boar dealt long ago with his white tusk, when I once journeyed to Parnassus with Autolycus' sons."

So saying, he drew aside his rags from the great scar. And when the two beheld and understood it all, their tears burst forth; they threw their arms round wise Odysseus and passionately kissed his face and neck. So likewise did Odysseus kiss their heads and hands. And daylight had gone down upon their weeping had not Odysseus stayed their tears and said:

"Have done with grief and wailing, or somebody in coming from the hall may see, and tell the tale indoors. Nay, go in one by one, not all together. I will go first, you after. And let this be agreed: the rest within, the lordly suitors, will not allow me to receive the bow and quiver. But, noble Eumaeus, bring the bow along the room and lay it in my hands. Then tell the women to lock the hall's close-fitting doors; and if from their inner room they hear a moaning or a strife within our walls, let no one venture forth, but stay in silence at her work. And, noble Philoetius, in your care I put the court-yard gates. Bolt with the bar and quickly lash the fastening."

So saying, Odysseus made his way into the stately house, and went and took the seat from which he first arose. And soon the serving-men of princely Odysseus entered too.

Now Eurymachus held the bow and turned it up and down, trying to heat it at the glowing fire. But still, with all his pains, he could not bend it; his proud soul groaned aloud. Then bitterly he spoke; these were the words he said:

"Ah! here is woe for me and woe for all! Not that I so much mourn missing the marriage, though vexed I am at that. Still, there are enough more women of Achaea, both here in sea-girt Ithaca and in the other cities. But if in strength we fall so short of princely Odysseus that we cannot bend his bow—oh, the disgrace for future times to know!"

Then said Antinoüs, Eupeithes' son: "Not so, Eurymachus, and you yourself know better. To-day throughout the land is the archer-god's high feast. Who then could bend a bow? Nay, quietly lay it by; and for the axes, what if we leave them standing? Nobody, I am sure, will carry one away and trespass on the house of Laërtes' son, Odysseus. Come then, and let the wine-pourer give pious portions to our cups, that after a libation we may lay aside curved bows. To-morrow morning tell Melanthius, the goatherd, to drive us here the choicest goats of all his flock; and we will set the thighs before the archer-god, Apollo, then try the bow and end the contest."

So said Antinoüs, and his saying pleased them. Pages poured water on their hands; young men brimmed bowls with drink and served to all, with a first pious portion for the cups. And after they had poured and drunk as their hearts would, then in his subtlety said wise Odysseus:

"Hearken, you suitors of the illustrious queen, and let me tell you what the heart within me bids. I beg a special favor of Eurymachus, and great Antinoüs too; for his advice was wise, that you now drop the bow and leave the matter with the gods, and in the morning God shall grant the power to whom he may. But give me now the polished bow, and let me in your presence prove my skill and power and see if I have yet such vigor left as once there was within my supple limbs, or whether wanderings and neglect have ruined all."

At these his words all were exceeding wroth, fearing that he might bend the polished bow. But Antinoüs rebuked him, and spoke to him and said: "You scurvy stranger, with not a whit of sense, are you not satisfied to eat in peace with us, your betters, unstinted in your food and hearing all we say? Nobody else, stranger or beggar, hears our talk. 'Tis wine that goads you, honeyed wine, a thing that has brought others trouble, when taken greedily and drunk without due measure. Wine crazed the Centaur, famed Eurytion, at the house of bold Peirithoüs, on his visit to Lapithae. And when his wits were crazed with wine, he madly wrought foul outrage on the household of Peirithoüs. So indignation seized the heroes. Through the porch and out of doors they rushed, dragging Eurytion forth, shorn by the pitiless sword of ears and nose. Crazed in his wits, he went his way, bearing in his bewildered heart the burden of his guilt. And hence arose a feud between the Centaurs and mankind; but the beginning of the woe he himself caused by wine. Even so I prophesy great harm to you, if you shall bend the bow. No kindness will you meet from any in our land, but we will send you by black ship straight to king Echetus, the bane of all mankind, out of whose hands you never shall come clear. Be quiet, then, and take your drink! Do not presume to vie with younger men!"

Then said to him heedful Penelope: "Antinoüs, it is neither honorable nor fitting to worry strangers who may reach this palace of Telemachus. Do you suppose the stranger, if he bends the great bow of Odysseus, confident in his skill and strength of arm, will lead me home and take me for his wife? He in his inmost soul imagines no such thing. Let none of you sit at the table disturbed by such a thought; for that could never, never be!"

Then answered her Eurymachus, the son of Polybus: "Daughter of Icarius, heedful Penelope, we do not think the man will marry you. Of course that could not be. And yet we dread the talk of men and women, and fear that one of the baser sort of the Achaeans say: 'Men far inferior sue for a good man's wife, and cannot bend his polished bow. But somebody else,—a wandering beggar,—came, and easily bent the bow and sent an arrow through the steel.' This they will say, to us a shame indeed."

Then said to him heedful Penelope: "Eurymachus, men cannot be in honor in the land and rudely rob the household of their prince. Why then count this a shame? The stranger is right tall, and well-knit too, and calls himself the son of a good father. Give him the polished bow, and let us see. For this I tell you, and it shall be done: if he shall bend it and Apollo grants his prayer, I will clothe him in a coat and tunic, goodly garments, give him a pointed spear to keep off dogs and men, a two-edged sword, and sandals for his feet, and I will send him where his heart and soul may bid him go."

Then answered her discreet Telemachus: "My mother, no Achaean has better right than I to give or to refuse the bow to any as I will. And out of all who rule in rocky Ithaca, or in the islands off toward grazing Elis, none may oppose my will, even if I wished to put the bows into the stranger's hands and let him take them once for all away. Then seek your chamber and attend to matters of your own,—the loom, the distaff,—and bid the women ply their tasks. Bows are for men, for all, especially for me; for power within this house rests here."

Amazed, she turned to her own room again, for the wise saying of her son she laid to heart. And coming to the upper chamber with her maids, she there bewailed Odysseus, her dear husband, till on her lids clear-eyed Athene caused a sweet sleep to fall.

Meanwhile the noble swineherd, taking the curved bow, was bearing it away. But the suitors all broke into uproar in the hall, and a rude youth would say: "Where are you carrying the curved bow, you miserable swineherd? Crazy fool! Soon out among the swine, away from men, swift dogs shall eat you,—dogs you yourself have bred,—will but Apollo and the other deathless gods be gracious!"

At these their words the bearer of the bow laid it down where he stood, frightened because the crowd within the hall cried out upon him. But from the other side Telemachus called threateningly aloud: "Nay, father! Carry on the bow! You cannot well heed all. Take care, or I, a nimbler man than you, will drive you to the fields with pelting stones. Superior in strength I am to you. Ah, would I were as much beyond the others in the house, beyond these suitors, in my skill and strength of arm! Then would I soon send somebody away in sorrow from my house; for men work evil here."

He spoke, and all burst into merry laughter and laid aside their bitter anger with Telemachus. And so the swineherd, bearing the bow along the hall, drew near to wise Odysseus and put it in his hands; then calling aside nurse Eurycleia, thus he said:

"Telemachus bids you, heedful Eurycleia, to lock the hall's close-fitting doors; and if a woman from the inner room hears moaning or a strife within our walls, let her not venture forth, but stay in silence at her work."

Such were his words; unwinged, they rested with her. She locked the doors of the stately hall. Then silently from the house Philoetius stole forth and straightway barred the gates of the fenced court. Beneath the portico there lay a curved ship's cable, made of byblus plant. With this he lashed the gates, then passed indoors himself, and went and took the seat from which he first arose, eying Odysseus. Now Odysseus already held the bow and turned it round and round, trying it here and there to see if worms had gnawed the horn while its lord was far away. And glancing at his neighbor one would say:

"A sort of fancier and a trickster with the bow this fellow is. No doubt at home he has himself a bow like that, or means to make one like it. See how he turns it in his hands this way and that, ready for mischief,—rascal!"

Then would another rude youth answer thus: "Oh may he always meet with luck as good as when he is unable now to bend the bow!"

So talked the suitors. Meantime wise Odysseus, when he had handled the great bow and scanned it closely,—even as one well-skilled to play the lyre and sing stretches with ease round its new peg a string, securing at each end the twisted sheep-gut; so without effort did Odysseus string the mighty bow. Holding it now with his right hand, he tried its cord; and clear to the touch it sang, voiced like the swallow. Great consternation came upon the suitors. All faces then changed color. Zeus thundered loud for signal. And glad was long-tried royal Odysseus to think the son of crafty Kronos sent an omen. He picked up a swift shaft which lay beside him on the table, drawn. Within the hollow quiver still remained the rest, which the Achaeans soon should prove. Then laying the arrow on the arch, he drew the string and arrow notches, and forth from the bench on which he sat let fly the shaft, with careful aim, and did not miss an axe's ring from first to last, but clean through all sped on the bronze-tipped arrow; and to Telemachus he said:

"Telemachus, the guest now sitting in your hall brings you no shame. I did not miss my mark, nor in the bending of the bow make a long labor. My strength is sound as ever, not what the mocking suitors here despised. But it is time for the Achaeans to make supper ready, while it is daylight still; and then for us in other ways to make them sport,— with dance and lyre; for these attend a feast."

He spoke and frowned the sign. His sharp sword then Telemachus girt on, the son of princely Odysseus; clasped his right hand around his spear, and close beside his father's seat he took his stand, armed with the gleaming bronze.

XXII.

THE SLAUGHTER OF THE SUITORS

THEN WISE Odysseus threw off his rags and sprang to the broad threshold, bow in hand and quiver full of arrows. Out he poured the swift shafts at his feet, and thus addressed the suitors:

"So the dread ordeal ends! Now to another mark I turn, to hit what no man ever hit before, will but Apollo grant my prayer."

He spoke, and aimed a pointed arrow at Antinoüs. The man was in the act to raise his goodly goblet,—gold it was and double-eared,—and even now guided it in his hands to drink the wine. Death gave his heart no care. For who could think that in this company of feasters one of the crowd, however strong, could bring upon him cruel death and dismal doom? But Odysseus aimed an arrow and hit him in the throat; right through his tender neck the sharp point passed. He sank down sidewise; from his hand the goblet fell when he was hit, and straightway from his nose ran a thick stream of human blood. Roughly he pushed his table back, kicking it with his foot, and scattered off the food upon the floor. The bread and roasted meat were thrown away. Into a tumult broke the suitors round about the hall when they saw the fallen man. They sprang from their seats and, hurrying through the hall, peered at the massive walls on every side. But nowhere was there shield or ponderous spear to seize. Then they assailed Odysseus with indignant words:

"Stranger, to your sorrow you turn your bow on men! You never shall take part in games again. Swift death awaits you; for you have killed the leader of the noble youths of Ithaca. To pay for this, vultures shall eat you here!"

So each one spoke; they thought he had not meant to kill the man. They foolishly did not see that for them one and all destruction's cords were knotted. But looking sternly on them wise Odysseus said:

"Dogs! You have been saying all the time I never should return out of the land of Troy; and therefore you destroyed my home, outraged my women-servants, and,—I alive,—covertly wooed my wife, fearing no gods that hold the open sky, nor that the indignation of mankind would fall on you hereafter. Now for you one and all destruction's cords are knotted!"

As he spoke thus, pale fear took hold on all. Each peered about to flee from instant death. Only Eurymachus made answer, saying:

"If you indeed be Ithacan Odysseus, now returned, justly have you described what the Achaeans have been doing,—full many crimes here at the hall and many in the field. But there at last lies he who was the cause of all, Antinoüs; for it was he who set us on these deeds, not so much needing and desiring marriage, but with this other purpose,— which the son of Kronos never granted,—that in the settled land of Ithaca he might himself be king, when he should treacherously have slain your son. Now he is justly slain. But spare your people, and we hereafter, making you public recompense for all we drank and ate here at the hall, will pay a fine of twenty oxen each and give you bronze and gold enough to warm your heart. Till this is done, we cannot blame your wrath."

But looking sternly on him, wise Odysseus said: "Eurymachus, if you would give me all your father's goods, and all your own, and all that you might gather elsewhere, I would not stay my hands from slaying until the suitors paid the price of all their lawless deeds. It lies before you then to fight or flee, if any man will save himself from death and doom. But some here will not flee, I think, from instant death."

As he spoke thus, their knees grew feeble and their very souls; but Eurymachus called out a second time: "Come, friends, the man will not hold back his ruthless hands; but having got possession of a polished bow and quiver, he will shoot from the smooth threshold until he kills us all. Let us then turn to fighting. Draw swords, and hold the tables up against his deadly arrows! Have at him all together! Perhaps we may dislodge him from the threshold and the door, then reach the town and quickly raise the alarm. So would the fellow soon have shot his last."

So saying, he drew his sharp two-edged bronze sword and sprang upon Odysseus with a fearful cry. But on the instant royal Odysseus shot an arrow and hit him in the breast beside the nipple, fixing the swift bolt in his liver. Out of his hand his sword dropped on the ground, and he himself, sprawling across the table, bent and fell, spilling the food and double cup upon the floor. With his brow he beat the pavement in his agony of heart, and with his kicking shook the chair. Upon his eyes gathered the mists of death.

But Amphinomus assaulted glorious Odysseus, and dashing headlong forward drew his sharp sword, hoping to make Odysseus yield the door. But Telemachus was quick and struck him with his brazen spear upon the back, between the shoulders, and drove the spear-point through his chest. He fell with a thud and struck the ground flat with his forehead. Telemachus sprang back and left the long spear sticking in Amphinomus; for he feared if he should draw the long spear out, an Achaean might attack him, rushing on him with his sword, and as he stooped might stab him. So off he ran and hastily went back to his dear father; and standing close beside him, he said in winged words:

"Now, father, I will fetch a shield and pair of spears, and a brazen helmet also, fitted to your brow. And I will go and arm myself, and give some armor to the swineherd and to the neatherd too; for to be armed is better."

Then wise Odysseus answered him and said: "Run! Bring the arms while I have arrows to defend me, or they will drive me from the door when I am left alone."

He spoke, and Telemachus heeded his dear father, and hastened to the chamber where the glittering armor lay. Out of the store he chose four shields, eight spears, and four bronze helmets having horsehair plumes. These he bore off and hastily went back to his dear father. Telemachus first girt his body with the bronze, then the two servants likewise girt themselves in goodly armor, and so all took their stand by Odysseus, keen and crafty.

He, just as long as he had arrows to defend him, shot down a suitor in the hall with every aim, and side by side they fell. Then when his arrows failed the princely bowman, he leaned the bow against the door-post of the stately room, letting it stand beside the bright face-wall, and he too slung a fourfold shield about his shoulders, put on his sturdy head a shapely helmet, horsehair-plumed,—grimly the crest above it nodded,—and took in hand two ponderous spears pointed with bronze.

Now in the solid wall there was a postern-door; and level with the upper threshold of the stately hall, an opening to a passage, closed with jointed boards. Odysseus ordered the noble swineherd to guard this postern-door and in its neighborhood to take his stand, since this was the only exit. But to the suitors said Agelaüs, speaking his words to all:

"Friends, could not one of you climb by the postern-door and tell our people, and quickly raise the alarm? So would the fellow soon have shot his last."

Then said to him Melanthius the goatherd: "No, heaven-descended Agelaüs, that may in no wise be; for the good court-yard door is terribly near at hand, and the mouth of the passage-way is narrow. One person there, if resolute, could bar the way for all. Yet I will fetch you from the chamber arms to wear; for there, I think, and nowhere else, Odysseus stored the armor,—he and his gallant son."

So having said, Melanthius, the goatherd, climbed to the chambers
of Odysseus through the vent-holes of the hall. Out of the store he
chose twelve shields, as many spears, and just as many brazen helmets
having horsehair plumes; then turning back, he brought them very
quickly and gave them to the suitors. And now did Odysseus' knees
grow feeble and his very soul, when he saw them donning arms and
waving in their hands long spears. Large seemed his task; and straightway to Telemachus he spoke these winged words:

"Surely, Telemachus, a woman of the house aids the hard fight
against us; or else it is Melanthius."

Then answered him discreet Telemachus: "Father, the fault is mine;
no other is to blame; for I it was who opened the chamber's tight-shut
door and left it open. Their watchman was too good. But, noble
Eumaeus, go and close the chamber-door, and see if any woman has a
hand in this, or if,—as I suspect,—it is the son of Dolius, Melanthius."

So they conversed together. And now Melanthius, the goatherd,
went to the room again to fetch more goodly armor. The noble swineherd spied him, and quickly to Odysseus, standing near, he said:

"High-born son of Laërtes, ready Odysseus, there is the knave whom
we suspected, just going to the chamber. Speak plainly; shall I kill him
if I prove the better man, or shall I bring him here to pay for all the
crimes he plotted in your house?"

Then wise Odysseus answered him and said: "Here in the hall
Telemachus and I will hold the lordly suitors, rage they as they may.
You two tie the man's feet and hands and drag him within the chamber; there fasten boards upon his back, and lashing a twisted rope
around him hoist him aloft, up the tall pillar, and bring him to the
beams, that he may keep alive there long and suffer grievous torment."

So he spoke, and willingly they heeded and obeyed. They hastened to
the chamber, unseen of him within. He was engaged in searching after
armor in a corner of the room, while the pair stood beside the door-posts,
one on either hand, and waited. Soon as Melanthius the goatherd crossed
the threshold, in one hand bearing a goodly helmet and in the other a
broad old shield beflecked with mould,—the shield of lord Laërtes,
which he carried in his youth, now laid away, its strap-seams parted,—
then on him sprang the two and dragged him by the hair within the door,
threw him all horror-stricken to the ground, bound hands and feet together with a galling cord, which tight and fast they tied, as they were ordered by Laërtes' son, long-tried royal Odysseus; then they lashed a
twisted rope around and hoisted him aloft, up the tall pillar, and brought
him to the beams; and mocking him said you, swineherd Eumaeus:

"Now then, Melanthius, you shall watch the whole night long,
stretched out on such a comfortable bed as suits you well. The early

dawn out of the Ocean-stream shall not in golden splendor slip unheeded by, when you should drive goats for the suitors at the hall to make their meal."

Thus was he left there, fast in deadly bonds. The pair put on their armor, closed the shining door and went to join Odysseus, keen and crafty. Here they stood, breathing fury, four of them on the threshold, although within the hall were many men of might. But near them came Athene, the daughter of Zeus, likened to Mentor in her form and voice. To see her made Odysseus glad, and thus he spoke:

"Mentor, save us from ruin! Remember the good comrade who often aided you. You are of my own years."

He said this, though he understood it was Athene, the summoner of hosts. But the suitors shouted from the other side, down in the hall; and foremost in abuse was Agelaüs, son of Damastor:

"Mentor, do not let Odysseus lure you by his words to fight the suitors and to lend him aid; for I am sure even then we still shall work our will. And after we have slain these men, father and son, you too shall die beside them for deeds you thought to do within the hall. Here with your head you shall make due amends. And when with the sword we have cut short your power, whatever goods you have, within doors and without, we will confound with the possessions of Odysseus. We will not let your sons and daughters live at home, nor let your true wife linger in the town of Ithaca."

As he spoke thus, Athene grew more wroth in spirit and chid Odysseus with these angry words: "Odysseus, you have no longer such firm power and spirit as when for the sake of white-armed high-born Helen you fought the Trojans nine years long unflinchingly, and vanquished many men in mortal combat, and by your wisdom Priam's wide-wayed city fell. Why, now returned to home and wealth and here confronted with the suitors, do you shrink from being brave? Nay, nay, good friend, stand by my side, watch what I do, and see how, in the presence of the foe, Mentor, the son of Alcimus, repays a kindness."

She spoke, but gave him not quite yet the victory in full. Still she made trial of the strength and spirit both of Odysseus and his valiant son. Up to the roof-beam of the smoky hall she darted like a swallow, resting there.

Now the suitors were led by Agelaüs, son of Damastor, by Eurynomus, Amphimedon, and Demoptolemus, by Peisander, son of Polyctor, and wise Polybus; for these in manly excellence were quite the best of all who still were living, fighting for their lives. The rest the bow and storm of arrows had laid low. So to these men said Agelaüs, speaking his words to all:

"Now, friends, at last the man shall hold his ruthless hands; for Mentor has departed after uttering idle boasts, and the men at the front door are left alone. So hurl your long spears, but not all together! Now then, six let fly first; and see if Zeus allows Odysseus to be hit and us to win an honor. No trouble about the rest when he is down!"

He said, and all to whom he spoke let fly their spears with power. Athene made all vain. One struck the doorpost of the stately hall; one the tight-fitting door; another's ashen shaft, heavy with bronze, crashed on the wall. And when the men were safe from the suitors' spears, then thus began long-tried royal Odysseus:

"Friends, let me give the word at last to our side too. Let fly your spears into the crowd of suitors, men who seek to slay and strip us, adding this to former wrongs!"

He spoke, and all with careful aim let fly their pointed spears. Odysseus struck down Demoptolemus; Telemachus, Euryades; the swineherd, Elatus; and the herdsman of the cattle, Peisander. All these together bit the dust of the broad floor, the other suitors falling back from hall to deep recess. Odysseus' men sprang forward and from the bodies of the dead pulled out the spears.

And now the suitors again let fly their pointed spears with power. Athene made them for the most part vain. One struck the doorpost of the stately hall; one the tight-fitting door; another's ashen shaft, heavy with bronze, crashed on the wall. But Amphimedon wounded Telemachus on the wrist of the right hand, though slightly; the metal tore the outer skin. And Ctesippus with his long spear grazed Eumaeus on the shoulder which showed above his shield; the spear flew past and fell upon the ground.

Once more the men beside Odysseus, keen and crafty, let fly their sharp spears on the crowd of suitors. And now by Odysseus, the spoiler of cities, Eurydamas was hit; by Telemachus, Amphimedon; by the swineherd, Polybus; and afterwards the herdsman of the cattle hit Ctesippus in the breast and cried in triumph:

"Ha, son of Polytherses, ready mocker, never again give way to folly and big words! Leave boasting to the gods; they are stronger far than you. This gift offsets the hoof you gave to great Odysseus a little while ago, when in his house he played the beggar man."

So spoke the herdsman of the crook-horned kine. Then Odysseus wounded Damastor's son with his long spear, when fighting hand to hand. Telemachus wounded Evenor's son, Leiocritus, with a spear-thrust in the middle of the waist, and drove the point clean through. He fell on his face and struck the ground flat with his forehead. And now Athene from the roof above stretched forth her murderous aegis. Their souls were panic-stricken. They scurried through the hall like herded cows, on whom the glancing gadfly falls and maddens them, in spring-time when the days are long. And as the crook-clawed hook-beaked vultures, descending from the hills, dart at the birds which fly the clouds and skim the plain, while the vultures pounce and kill them; defense they have not and have no escape, and men are merry at their capture; so the four chased the suitors down the hall and smote them right and left. There went up moans, a dismal sound, as skulls were crushed and all the pavement ran with blood.

But Leiodes, rushing forward, clasped Odysseus by the knees, and spoke imploringly these winged words: "I clasp your knees, Odysseus! Oh, respect and spare me! For I protest I never harmed a woman of the house by wicked word or act. No! and I used to try to stop the rest,—the suitors,—when one of them would do such deeds. But they were not inclined to hold their hands from wrong. So through their own perversity they met a dismal doom; and I, their soothsayer, although I did no ill, must also fall. There is no gratitude for good deeds done!"

Then looking sternly on him wise Odysseus said: "If you avow yourself their soothsayer, many a time you must have prayed within the hall that the issue of a glad return might be delayed for me, while my dear wife should follow you and bear you children. Therefore you shall not now avoid a shameful death."

So saying, he seized in his sturdy hand a sword that lay near by, a sword which Agelaüs had dropped upon the ground when he was slain, and drove it through the middle of Leiodes' neck. While he yet spoke, his head rolled in the dust.

But the bard, the son of Terpes, still had escaped dark doom,—Phemius, who sang perforce among the suitors. He stood, holding the tuneful lyre in his hands, close to the postern-door; and in his heart he doubted whether to hasten from the hall to the massive altar of great Zeus, guardian of courts, and take his seat where oftentimes Laërtes and Odysseus had burned the thighs of beeves; or whether he should run and clasp Odysseus by the knees. Reflecting thus, it seemed the better way to touch the knees of Laërtes' son, Odysseus. He laid his hollow lyre upon the ground, midway between the mixer and the silver-studded chair, ran forward to Odysseus, clasped his knees, and spoke imploringly these winged words:

"I clasp your knees, Odysseus! Oh, respect and spare me! To you yourself hereafter grief will come, if you destroy a bard who sings to gods and men. Self-taught am I; God planted in my heart all kinds of song; and I had thought to sing to you as to a god. Then do not seek to slay me. Telemachus, your own dear son, will say how not through will of mine, nor seeking gain, I lingered at your palace, singing to the suitors at their feasts; for being more and stronger men than I, they brought me here by force."

What he had said revered Telemachus heard, and he quickly called to his father who was standing near: "Hold! For the man is guiltless. Do not stab him with the sword! And let us also spare Medon, the page, who here at home used to have charge of me while I was still a child,— unless indeed Philoetius or the swineherd slew him, or he encountered you as you stormed along the hall."

What he was saying Medon, that man of understanding, heard; for he lay crouching underneath a chair, wrapped in a fresh-flayed ox's hide, seeking to shun dark doom. Straightway he rose from underneath the chair, quickly cast off the hide, sprang forward to Telemachus, clasped his knees, and cried imploringly in winged words:

"Friend, stay your hand! It is I! And speak to your father, or exulting in his sharp sword he will destroy me out of indignation at the suitors, who wasted the possessions in his halls and in their folly paid no heed to you."

But wise Odysseus, smiling, said: "Be of good cheer, for he has cleared and saved you; that in your heart you may perceive and may report to others how much more safe is doing good than ill. But both of you leave the hall and sit outside, out of this bloodshed, in the court,— you and the full-voiced bard,—till I have accomplished in the house all that I still must do."

Even as he spoke, the pair went forth and left the hall, and both sat down by the altar of great Zeus, peering about on every side as still expecting death. Odysseus too peered round his hall to see if any living man were lurking there, seeking to shun dark doom. He found them all laid low in blood and dust, and in such numbers as the fish which fishermen draw to the shelving shore out of the foaming sea in meshy nets; these all, sick for the salt sea wave, lie heaped upon the sands, while the resplendent sun takes life away; so lay the suitors, heaped on one another. And now to Telemachus said wise Odysseus:

"Telemachus, go call nurse Eurycleia, that I may speak to her the thing I have in mind."

He spoke, and Telemachus heeded his dear father and, shaking the door, said to nurse Eurycleia: "Up! aged woman, who have charge of all the damsels in our hall! Come hither! My father calls and wants to speak with you."

Such were his words; unwinged, they rested with her. Opening the doors of the stately hall, she entered. Telemachus led the way. And there among the bodies of the slain she found Odysseus, dabbled with blood and gore, like a lion come from feeding on some stall-fed ox; its whole breast and its cheeks on either side are bloody; terrible is the beast to see; so dabbled was Odysseus, feet and hands. And when she saw the bodies and the quantity of blood, she was ready to cry aloud at the sight of the mighty deed. But Odysseus held her back and stayed her madness, and speaking in winged words he said:

"Woman, be glad within; but hush, and make no cry. It is not right to glory in the slain. The gods' doom and their reckless deeds destroyed them; for they respected nobody on earth, bad man or good, who came among them. So through their own perversity they met a dismal doom. But name me now the women of the hall, and tell me who dishonor me and who are guiltless."

Then said to him his dear nurse Eurycleia: "Then I will tell you, child, the very truth. You have fifty women-servants at the hall whom we have taught their tasks, to card the wool and bear the servant's lot. Out of these women, twelve in all have gone the way of shame, paying no heed to me nor even to Penelope. It is but lately Telemachus has come to manhood, and his mother has never suffered him to rule the maids. But let me go above, to the bright upper chamber, and tell your wife, whom a god has laid asleep."

Then wise Odysseus answered her and said: "Do not awake her yet; tell those women to come here who in the past behaved unworthily."

So he spoke, and through the hall forth the old woman went, to give the message to the maids and bid them come with speed. Meanwhile Odysseus, calling to his side Telemachus, the neatherd, and the swine-herd, spoke to them thus in winged words:

"Begin to carry off the dead, and bid the women aid you; then let them clean the goodly chairs and tables with water and porous sponges. And when you have set in order all the house, lead forth these serving-maids out of the stately hall to a spot between the round-house and the neat court-yard wall, and smite them with your long swords till you take life from all; and so they may forget the love they had among the suit-ors, when they would meet them unobserved."

He spoke, and the women came, trooping along together, in bitter lamentation, letting the big tears fall. First they carried out the bodies of the dead and laid them by the portico of the fenced court, piling them there one on another. Odysseus gave the orders and hastened on the work, and only because compelled the maids bore off the bodies. Then afterwards they cleaned the goodly chairs and tables with water and porous sponges. Telemachus, the neatherd and the swineherd with shovels scraped the pavement of the strong-built room, and the maids took up the scrapings and threw them out of doors. And when they had set in order all the hall, they led the serving-maids out of the stately hall to a spot between the round-house and the neat court-yard wall, and there they shut them in a narrow space whence there was no escape. Then thus began discreet Telemachus:

"By no honorable death would I take away the lives of those who poured reproaches on my head and on my mother, and lay beside the suitors."

He spoke, and tied the cable of a dark-bowed ship to a great pillar, then lashed it to the round-house, stretching it high across, too high for one to touch the feet upon the ground. And as the wide-winged thrushes or the doves strike on a net set in the bushes; and when they think to go to roost a cruel bed receives them; even so the women held their heads in line, and around every neck a noose was laid, that they might die most vilely. They twitched their feet a little, but not long.

Then forth they led Melanthius across the porch and yard. With rustless sword they lopped off his nose and ears, pulled out his bowels to be eaten raw by dogs, and in their rage cut off his hands and feet.

Afterwards washing clean their own hands and their feet, they went to meet Odysseus in the house, and all the work was done. But to his dear nurse Eurycleia said Odysseus: "Woman, bring sulphur, a protection against harm, and bring me fire to fumigate the hall. And bid Penelope come hither with her women, and order all the maids throughout the house to come."

Then said to him his dear nurse Eurycleia: "Truly, my child, in all this you speak rightly. Yet let me fetch you clothes, a coat and tunic. And do not, with this covering of rags on your broad shoulders, stand in the hall. That would be cause for blame."

But wise Odysseus answered her and said: "First let a fire be lighted in the hall."

At these his words, his dear nurse Eurycleia did not disobey; but brought the fire and sulphur. Odysseus fumigated all the hall, the buildings and the court.

And now the old woman passed through the goodly palace of Odysseus to take his message to the maids and bid them come with speed. Out of their room they came, with torches in their hands. They gathered round Odysseus, hailing him with delight. Fondly they kissed his face and neck, and held him by the hand. Glad longing fell upon him to weep and cry aloud. All these he knew were true.

XXIII.

THE RECOGNITION BY PENELOPE

SO THE old woman, full of glee, went to the upper chamber to tell her mistress her dear lord was in the house. Her knees grew strong; her feet outran themselves. By Penelope's head she paused, and thus she spoke:

"Awake, Penelope, dear child, to see with your own eyes what you have hoped to see this many a day! Odysseus is here! He has come home at last, and slain the haughty suitors,—the men who vexed his house, devoured his substance, and oppressed his son."

Then heedful Penelope said to her: "Dear nurse, the gods have crazed you. They can befool one who is very wise, and often they have set the simple in the paths of prudence. They have confused you; you were sober-minded heretofore. Why mock me when my heart is full of sorrow, telling wild tales like these? And why arouse me from the sleep that sweetly bound me and kept my eyelids closed? I have not slept so soundly since Odysseus went away to see accursed Ilios,—name never to be named. Nay then, go down, back to the hall. If any other of my maids had come and told me this and waked me out of sleep, I would soon have sent her off in sorry wise into the hall once more. This time age serves you well."

Then said to her the good nurse Eurycleia: "Dear child, I do not mock you. In very truth it is Odysseus; he is come, as I have said. He is the stranger whom everybody in the hall has set at naught. Telemachus knew long ago that he was here, but out of prudence hid his knowledge of his father till he should have revenge from these bold men for wicked deeds."

So spoke she; and Penelope was glad, and, springing from her bed, fell on the woman's neck, and let the tears burst from her eyes; and, speaking in winged words, she said: "Nay, tell me, then, dear nurse, and tell me truly; if he is really come as you declare, how was it he laid hands upon the shameless suitors, being alone, while they were always here together?"

Then answered her the good nurse Eurycleia: "I did not see; I did not ask; I only heard the groans of dying men. In a corner of our protected chamber we sat and trembled,—the doors were tightly closed,—until your son Telemachus called to me from the hall; for his father bade him call. And there among the bodies of the slain I found Odysseus standing. All around, covering the trodden floor, they lay, one on another. It would have warmed your heart to see him, like a lion, dabbled with blood and gore. Now all the bodies are collected at the courtyard gate, while he is fumigating the fair house by lighting a great fire. He sent me here to call you. Follow me, then, that you may come to gladness in your true hearts together, for sorely have you suffered. Now the long hope has been at last fulfilled. He has come back alive to his own hearth, and found you still, you and his son, within his hall; and upon those who did him wrong, the suitors, on all of them here in his home he has obtained revenge."

Then heedful Penelope said to her: "Dear nurse, be not too boastful yet, nor filled with glee. You know how welcome here the sight of him would be to all, and most to me and to the son we had. But this is no true tale you tell. Nay, rather some immortal slew the lordly suitors, in anger at their galling insolence and wicked deeds; for they respected nobody on earth, bad man or good, who came among them. So for their sins they suffered. But Odysseus, far from Achaea, lost the hope of coming home; nay, he himself was lost."

Then answered her the good nurse Eurycleia: "My child, what word has passed the barrier of your teeth, to say your husband, who is now beside your hearth, will never come! Your heart is always doubting. Come, then, and let me name another sign most sure,—the scar the boar dealt long ago with his white tusk. I found it as I washed him, and I would have told you then; but he laid his hand upon my mouth, and in his watchful wisdom would not let me speak. But follow me. I stake my very life; if I deceive you, slay me by the vilest death."

Then heedful Penelope answered her: "Dear nurse, 'tis hard for you to trace the counsels of the everlasting gods, however wise you are. Nevertheless, let us go down to meet my son, and see the suitors who are dead, and him who slew them."

So saying, she went from her chamber to the hall, and much her heart debated whether aloof to question her dear husband, or to draw near and kiss his face and take his hand. But when she entered, crossing the stone threshold, she sat down opposite Odysseus, in the firelight, beside the farther wall. He sat by a tall pillar, looking down, waiting to hear if his stately wife would speak when she should look his way. But she sat silent long; amazement filled her heart. Now she would gaze with a long look upon his face, and now she would not know him for the mean clothes that he wore. But Telemachus rebuked her, and spoke to her and said:

"Mother, hard mother, of ungentle heart, why do you hold aloof so from my father, and do not sit beside him, plying him with words and questions? There is no other woman of such stubborn spirit to stand off from the husband who, after many grievous toils, comes in the twentieth year home to his native land. Your heart is always harder than a stone!"

Then said to him heedful Penelope: "My child, my soul within is dazed with wonder. I cannot speak to him, nor ask a question, nor look him in the face. But if this is indeed Odysseus, come at last, we certainly shall know each other better than others know; for we have signs which we two understand,—signs hidden from the rest."

As she, long tried, spoke thus, royal Odysseus smiled, and said to Telemachus forthwith in winged words: "Telemachus, leave your mother in the hall to try my truth. She soon will know me better. Now, because I am foul and dressed in sorry clothes, she holds me in dishonor, and says I am not he. But you and I have yet to plan how all may turn out well. For whoso kills one man among a tribe, though the man leaves few champions behind, becomes an exile, quitting king and country. We have destroyed the pillars of the state, the very noblest youths of Ithaca. Form, then, a plan, I pray."

Then answered him discreet Telemachus: "Look you to that, dear father. Your wisdom is, they say, the best among mankind. No mortal man can rival you. Zealously will we follow, and not fail, I think, in daring, so far as power is ours."

Then wise Odysseus answered him and said: "Then I will tell you what seems best to me. First wash and put on tunics, and bid the maids about the house array themselves. Then let the sacred bard with tuneful lyre lead us in sportive dancing, that men may say, hearing us from without, 'It is a wedding,' whether such men be passers-by or neighboring folk; and so broad rumor may not reach the town about the suitors' murder till we are gone to our well-wooded farm. There will we plan as the Olympian shall grant us wisdom."

So he spoke, and willingly they heeded and obeyed. For first they washed themselves and put on tunics, and the women also put on their attire. And then the noble bard took up his hollow lyre, and in them stirred desire for merry music and the gallant dance; and the great house resounded to the tread of lusty men and gay-girt women. And one who heard the dancing from without would say, "Well, well! some man has married the long-courted queen. Hard-hearted! For the husband of her youth she would not guard her great house to the end, till he should come." So they would say, but knew not how things were.

Meanwhile within the house Eurynome, the housekeeper, bathed resolute Odysseus and anointed him with oil, and on him put a goodly robe and tunic. Upon his face Athene cast great beauty; she made him taller than before, and stouter to behold, and made the curling locks to fall around his head as on the hyacinth flower. As when a man lays gold on silver,—some skillful man whom Hephaestus and Pallas Athene have trained in every art, and he fashions graceful work; so did she cast a grace upon his head and shoulders. Forth from the bath he came, in bearing like the immortals, and once more took the seat from which he first arose, facing his wife, and spoke to her these words:

"Lady, a heart impenetrable beyond the sex of women the dwellers on Olympus gave to you. There is no other woman of such stubborn spirit to stand off from the husband who, after many grievous toils, comes in the twentieth year home to his native land. Come, then, good nurse, and make my bed, that I may lie alone. For certainly of iron is the heart within her breast."

Then said to him heedful Penelope: "Nay, sir, I am not proud, nor contemptuous of you, nor too much dazed with wonder. I very well remember what you were when you went upon your long-oared ship away from Ithaca. However, Eurycleia, make up his massive bed outside that stately chamber which he himself once built. Move the massive frame out there, and throw the bedding on,—the fleeces, robes, and bright-hued rugs."

She said this in the hope to prove her husband; but Odysseus spoke in anger to his faithful wife: "Woman, these are bitter words which you have said! Who set my bed elsewhere? A hard task that would be for one, however skilled,—unless a god should come and by his will set it with ease upon some other spot; but among men no living being, even in his prime, could lightly shift it; for a great token is inwrought into its curious frame. I built it; no one else. There grew a thick-leaved olive shrub inside the yard, full-grown and vigorous, in girth much like a pillar. Round this I formed my chamber, and I worked till it was done, building it out of close-set stones, and roofing it over well. Framed and tight-fitting doors I added to it. Then I lopped the thick-leaved olive's crest, cutting the stem high up above the roots, neatly and skillfully smoothed with my axe the sides, and to the line I kept all true to shape my post, and with an auger I bored it all along. Starting with this, I fashioned me the bed till it was finished, and I inlaid it well with gold, with silver, and with ivory. On it I stretched a thong of ox-hide, gay with purple. This is the token I now tell. I do not know whether the bed still stands there, wife, or whether somebody has set it elsewhere, cutting the olive trunk."

As he spoke thus, her knees grew feeble and her very soul, when she recognized the tokens which Odysseus exactly told. Then bursting into tears, she ran straight toward him, threw her arms round Odysseus' neck and kissed his face, and said:

"Odysseus, do not scorn me! Ever before, you were the wisest of mankind. The gods have sent us sorrow, and grudged our staying side by side to share the joys of youth and reach the threshold of old age. But do not be angry with me now, nor take it ill that then when I first saw you I did not greet you thus; for the heart within my breast was always trembling. I feared some man might come and cheat me with his tale. Many a man makes wicked schemes for gain. Nay, Argive Helen, the daughter of Zeus, would not have given herself to love a stranger if she had known how warrior sons of the Achaeans would bring her home again, back to her native land. And yet it was a god prompted her deed of shame. Before, she did not cherish in her heart such sin, such grievous sin, from which began the woe which stretched to us. But now, when you have clearly told the tokens of our bed, which no one else has seen, but only you and I and the single servant, Actoris, whom my father gave me on my coming here to keep the door of our closed chamber,—you make even my ungentle heart believe."

So she spoke, and stirred still more his yearning after tears; and he began to weep, holding his loved and faithful wife. As when the welcome land appears to swimmers, whose sturdy ship Poseidon wrecked at sea, confounded by the winds and solid waters; a few escape the foaming sea and swim ashore; thick salt foam crusts their flesh; they climb the welcome land, and are escaped from danger; so welcome to her gazing eyes appeared her husband. From round his neck she never let her white arms go. And rosy-fingered dawn had found them weeping, but a different plan the goddess formed, clear-eyed Athene. She checked the long night in its passage, and at the Ocean-stream she stayed the gold-throned dawn, and did not suffer it to yoke the swift-paced horses which carry light to men, Lampus and Phaëton which bear the dawn. And now to his wife said wise Odysseus:

"O wife, we have not reached the end of all our trials yet. Hereafter comes a task immeasurable, long and severe, which I must needs fulfill; for so the spirit of Teiresias told me, that day when I descended to the house of Hades to learn about the journey of my comrades and myself. But come, my wife, let us to bed, that there at last we may refresh ourselves with pleasant sleep."

Then said to him heedful Penelope: "The bed shall be prepared whenever your heart wills, now that the gods have let you reach your stately house and native land. But since you speak of this, and God inspires your heart, come, tell that trial. In time to come, I know, I shall experience it. To learn about it now, makes it no worse."

Then wise Odysseus answered her and said: "Lady, why urge me so insistently to tell? Well, I will speak it out; I will not hide it. Yet your heart will feel no joy; I have no joy myself; for Teiresias bade me go to many a peopled town, bearing in hand a shapely oar, till I should reach the men that know no sea and do not eat food mixed with salt. These, therefore, have no knowledge of the red-cheeked ships, nor of the shapely oars which are the wings of ships. And this was the sign, he said, easy to be observed. I will not hide it from you. When another traveler, meeting me, should say I had a winnowing-fan on my white shoulder, there in the ground he bade me fix my oar and make fit offerings to lord Poseidon,—a ram, a bull, and the sow's mate, a boar,—and, turning homeward, to offer sacred hecatombs to the immortal gods who hold the open sky, all in the order due. And on myself death from the sea shall very gently come and cut me off, bowed down with hale old age. Round me shall be a prosperous people. All this, he said, should be fulfilled."

Then said to him heedful Penelope: "If gods can make old age the better time, then there is hope there will be rest from trouble."

So they conversed together. Meanwhile, Eurynome and the nurse prepared their bed with clothing soft, under the light of blazing torches. And after they had spread the comfortable bed, with busy speed, the old woman departed to her room to rest; while the chamber-servant, Eurynome, with torch in hand, walked on before, as they two came to bed. She brought them to their chamber, and then she went her way. So they came gladly to their old bed's rites. And now Telemachus, the neatherd and the swineherd stayed their feet from dancing, and bade the women stay, and all betook themselves to rest throughout the dusky halls.

So when the pair had joyed in happy love, they joyed in talking too, each one relating: she, the royal lady, what she endured at home, watching the wasteful throng of suitors, who, making excuse of her, slew many cattle, beeves, and sturdy sheep, and stores of wine were drained from out the casks; he, high-born Odysseus, what miseries he brought on other men and what he bore himself in anguish,—all he told, and she was glad to listen. No sleep fell on her eyelids till he had told her all.

He began with how at first he conquered the Ciconians, and came thereafter to the fruitful land of Lotus-eaters; then what the Cyclops did, and how he took revenge for the brave comrades whom the Cyclops ate and never pitied; then how he came to Aeolus, who gave him hearty welcome and sent him on his way; but it was fated that he should not reach his dear land yet, for a sweeping storm bore him once more along the swarming sea, loudly lamenting; how he came to Telepylus in Laestrygonia, where the men destroyed his ships and his mailed comrades, all of them; Odysseus fled in his black ship alone. He told of Circe, too, and all her crafty guile; and how on a ship of many oars he came to the mouldering house of Hades, there to consult the spirit of Teiresias of Thebes, and looked on all his comrades, and on the mother who had borne him and cared for him when little; how he had heard the full-voiced Sirens' song; how he came to the Wandering Rocks, to dire Charybdis and to Scylla, past whom none goes unharmed; how then his crew slew the Sun's kine; how Zeus with a blazing bolt smote his swift ship,—Zeus, thundering from on high,—and his good comrades perished, utterly, all, while he escaped their evil doom; how he came to the island of Ogygia and to the nymph Calypso, who held him in her hollow grotto, wishing him to be her husband, cherishing him, and saying she would make him an immortal, young forever, but she never beguiled the heart within his breast; then how he came through many toils to the Phaeacians, who honored him exceedingly, as if he were a god, and brought him on his way to his own native land, giving him stores of bronze and gold and clothing. This was the latest tale he told, when pleasant sleep fell on him, easing his limbs and from his heart removing care.

Now a new plan the goddess formed, clear-eyed Athene, when in her mind she judged Odysseus had enough of love and sleep. Straightway from out the Ocean-stream she roused the gold-throned dawn, to bring the light to men. Odysseus was aroused from his soft bed, and gave his wife this charge:

"Wife, we have had in days gone by our fill of trials: you, mourning here my grievous journey home; me, Zeus and the other gods bound fast in sorrow, all eager as I was, far from my native land. But since we now have reached the rest we long desired together, do you protect whatever wealth is still within my halls. As for the flocks which the audacious suitors wasted, I shall myself seize many, and the Achaeans shall give me more besides, until they fill my folds. But now I go to the well-wooded farm, to visit my good father, who for my sake has been in constant grief. On you, my wife, wise as you are, I lay this charge. Straight with the sunrise a report will go abroad about the suitors whom I slew here in the hall. Then go to the upper chamber with your waiting-women. There abide. Give not a look to any one, nor ask a question."

He spoke, and girt his beautiful arms about his shoulders; and he awoke Telemachus, the neatherd and the swineherd, and bade them all take weapons in their hands for fighting. They did not disobey, but took their brazen harness. They opened the doors; they sallied forth; Odysseus led the way. Over the land it was already light, but Athene, hiding them in darkness, led them swiftly from the town.

XXIV.

PEACE

Meanwhile Cyllenian Hermes summoned hence the spirits of the suitors. In his hand he held a wand, beautiful, made of gold, with which he charms to sleep the eyes of whom he will, while again whom he will he wakens out of slumber. With this he started them and led them forth; they followed gibbering after. As in a corner of a monstrous cave the bats fly gibbering, when one tumbles from the rock out of the cluster as they cling together; so gibbering, these moved together. Protecting Hermes was their guide down the dank pathway. Past the Ocean-stream they went, past the White Rock, past the portals of the Sun and land of dreams, and soon they reached the field of asphodel, where spirits dwell, spectres of worn-out men.

Here they came upon the spirit of Achilles, son of Peleus, and of Patroclus too, of gallant Antilochus, and of Ajax, who was first in beauty and in stature of all the Danaäns after the gallant son of Peleus. These formed a group around Achilles; to whom approached the spirit of Agamemnon, son of Atreus, sorrowing. Around thronged other spirits of men who by his side had died in the house of Aegisthus and there had met their doom. And the spirit of the son of Peleus first addressed him:

"O son of Atreus, throughout your life we said you were exceeding dear to Zeus, the Thunderer, beyond all other heroes, because you were the lord of many mighty men there in the land of Troy where we Achaeans suffered; yet all too early you were doomed to meet fell fate, which no one that is born avoids. Ah, would that, in the pride of your full power, there in the land of Troy you had met death and doom! Then would the whole Achaean host have made your grave, and for your son in after days a great name had been gained. Now you must be cut off by an inglorious death."

Then said to him the spirit of the son of Atreus: "Fortunate son of Peleus, godlike Achilles, who died at Troy, afar from Argos! Around you others fell, the Trojans' and Achaeans' bravest sons, battling because of you; while in a cloud of dust proud you lay proudly, all your horse-manship forgotten. All through the day we battled, and never would have stopped our fighting had Zeus himself not stopped us with a storm. And after we had borne you to the ships from out the fight, we laid you on a bier and washed your comely body with warm water and with oil. The Danaäns standing round you shed many burning tears, and cut their hair. Out of the sea came forth your mother, with the immortal sea nymphs, when she heard the tale, while over the water ran a wondrous wail, and secret trembling fell on all the Achaeans. Then all had hastened off and boarded the hollow ships, if one had not detained them who was wise in ancient lore, Nestor, whose counsel had before been proved the best. He with good will addressed them thus, and said: 'Hold, Argives! Do not flee, you young Achaeans! It is his mother coming from the sea with the immortal nymphs to look on her dead son.' By these his words the bold Achaeans were withheld from flight; while round you stood the daughters of the old man of the sea, lamenting bitterly, and with immortal robes they clad your body. Meantime the Muses, nine in all, with sweet responsive voices sang your dirge. Then not an Argive could you see but was in tears; the piercing song so deeply moved them. For seventeen days, alike by night and day, we mortal men and deathless gods continued mourning. On the eighteenth we gave you to the flames. Many fat sheep we slew beside you, and many crook-horned kine. In vesture of the gods you burned, with much anointing oil and much sweet honey. Many Achaean heroes moved in their armor round your blazing pyre, footmen and chario-teers, and a loud din arose. And when at length Hephaestus' flame had made an end of you, at dawn we gathered your white bones, Achilles, laid in pure wine and oil. Your mother gave the golden urn; a gift, she said, of Dionysus, and handiwork of famed Hephaestus. In this your white bones lie, illustrious Achilles, mingled with those of dead Patroclus, son of Menoetius, and parted from Antilochus, whom you regarded more than all your other comrades, excepting dead Patroclus. Over them all the powerful host of Argive spearmen built a great stately tomb at a projecting point on the broad Hellespont, so that it might be seen far off upon the sea by men who now are born or shall be born hereafter. Your mother, having besought the gods for splendid prizes, offered them in the open lists to the bravest of the Achaeans. In former days you have been present at the burial of many a hero, when at a king's death young men girt themselves and strove for prizes; but here you would have marveled in your heart far more to see the splendid prizes offered in your honor by silver-footed Thetis; for you were very dear to all the gods. Thus though you died, you did not lose your name; but ever among mankind, Achilles, your glory shall be great. While as for me, what gain had I in winding up the war? On my return Zeus purposed me a miserable end, at the hands of Aegisthus and my accursed wife."

So they conversed together. And now the Guide approached, the Speedy-comer, leading the spirits of the suitors whom Odysseus slew. Amazed, the two drew near to see; and the spirit of Agamemnon, son of Atreus, perceived the son of Melaneus, renowned Amphimedon; for Melaneus of Ithaca was once his entertainer. Then thus began the spirit of the son of Atreus:

"Amphimedon, what has happened that you come to this dreary land, all of you chosen men and all alike in years? One who would pick the best men of a town would choose no others. Was it on shipboard that Poseidon smote you, raising ill winds and heavy seas? Or did fierce men destroy you on the land, while you were cutting off their kine or their fair flocks of sheep, or while you fought to win their town and carry off their women? Tell what I ask! I call myself your friend. Do you not recollect how I, with godlike Menelaus, came to your house to urge Odysseus to follow us to Ilios on the well-benched ships? A whole month long we spent, crossing the open sea, and found it hard to win the spoiler of towns, Odysseus."

Then answered him the spirit of Amphimedon: "Great son of Atreus, Agamemnon, lord of men, all that you say, heaven-favored one, I recollect; and I in turn will very plainly tell how a cruel end of death befell us. We wooed the wife of long gone Odysseus. She neither declined the hated suit nor did she end it, because she planned for us death and dark doom. This was the last pretext she cunningly devised: within the hall she set up a great loom and went to weaving; fine was the web and very large; and then to us said she: 'Young men who are my suitors, though royal Odysseus now is dead forbear to urge my marriage till I complete this robe,—its threads must not be wasted,—a shroud for lord Laërtes, against the time when the fell doom of death that lays men low shall overtake him. Achaean wives about the land, I fear, might give me blame if he should lie without a shroud, he who had great possessions.' Such were her words, and our high hearts assented. Then in the daytime would she weave at the great web, but in the night unravel, after her torch was set. Thus for three years she hid her craft and cheated the Achaeans. But when the fourth year came, as time rolled on, when the months waned and the long days were done, then at the last one of her maids, who knew full well, confessed, and we discovered her unraveling the splendid web; so then she finished it, against her will, perforce. When she displayed the robe, after weaving the great web and washing it, like sun or moon it shone. And then some hostile god guided Odysseus,—whence I know not,—to the confines of our country, where the swineherd has his home. Thither the son of royal Odysseus also came, returning by black ship from sandy Pylos. And when the two had planned the suitors' cruel death, they entered our famous town; Odysseus later, Telemachus coming on before. The swineherd brought Odysseus, who wore a sorry garb, like an old and wretched beggar, leaning upon a staff. Upon his back were miserable clothes, and none of us could know him as he suddenly appeared, not even our older men; but we assailed him with harsh words and missiles. A while he bore with patience this pelting and abuse in his own house; but when at last the will of aegis-bearing Zeus aroused him, he and Telemachus gathered the goodly weapons and put them in the store-room, fastening the bolts. Then, full of craft, he bade his wife deliver to the suitors the bow and the gray steel, to be to us ill-fated men means for our sport and harbingers of death. Not one of us could draw the string of the strong bow; we fell far short of power. But when the great bow reached Odysseus' hands, we shouted all together not to give the bow, whatever he might say. Telemachus alone urgently bade him take it. Then long-tried royal Odysseus took the bow in hand, bent it with ease, and sent an arrow through the steel. Advancing to the threshold, there he stood and poured out the swift arrows, glaring terribly around. He shot down prince Antinoüs, and then on others turned his grievous shafts, with careful aim, and side by side they fell. Soon it was seen some god was the men's ally; for straightway rushing down the hall, with all their might they smote us right and left. Then went up moans, a dismal sound, as skulls were crushed and all the pavement ran with blood. Thus we died, Agamemnon; and still uncared-for in Odysseus' halls our bodies lie. Our friends at home have had no tidings, or they had washed the dark clots from our wounds and laid us out with wailing; for that is the dead man's due."

Then answered the spirit of the son of Atreus: "Fortunate son of Laërtes, ready Odysseus! You won a wife full of all worth. How upright was the heart of true Penelope, the daughter of Icarius! How faithful to Odysseus, the husband of her youth! Wherefore the story of her worth shall never die; but for all humankind immortal ones shall make a gladsome song in praise of steadfast Penelope. Not like the daughter of Tyndareus did she contrive vile deeds and slay the husband of her youth. Of her a loathsome song shall spread among mankind, and bring an ill repute on all the sex of women, even on well-doers too."

So they conversed together, where they stood within the house of Hades, in the secret places of the earth.

But Odysseus and his men, after departing from the town, soon reached the rich well-ordered farmstead of Laërtes. This place Laërtes had acquired for himself in days gone by, after much patient toil. Here was his house; round it on every side there ran a shed, in which ate, sat, and slept the slaves who did his pleasure. Within, there lived an old Sicilian woman, who tended carefully the aged man here at his farm, far from the town. Arriving here, Odysseus thus addressed his servants and his son:

"Go you at once into the stately house and slay forthwith for dinner the fattest of the swine. But I will put my father to the proof, and try if he will recognize and know me by the sight, or if he will fail to know me who have been absent long."

So saying, he gave his armor to his men, who then went quickly in, while Odysseus approached the fruitful vineyard, to make his trial there. Dolius he did not find, in crossing the long garden, nor any slaves or men; for they were gone to gather stones to make a vineyard wall, and Dolius was their leader. His father he found alone in the well-ordered vineyard, hoeing about a plant. He wore a dirty tunic, patched and coarse, and round his shins had bound sewed leather leggings, a protection against scratches. Upon his hands were gloves, to save him from the thorns, and on his head a goatskin cap; and so he nursed his sorrow.

When long-tried royal Odysseus saw his father, worn with old age and in great grief of heart, he stopped beneath a lofty pear-tree and shed tears. Then in his mind and heart he doubted much whether to kiss his father, to clasp him in his arms and tell him all, how he had come and found his native land; or first to question him and prove him through and through. Reflecting thus, it seemed the better way to try him first with probing words. With this intent, royal Odysseus walked straight toward him. Laërtes, with his head bent low, was digging round the plant, and standing by his side his gallant son addressed him:

"Old man, you have no lack of skill in tending gardens. Of these your care is good. Nothing is here—shrub, fig-tree, vine, olive, or pear, or bed of earth,—in all the field uncared for. But one thing I will say; be not offended. No proper care is taken of yourself; for you are meeting hard old age, yet you are sadly worn and meanly clad. It is not as if for idleness your master had cast you by, and nothing of the slave shows in your face or form. Rather you seem a royal person; like one who after taking bath and food might sleep at ease, as is the due of age. Come, then, declare me this and plainly tell whose slave you are, whose farm you tend. And tell me truly this, that I may know full well, if this is really Ithaca to which we now are come, as the man said just now who met me on my way. He was not otherwise, however; for he did not deign to talk at length, nor yet to hear my talk, when I inquired for my friend, and asked if he were living still or if he were already dead and in the house of Hades. But let me speak of that to you, and do you mark and listen. In my own country once I entertained a man who had come thither; and none among the traveling strangers was more welcome at my house. He called himself by birth a man of Ithaca, and said his father was Laërtes, son of Arceisius. I brought him home and entertained him well and gave him generous welcome from the abundance in my house. Such gifts I also gave as are fitting for a guest: of fine-wrought gold I gave him seven talents, gave him a flowered bowl of solid silver, twelve cloaks of single fold, as many rugs, as many goodly mantles, and as many tunics too. Further, I gave him women trained to faultless work, any four shapely damsels whom he himself might choose."

Then answered him his father, shedding tears: "Certainly, stranger, you are in the land for which you ask; but lawless impious men possess it now. Vain were the many gifts you gave. Yet had you found him living in the land of Ithaca, with fair return of gifts he had sent you on your way, and with a generous welcome; for that is just, when one begins a kindness. But come, declare me this, and plainly tell: how many years are passed since you received this guest, this hapless guest, my son,—if really it was he, ill-fated man!—whom, far from friends and home, fishes devoured in the deep or else on land he fell a prey to beasts and birds. No mother mourned for him and wrapped him in his shroud, nor father either,—we who gave him life! Nor did his richly-dowered wife, steadfast Penelope, wail by her husband's couch, as the wife should, and close his eyes, though that is the dead man's due. Tell me, however, truly, and let me know full well: who are you? of what people? Where is your town and kindred? Where is the swift ship moored which brought you hither, you and your gallant comrades? Or did you come a passenger on some strange ship, from which they landed you and sailed away?"

Then wise Odysseus answered him and said: "Well, I will very plainly tell you all. I come from Alybas, where I have a noble house, and am the son of lord Apheidas, the son of Polypemon. My own name is Eperitus. God drove me from Sicania and brought me here, against my will. Here my ship lies, just off the fields outside the town. As for Odysseus, five years ago he went away and left my land. Ill-fated man! And yet the birds were favorable at starting and came on his right hand. So I rejoiced and sent him forth, and he rejoicing went his way. Our hearts then hoped to meet again in friendship, and to give each other glorious gifts."

So he spoke, and on Laërtes fell a dark cloud of grief. He caught in his hands the powdery dust and strewed it on his hoary head with many groans. Odysseus' heart was stirred. Up through his nostrils shot a tingling pang as he beheld his father. Forward he sprang and clasped and kissed him, saying:

"Lo, father, I am he for whom you seek, now in the twentieth year come to my native land! Then cease this grief and tearful sighing; for let me tell you,—and the need of haste is great,—I slew the suitors in our halls, and so avenged their galling insolence and wicked deeds."

Then in his turn Laërtes answered: "If you are indeed my son, Odysseus, now returned, tell me some trusty sign that so I may believe."

But wise Odysseus answered him and said: "Examine first this scar, which a boar inflicted with his gleaming tusk upon Parnassus, whither I had gone. You and my honored mother sent me thither, to see Autolycus, my mother's father, and to obtain the gifts which he, when here, agreed to give. Then come, and let me tell the trees in the well-ordered vineyard, which you once gave, when I, being still a child, begged you for this and that, as I followed about the garden. Among these trees we passed. You named them and described them. You gave me thirteen pear-trees, ten apples, forty figs. And here you marked off fifty rows of vines to give, each one in bearing order. Along the rows clusters of all sorts hang, whenever the seasons sent by Zeus give them their fullness."

As he spoke thus, Laërtes' knees grew feeble and his very soul, when he recognized the tokens which Odysseus exactly told. Round his dear son he threw his arms, and long-tried royal Odysseus drew him fainting toward him. But when he gained his breath, and in his breast the spirit rallied, finding his words once more Laërtes said:

"O father Zeus, surely you gods still live on high Olympus, if the suitors have indeed paid for their wanton sin! And yet I have great fear at heart that all the men of Ithaca may soon attack us here and may send tidings through the Cephallenian cities."

But wise Odysseus answered him and said: "Be of good courage! Let not these things vex your mind! But let us hasten to the house which stands beside the orchard. Thither I sent Telemachus, the neatherd and the swineherd, that there they straightway might prepare our meal."

So talked the two, and walked to the fair house. And when they reached the stately buildings, they found Telemachus, the neatherd and the swineherd, carving much meat and mixing sparkling wine. Soon in his room the Sicilian servant bathed brave Laërtes and anointed him with oil and round him wrapped a goodly cloak. And Athene, drawing nigh, filled out the limbs of the shepherd of the people, and made him taller than before and larger to behold. Out of the bath he came, and his son wondered to see how like the immortal gods his bearing was; and speaking in winged words he said:

"Certainly, father, one of the everlasting gods has made your face and figure nobler to behold."

Then in his turn said wise Laërtes: "O father Zeus, Athene, and

Apollo, would I were what I was when I took Nericus, the stately citadel
on the main shore, leading my Cephallenians; and would that thus I
yesterday had stood beside you in our hall, my armor on my shoulders,
beating back the suitors! Then had I shook the knees of many in the
hall, and you had felt your inmost heart grow warm!"

So they conversed together. Meanwhile the others, after ceasing
from their labor of laying out the meal, took seats in order on couches
and on chairs. They all were laying hands upon their food, when in
came aged Dolius and his sons, tired from their work. Their mother,
the old Sicilian woman, had gone and called them; for she provided for
them, and diligently tended the old man now that old age was on him.
When the men saw Odysseus and marked him in their minds, they
stood still in the hall, astonished; but Odysseus kindly accosting them,
spoke thus:

"Old man, sit down to dinner and lay aside surprise; for eager as we
were to take our food, we waited long about the hall, ever expecting you."

He spoke, and Dolius ran, both hands outstretched, and seizing
Odysseus' hand kissed it upon the wrist, and speaking in winged words
he said:

"Dear master, because you have come home to us who sorely missed
you and never thought to see you any more,—but gods themselves have
brought you,—hail and rejoice! Gods grant you blessings! And tell me
truly this, that I may know it well: does heedful Penelope understand
that you are here, or shall we send her tidings?"

Then wise Odysseus answered him and said: "Old man, she understands already. Why should you think of that?"

So he spoke, and Dolius took his seat upon a polished bench.
Likewise the sons of Dolius, gathering round renowned Odysseus,
greeted him with their words and clasped his hands, and then sat down
in order by Dolius, their father. Thus were they busied with their dinner in the hall.

Rumor, meanwhile, with tidings, ran swiftly through the town, reporting the suitors' awful death and doom; and those who heard gathered
from every side, with moans and groans, before the palace of Odysseus.
Out of the house they each brought forth his dead, and buried them;
and all that came from other towns they gave to fishermen to carry
home on their swift ships. Then they went trooping to the assembly, sad
at heart. And when they were assembled and all had come together,
Eupeithes rose and thus addressed them: for he cherished in his heart
a sorrow for his son that could not be appeased,—his son Antinoüs, the
first whom royal Odysseus slew. With tears for him, he thus addressed
them, saying:

"O friends, this man has wrought a monstrous deed on the Achaeans!

For some he carried off in ships,—good men and many,—and then he lost his hollow ships and lost his people too; and now he has come home and killed the very noblest men of Cephallenia. Up then! Let us set forth, before he swiftly goes to Pylos, and sacred Elis where the Epeians rule, or we shall be disgraced henceforth forever; for it will be a shame for future times to know, if we take no revenge on those who slew our sons and brothers. Life to my thinking then would be no longer sweet. Nay, I would die at once and join the men now slain. But forth, ere they escape from us across the sea!"

Tears in his eyes, he spoke; pity touched all the Achaeans. But Medon now drew near, and with him the sacred bard, from the palace of Odysseus; for slumber left them. They stood still in the midst, and wonder fell on all, while Medon, a man of understanding, thus addressed them:

"Hearken to me now, men of Ithaca; for not without consent of the immortal gods Odysseus planned these deeds. I myself saw a deathless god stand by Odysseus, in all points like to Mentor. And this immortal god appeared before Odysseus, cheering him on; then to the consternation of the suitors he stormed along the hall, and side by side they fell."

As he spoke thus, pale fear took hold on all. But to them spoke the old lord Halitherses, the son of Mastor; for he alone looked both before and after. He with good will addressed them thus, and said:

"Hearken now, men of Ithaca, to what I say. By your own fault, my friends, these deeds are done; because you paid no heed to me nor yet to Mentor, the shepherd of the people, in hindering your sons from foolish crime. They wrought a monstrous deed in wanton willfulness, when they destroyed the goods and wronged the wife of one who was their prince, saying that he would come no more. Let then the past be ended, and listen to what I say: do not set forth, or some may find a self-sought ill."

He spoke; but with a mighty cry up started more than half,—together in their seats remained the rest,—for his counsel had not pleased them. Eupeithes they approved, and they straightway ran for weapons. Then when they had arrayed themselves in glittering bronze, they gathered in a troop outside the spacious town. Eupeithes in his folly led them. He thought to avenge the murder of his son, yet was himself never to come back more, but there would meet his doom.

Meanwhile Athene said to Zeus, the son of Kronos: "Our father, son of Kronos, most high above all rulers, speak what I ask: what is your secret purpose? Will you still further stir up evil strife and the dread din of war, or do you stablish peace betwixt the two?"

Then answered her cloud-gathering Zeus and said: "My child, why question me of this? For was it not yourself proposed the plan to have

Odysseus crush these men by his return? Do as you will; I tell you what
is wise. Now royal Odysseus has avenged himself upon the suitors, let
a sure league be made and he be always king; while for the death of
sons and brothers we bring about oblivion. So shall all love each other
as before, and wealth and peace abound."

With words like these he roused Athene, eager enough before, and
she went dashing down the ridges of Olympus.

Now when the men had stayed desire for cheering food, then thus
began long-tried royal Odysseus: "Let some one go and see if our foes
are drawing near."

He spoke; and out the son of Dolius ran, as he was bidden, and went
and stood upon the threshold, and saw the men all near. Then straight
to Odysseus in winged words he called: "Here they are, close at hand!
Quick, let us arm!"

As soon as he spoke, there sprang to arms the four men with
Odysseus and the six sons of Dolius. Laërtes too and Dolius put on
armor; gray though they were, still warriors at need. Then when they
had arrayed themselves in glittering bronze, they opened the doors and
sallied forth, Odysseus leading.

But Athene now drew near, the daughter of Zeus, likened to Mentor
in her form and voice; whom long-tried royal Odysseus saw with joy,
and to Telemachus his son he straightway said: "Now shall you learn,
Telemachus, by taking part yourself while men are battling where the
best are proved, how not to bring disgrace upon your line of sires; for
they from ancient times were famed for strength and bravery through
all the land."

Then answered him discreet Telemachus: "In this my present mood,
dear father, you shall see me, if you will, bring no disgrace upon the
line of which you speak."

So said he, and Laërtes too was glad and said: "Oh, what a day for me
is this, kind gods! Right glad am I. My son and son's son vie in valor."

And standing by his side, clear-eyed Athene said: "Son of Arceisius,
far the dearest of my friends, call on the clear-eyed maid and father
Zeus; then swing your long spear and straight let it fly."   .

With words like these Pallas Athene inspired him with great power.
He prayed to the daughter of mighty Zeus; then swung his long spear
and straight let it fly, and struck Eupeithes on the helmet's brazen
cheek. This did not stay the spear; the point passed through. He fell
with a thud; his armor rattled round him. On the front ranks Odysseus
fell, he and his gallant son, and smote them with their swords and double-
pointed spears. And now they certainly had slain them all and cut them
off from coming home, had not Athene, daughter of aegis-bearing
Zeus, shouted aloud and held back all the host:

"Hold, men of Ithaca, from cruel combat, and without bloodshed straightway part!"

As thus Athene spoke, pale fear took hold on all. Their weapons all flew from their trembling hands and fell upon the ground, as the goddess gave her cry. To the town they turned, eager to save their lives. Fearfully shouted long-tried royal Odysseus, and gathering his might swooped like a soaring eagle. Then too the son of Kronos cast his blazing bolt, and down it fell by the dread father's clear-eyed child. And now to Odysseus said clear-eyed Athene:

"High-born son of Laërtes, ready Odysseus, stay! Cease from the struggle of uncertain war! Let not the son of Kronos, far-seeing Zeus, be moved to anger!"

So spoke Athene. Odysseus heeded, and was glad at heart. Then for all coming time betwixt the two a peace was made by Pallas Athene, daughter of aegis-bearing Zeus, likened to Mentor in her form and voice.

DOVER · THRIFT · EDITIONS

POETRY

THE CONGO AND OTHER POEMS, Vachel Lindsay. 96pp. 0-486-27272-9

EVANGELINE AND OTHER POEMS, Henry Wadsworth Longfellow. 64pp. 0-486-28255-4

FAVORITE POEMS, Henry Wadsworth Longfellow. 96pp. 0-486-27273-7

COMPLETE POEMS, Christopher Marlowe. 112pp. 0-486-42674-2

"TO HIS COY MISTRESS" AND OTHER POEMS, Andrew Marvell. 64pp. 0-486-29544-3

SPOON RIVER ANTHOLOGY, Edgar Lee Masters. 144pp. 0-486-27275-3

SELECTED POEMS, Claude McKay. 80pp. 0-486-40876-0

SONGS OF MILAREPA, Milarepa. 128pp. 0-486-42814-1

RENASCENCE AND OTHER POEMS, Edna St. Vincent Millay. 64pp. (Not available in Europe or the United Kingdom) 0-486-26873-X

SELECTED POEMS, John Milton. 128pp. 0-486-27554-X

CIVIL WAR POETRY: An Anthology, Paul Negri (ed.). 128pp. 0-486-29883-3

ENGLISH VICTORIAN POETRY: AN ANTHOLOGY, Paul Negri (ed.). 256pp. 0-486-40425-0

GREAT SONNETS, Paul Negri (ed.). 96pp. 0-486-28052-7

THE RAVEN AND OTHER FAVORITE POEMS, Edgar Allan Poe. 64pp. 0-486-26685-0

ESSAY ON MAN AND OTHER POEMS, Alexander Pope. 128pp. 0-486-28053-5

GOBLIN MARKET AND OTHER POEMS, Christina Rossetti. 64pp. 0-486-28055-1

CHICAGO POEMS, Carl Sandburg. 80pp. 0-486-28057-8

CORNHUSKERS, Carl Sandburg. 157pp. 0-486-41409-4

COMPLETE SONNETS, William Shakespeare. 80pp. 0-486-26686-9

SELECTED POEMS, Percy Bysshe Shelley. 128pp. 0-486-27558-2

AFRICAN-AMERICAN POETRY: An Anthology, 1773–1930, Joan R. Sherman (ed.). 96pp. 0-486-29604-0

NATIVE AMERICAN SONGS AND POEMS: An Anthology, Brian Swann (ed.). 64pp. 0-486-29450-1

SELECTED POEMS, Alfred Lord Tennyson. 112pp. 0-486-27282-6

AENEID, Vergil (Publius Vergilius Maro). 256pp. 0-486-28749-1

GREAT LOVE POEMS, Shane Weller (ed.). 128pp. 0-486-27284-2

CIVIL WAR POETRY AND PROSE, Walt Whitman. 96pp. 0-486-28507-3

SELECTED POEMS, Walt Whitman. 128pp. 0-486-26878-0

THE BALLAD OF READING GAOL AND OTHER POEMS, Oscar Wilde. 64pp. 0-486-27072-6

EARLY POEMS, William Carlos Williams. 64pp. (Available in U.S. only.) 0-486-29294-0

FAVORITE POEMS, William Wordsworth. 80pp. 0-486-27073-4

EARLY POEMS, William Butler Yeats. 128pp. 0-486-27808-5